Praise for
Cracked Open – Never Broken

D1538454

Iman has not just survived a life of obstacles that defy belief, she has done the work to triumph. In telling her story, she inspires others to believe that they, too, can find the courage to heal.

—Kate Swoboda, Author of The Courage Habit

Brave and raw, tender, and revealing—if you've experienced childhood challenges, you'll find a good friend in Cracked Open – Never Broken. Gatti's memoir is... WOW. Layered, real and ultimately, triumphant. Plus, the writing is exquisite.

—Rachael Maddox, Author of Secret Bad Girl

Cracked Open – Never Broken, transcends the personal story. My heart burst wide open from the very first page. The empowering concept of choosing love in the face of adversity is beautifully illustrated in this transformational story. In a world that demonstrates so much hurt and confusion, Iman's story has the power to comfort, heal, and empower.

—Suzanne Adams, Bestselling
Author of Musings of an Earth Angel

Iman Gatti is a writer that can't be ignored. I was sad I had to go out to be an adult in the real world and leave her pages as I was reading. The giddy feeling I got from being able to dive back in was rare, and the sign of a life-changing book. As a trauma survivor myself, I felt seen, heard, and understood, just by relating to Iman's experiences of surviving in the hopes of better days ahead. This book will leave you speechless, in awe, in tears, and in total head-nodding and appreciation for the strength of the human spirit. It'll remind you that whatever you are facing, you'll be able to make it through just like she did. If you're looking to be truly moved and inspired for a lifetime, *Cracked Open – Never Broken*, has to be your next book club pick. (I'm looking at you Oprah!)

—Emily Aube, Author of Love before Fear

Prepare yourself for a shocking, heart-breaking, and ultimately triumphant personal tale from Iman Gatti. Told with courage, grace, and ultra-fine detail, *Cracked Open – Never Broken* is at once "hard to read" due to the details of her story, and "can't put it down" because of how beautifully those details are written. Simply put—you can't stop reading because you want to know what happens next! You want to know how her story turns out. You want to discover if there is happiness, joy, love, and comfort at the end of the dark tunnel. And let me tell you—you won't be disappointed! A must read for anyone who loves to be inspired by an authentic, true-life story of love and loss, resilience, and redemption.

—Dana B. Myers, Author and Founder of Booty Parlor

Cracked Open – Never Broken is an open, honest memoir about unimaginable loss and hardship. But really, it's about so much more than that. Iman is an incredible example of strength, possibility, and resiliency, despite coming from deplorable and unthinkable circumstances. Her story honours that of so many children growing up without proper nurturing, being hurled from home to home and somehow making it out not only alive, but actually thriving. Iman's deep connection to her mother and herself is what I think saved her. I am proud to know her today and honoured to be a part of every step she takes towards her amazing future. Cracked Open – Never Broken is just the beginning of her incredible journey.

—Heidi Nicole, Certified Transition Life Coach

My heart is cracked open after reading this book! Iman bravely shares her story, and in doing so teaches us that through the greatest challenges of our life we do survive, we do recover, we do find healing, and we can live a life beyond our wildest dreams. We learn that the number one thing that makes us stronger is love, and grief is only about love. It is through Iman's courage and inspiration that she opens the door for us to explore our own story and to begin our work of healing and transformation. This book is heart-felt, soul-nurturing, inspiring and hopeful.

—Melanie Haraldson, Yoga Instructor and
Certified Women's Health Coach

CRACKED OPEN – NEVER BROKEN

CRACKED OPEN – NEVER BROKEN

A Memoir

Iman Gatti

PURPOSE
DRIVEN
PUBLISHING

Copyright © 2017 Iman Gatti. All rights reserved.

No part of this publication shall be reproduced, transmitted, or sold in whole or in part in any form without prior written consent of the author, except as provided by the United States of America copyright law. Any unauthorized usage of the text without express written permission of the publisher is a violation of the author's copyright and is illegal and punishable by law. All trademarks and registered trademarks appearing in this guide are the property of their respective owners.

For permission requests, write to the publisher, addressed "Attention: Permissions Coordinator," at the address below.
Purpose Driven Publishing
141 Weston Street, #155
Hartford, CT, 06141

The opinions expressed by the Author are not necessarily those held by Purpose Driven Publishing.

Ordering Information: Quantity sales and special discounts are available on quantity purchases by corporations, associations, and others. For details, contact the publisher at the address above.

Edited by: Jennifer Sintime, Heather B. Habelka
Cover design by: Donna Cunningham
Cover photography: Con Boland
Layout by: Medlar Publishing Solutions Pvt Ltd.

ISBN: 978-1-946384-20-1 (print)
ISBN: 978-1-946384-21-8 (ebook)
Library of Congress Control Number: 2017954829

First edition, November 2017.
The information contained within this book is strictly for informational purposes. The material may include information, products, or services by third parties. As such, the Author and Publisher do not assume responsibility or liability for any third party material or opinions. Readers are advised to do their own due diligence when it comes to making decisions.

The stories in this book have been written from the Author's recollections. They are not written to represent word-for-word transcripts of conversations or events. Rather, the Author has retold them in a way that evokes the feeling and meaning of what was said. In all instances the essence of the dialogue is accurate. However, names and identifying details have been changed to protect the privacy of the people involved.

Purpose Driven Publishing works with authors, and aspiring authors, who have a story to tell and a brand to build. Do you have a book idea you would like us to consider publishing? Please visit PurposeDrivenPublishing.com for more information.

Dear Reader,

Throughout writing this memoir, I have attempted to relay all the events portrayed to the best of my memory.

Because most of this book takes place when I was a child, it is with a child's perspective that I remember the events that occurred. As we all know, memory is always flawed. There were times when I couldn't recall exact words spoken in a conversation or the particular date that an event took place. For those times, I used my best judgment and my experience, as well as help from friends and family from my childhood to reconstruct the scenes and dialogue to the best of my ability.

I have changed many of the names of people and almost all of the towns and schools I attended to offer as much respect, anonymity, and privacy as I could to those involved, while still being able to share my story authentically.

It has taken me a great deal of courage to come to a place of healing and forgiveness in my life enough to share my story with the world. My life has been one of severe trauma, loss, overcoming, and triumph and I did my best to remain respectful and fair of everyone I included in this book. It is my greatest wish that the people portrayed herein feel good with my depiction of them.

Of course, there are people who may not feel good about how they are written about and to them I would like to share a quote by Anne Lamott:

> *"You own everything that happened to you. Tell your stories. If people wanted you to write warmly about them, they should have behaved better."*

That is to say that not everything that happened to me was good; nor were some of the people I encountered good to me. Throughout everything I have shared and everyone with whom I have included in this work, I have put my sincerest efforts forward to treat each character and situation with a compassionate and delicate nature.

While reading through my memoir, I hope you can find the humanity, tenacity, and grace with which this book was written.

Sincerely,

Aman

Dedication

TO MY MOTHER,
THANK YOU FOR YOUR ETERNAL SACRIFICE.
YOUR LOVE IS FOREVER MY FUEL.

TO MY BELOVED RON,
THANK YOU FOR CHOOSING ME AND SHINING
YOUR LIGHT TO ILLUMINATE MY PATH. I LOVE YOU.

Foreword

I first met Iman at my Spirit Junkie Masterclass Level 2 training. At the training I invited the students to get in front of the group to share their inspirational stories. These stories allow the students to show how they'd turned their pain into their purpose. I wanted them to be authentic, vulnerable, and provide an inspirational lesson. I knew that while this request was challenging, it would also be transformational for each person to share their story out loud in a room full of strangers. Most of the students had never publicly shared their stories before, so there was a lot of nervous energy in the room.

On the first day of the speaking training Iman fearlessly stood up to share her story. On the stage I saw a confident, kind, and gentle woman. Even though she was so relaxed I could tell that there was a strong desire behind her need to share. She spoke at a slow pace and painted a beautiful picture of her childhood. She spoke of innocence and peace. Then the story shifted direction and the truth was revealed. Iman stood in front of a room full of strangers and uttered words I didn't expect to hear. The story she revealed that day was haunting, yet somehow she was able to turn it into a message of empowerment.

What I admired most about Iman was how safe she felt in her vulnerability. She was confident in her personal recovery, which inspired us to feel as though we could overcome anything. She delivered a message of hope that helped us remember our own. Throughout these pages you will learn Iman's story. She will inspire you to face your own darkness and bring it to the light. She will guide you to accept your circumstances and rely on a higher power no matter what. And most importantly she will remind you of the power of recovery and grace.

I'm proud to call Iman my student and my friend. I knew she would put her story into print, and today you can celebrate her journey and recognize your own. May these pages bless you and guide you to awaken to your own authentic story of hope.

—*Gabrielle Bernstein*

Survival of the Fittest

Take one step forward
Get thrown three back
Every second on guard
Waiting for the attack
Their words try to break me
Their violence only wounds my skin
They raise their weapons
But they'll never get in
This torture makes me stronger
Gives me reason to believe
All the pain I endure
Will only help me when I leave
This wretched prison, built around my soul
They think I am breaking, but will never truly know
That deep inside a light shines on
Visible through the shattered pieces of my heart
This single flame which cannot go out
But burns stronger when they beat me
And hotter when they yell
Yet, in my torment, I cannot help but smile
For only paradise can await
A child forced into hell

Aman

Chapter One

Age 6: Home

I remember the way the moon looked—an illuminating crescent, glowing a peaceful white. Its glimmer instilled a tranquil undertone amid all the chaos. I had not fully come to understand what was happening. I was aware of only two things: my mother was dead, and I would never be the same. No one told me the latter, of course. It would be barbaric to admit such a terrible reality to a six-year-old—especially one who had just borne witness to the wicked cruelty of death. The horror itself is silencing. In situations so gruesome, people are unaware of how to comfort you, let alone themselves. Only the lullabies of still silence bring serenity. My body was going into shock, it felt as though my innocence was being ripped away from me as a strange calming sensation washed over. The spinning room, the inevitable tick of time, the beating of my heart; it had all stopped—an astonishing contrast to the loud, shattering reality of my surroundings.

In the seconds that the light had gone on, my eyes adjusted to the brightness. I saw his face, calling out to him with excitement. But holding a finger to his dark, moustachioed lip, he hushed me to silence. Obedient and not wanting to wake my mother, my hands covered my mouth. As my father turned off the light, the moon's glimmer reflected off the butcher's knife held in his hand, catching my eye. Quietly, he inched closer to the right side of the bed, where my mother slept soundly. The knife rose above his head, clutched between his brown-skinned hands. A shriek escaped my lips in the

1

brief seconds as I reached out, grasping my mother's arm. Eyes jolting open as the cold knife entered her, she cried out, begging him to stop. With the mild strength of a fifteen-year-old boy, my brother Adam rushed into the room, grabbing my father's arm in an earnest attempt to stop him. Weak by comparison, he was thrown into the hall. Without losing a moment, my father continued, repeatedly thrusting the knife into my mother. My white satin nightgown transformed into the same putrid red that cloaked every-thing around me.

I watched as my father fled. He had done what he had come for, leaving me, my mother, and my treasured stuffed teddy bears, saturated in her blood. Climbing off the bed, I took slow steps to the window. Pushing the sheer white curtains aside, I looked out into our front yard. The same undisturbed moon illuminated our room; the heavy weight of silence looming.

They grew up as neighbours in Tunisia, North Africa. My father, Maazir, a stalky, five-foot-five, dark-featured man, had loved my mother her whole life. It was no surprise he loved her. My mother, Rafia, had a radiant smile, a soulful laugh, long dark hair, and a kindness that exuded all around her. But she was in love with another man whose parents disliked the notion of their marriage. And so, all those years ago, she settled for my father.

After their marriage, they moved to Paris, France. With aspirations of becoming an Executive Chef, my father studied culinary arts at the esteemed Le Cordon Bleu Paris while my mother worked as a seamstress. Eventually, a few years after the birth of Adam, their first child, they decided to move to the far-off prairies of Canada. My mother's sister, Samira, had convinced them to do so after vocalizing how lonely she was in Alberta, alone with her Canadian husband. Soon after, my mother with her small family in tow, headed to Edmonton. First arriving in Ontario, my family stayed there for a brief amount of time. It was here, during the late fall of 1976, that my second brother Chokri was born.

My mother cried when she had a second son. The tears sprouted from joy, but also out of her desperation for a daughter. Her desire was so intense that she used to let Adam's wavy black locks grow a little too long, and dress him in shirts that would slightly err on the side of feminine. But it wasn't until the late summer of 1981 that her prayers were finally answered. And for this reason, she named me Shahia, meaning *intense desire or craving* in Arabic. It was weeks later in a dream when a man came to her, telling her that my name was meant to be Iman, meaning *faith in God,* and this faith is what I would need. Being superstitious, she legally changed my name, having her own faith in the words spoken to her.

She was beautiful, my mother. She had long dark hair, an olive complexion, brown eyes, a big smile and an even bigger laugh. Beauty radiated all around her—from the waves of her hair, to the gentleness in her heart. During their move to Paris for my father's schooling, my mother wanted to work as a seamstress in a factory. True to her diligent character, she found a factory that was seeking seamstresses and she went to work. She was so proud of herself, and for good reason. Like many other women from Tunisia, she had never had a job before. It was during the first few weeks of her newfound position in the workplace, after settling in, that one of the seamstresses took a brief leave of absence. Unaware of workplace politics, my mother took over the absent employee's sewing station. When returning from her leave, the coworker came in to find my mother working at her station. It was then that she became abrasive, as many do when their territory is being encroached upon, and lashed out at my mother. Yelled at and scolded, my mother burst into tears. She had never had a job before and was unaware of the mild cruelties that are endured in the work place. She didn't understand office politics, nor was it in her nature to speak poorly of others—she was just too kind. And so, returning home, face full of tears, she told my father she never wanted to work again. She was frightened and afraid of trying to be independent. My father simply told her that she didn't have to work, and she didn't have to in the first place.

My mother settled in to the life of a homemaker with ease. Being too young for school, I would be with her from morning until night. We would wake up, and after endless attempts to wake Chokri, she would send my brothers off to Belmead Elementary School, which was just across the street from our townhouse. Mere minutes past 7:00 a.m., she would begin preparing dinner, filling our house with the succulent aroma of garlic and onion. The lingering scent of bleach would soon add to the bouquet as she cleaned every washroom, swept every floor, and dusted every shelf. She was meticulous about her home. If a speck on the carpet came into her line of vision, she was quick to bend over and snatch it up. Nothing could be out of place—not even a hair on my head. But even when I would return from playing, hair embedded with leaves, knees of my tights torn, covered in mud and scrapes, she would never react as though I had done something wrong. It was almost comical. She would look at me, covered in dirt and disheveled, and laugh, "Oh, Iman—really?"

It wasn't that she spoiled us, but the evidence of her love was in everything she did. Every morning she would spend hours twirling my brown tangled tresses around her fingers, patiently ensuring each lock curled to perfection. She would sit with me every day, even before I had started school, at my little desk in the kitchen, teaching me to read. My brothers taught me too, though, their maturing vernacular was headed in a fouler direction. During my reading lesson one afternoon, I asked her what an F looked like. She showed me. "What about U?" I questioned. She showed me. I continued until I had spelled *Fuck You*. Finally registering what she had written out for me—after a ten second delay—she gasped. I leaped up from the couch, sprinting to find refuge behind a wall. Peering at my mother, she looked at me with the same face she always did, "Iman, that's not nice," she said. Then she called me over, and all was forgiven.

I suppose that's the role of older siblings—they teach you taboo phrases, make jokes at your expense, and play games that leave you in tears. Despite all this, Adam was the responsible one. By fate of being the firstborn, and a male, he was enrolled in cadets. Though bred to be a man's man, his heart was soft and sensitive. As a child, he would raise birds, and care for me—changing my diapers, bathing me, watching over me. His brown skin and dark features mirrored my father's. Though, unlike my father's strict, hard demeanour, Adam was caring, and generous. Chokri, on the other hand, was the jester of our family. With endless jokes, a mischievous air, and the finesse and good looks of a ladies' man, laughter would always erupt around him. A charming schemer, he would manipulate me into handing over my allowance, or trading five Halloween treats for his measly one, without a shred of effort. He was the Keeper of the Cookies, or so I would call him. Chokri being a name far too difficult for me to pronounce at such a young age, I would call him Cookie. And, to the logic of a small child, if his name was Cookie, he must have known where all the cookies were. "Cookie, can I have a cookie?" became an ongoing joke over the years. Even in my mid-thirties, I continue to call him by the pet name. Regardless of the surprise slaps to my arm, attempts to push me over, or the blatant thievery of my Halloween candies, I loved him. And he would get me the cookies, every time I asked.

Being nine and five years older than me, my brothers and I didn't have very much in common. When they would leave in the mornings for school, I would stay at home all day with my mother, without a complaint, of course. My mother and I shared an attachment like no other. Kisses and coos from extended family and friends were lost on me. Shy, I would cling to my mother. If she was standing, I would hide behind her legs. Even as others beckoned or when she requested I give my aunt a hug, I would cling to my mother's thigh with all the strength a child could harness. If she sat down, I would be sitting beside her. When she would lie on the couch, watching TV, I would nestle in the warm nook behind her bent knees. My mother was my safe fortress, my keeper, my friend.

Extending to the capacity at which a six-year-old could comprehend, my mother would teach me to bake and cook meals. Standing beside her, learning the culinary arts, I declared my disgust for touching raw meat.

"Mom, it's gross," I announced with conviction, "It looks disgusting. I'm never touching meat!" I was firm in my decision.

"Well what about when you get married?" she questioned. "When you have a family and kids, you have to feed them!"

Looking down at the raw, exposed flesh she touched with her bare hands, I shook my head, "I just don't think I could." And her response wasn't one that would shatter my dreams, or dismiss my resolve.

"Well, you'll just have to wear gloves," was all she said. That was the thing with my mother; she was always so encouraging of everything I did, even when I realize now, how much of a handful I may have been.

It was mid-fall, and dried leaves and dirt covered me as I ran inside from playing in the fallen foliage. Seeing my mother in the bathtub, too excited to contain myself, I stripped off all my clothes and I jumped in without hesitation. The water was clouded with floating fragments of leaves that were once woven into my curls. I could only imagine how startled or dismayed she was that I had ruined this small luxury that she had made for herself.

She got out of the tub, "You go ahead, honey, let me put some more water in there for you." I responded with the innocent desire to just be with her, "Why are you leaving?" I asked. "I want to have a bath with you!" And with a calm, loving reply, she told me she had to do something else.

Our bond was celestial. When I was finally old enough to attend school, our morning routine was akin to that of an actress before filming, or a dancer backstage before stepping onto the stage. My tights, dress, and shoes matched perfectly, my nails were painted, and my little purse was filled with the flavoured lip glosses my mother bought for me. After spending her morning pampering her little girl, she would walk me across the street to my school. One time, after decorating me in newly bought earrings shaped into miniature hearts, we arrived at my kindergarten class. She briefly spoke to my kindergarten teacher, "Can you make sure that her hearts are always right side up?" She requested. "They must never be upside down, because sometimes Iman twirls them—but can you make sure they're always staying the same way?"

I remember being cared for in such a deep way. I felt precious. I felt special. And I know my mother waited a long time to have me. My father, though stern and strict, had his moments of paternal love as well. He called me "princess." Though rarely home, every week he bought me a new nail polish to add to my abundant collection, gave me an allowance for my piggy bank, and performed magic tricks for us. As a family, we would go camping and fishing. We could cook and just be together. Cooking was very prominent in our household. My mother was an excellent cook, and my father was a professional. Being an executive chef and having connections with local farmers, my father would take us to local farms. Reminiscent of the old country, they would buy whole animals to have slaughtered, frozen, and kept for the winter months. Purchasing sheep one summer, my mother and I sat on the farm, the fresh air surrounding us, the sun beaming a heavenly heat upon our skin. The sounds of farm life echoed in the background. A warm breeze carried the fragrant scent of sweet grass to the step where we sat. A bucket of wool from the sheep she had sheered and a bucket of water were beside us. Meticulously and patiently, we picked the grass embedded in the handfuls of softly curled fleece, submerging them into the bucket of water, and drying them in the sunlight. With this fleece, she would stuff our pillows, and make me teddy bears.

Those sun-filled moments were few and far between. Despite these trips to the farm and our occasional nuclear bliss, my father's anger and grim energy shrouded him. Decorated with scars that they still have to this day, my brothers would constantly find themselves on the wrong end of my father's belt, victim to his abusive nature. Though I was fortunate to never have felt his wrath in a physical manner, he would often yell at me. There were times when I didn't even know what I had done and I would be put in a time-out. Sobbing after being sentenced to stand alone in the dark corridor of the upstairs, I heard my mother refuting my punishment. He stood firm, "Leave her there! Don't you dare touch her, Rafia. You spoil her." And so, my mother came upstairs and stood beside me, supporting me in the dark, as my sobs subsided.

The physical abuse wasn't limited to my siblings. My father would throw both verbal and physical punches at my mother—slapping her, kicking her, and throwing her off chairs. Peering into the kitchen one evening, I saw him repeatedly slapping her face with ferocity. And there she was, returning from each blow with a smile on her face—a perfect illustration of their contrasting dispositions—she refused to be broken.

My father was having an affair. Unfortunately, he had met a young blonde in Canada and thought it wise to have his cake and eat it too. No fool, my mother caught on—the late hours and erratic schedule of a chef was only plausible to an extent. It was very hard for Adam, Chokri, and I, after my father was kicked out. Despite our dislike for him, we still loved him. Though saddening, the reality that he would not be around as often brought a sense of relief. We no longer had to watch him beat our mother. She was our sun, moon, and stars and the violence and tears were something we would happily live without. Left with a key to visit us as needed, my father would come into our house in the middle of the night. After he finished work he would come into our home and eat our mother's food, leaving his soiled dishes on the kitchen table. In the morning, we would see that he had been there. He had made his presence known. But my mother, without the bat of a lash, would do the dishes and move on with her day.

My father leaving sparked a change in my mother. She was empowered. Dismissing her past self, who fled her first job in tears, she started to attend school. Enrolling in a class for English as a Second Language, she was driven to develop life skills to better herself. Her second youngest sister, Fatima, who was a spitting image of my mother, soon joined us in Edmonton with her family. Tarek, her husband, was a handsomely tall and slim, lighter-toned Tunisian man with a European air to him. Her son, Ali, was affectionate and loving, with a sweetness that radiated around him. They were vibrant, my mother and Fatima. Their laughter echoed in our house, more friends than sisters. My mother had surrounded herself with family, creating a close support system, inspiring her and giving her strength to live on her own.

Deciding she was ready to move on, my mother began dating. Devastated that my aunt would be babysitting me as my mother went out one evening, I began screaming and crying—unable to accept that I would be with anyone other than my precious mother. I would wail and squeal, asking her why she had to leave me. But with her hair feathered to suit the '80s trend, her lipstick applied, and her coat on, she kissed me and left. Though it wasn't long before she returned; perhaps only an hour had passed. She told Fatima that she couldn't do it—*she couldn't leave us*. A tinge of guilt creeps in when I look back at this moment, but I don't regret a single minute that I spent with her because, in the long run, I didn't get very many.

I unflinchingly moved in on the opportunity to sleep with my mother the moment my father left. Shrouded in the lingering scent of Chanel No. 5, I would nestle myself in with my pile of teddy bears, the beige duvet with embellished red hearts and leaves would make a crinkling sound as I settled in. She would sleep to my left, with a small, ten-inch black and white TV resting on the night table. The flicker of the screen would add flashes of light against the white walls of the room. The sheer white curtain to the right of me would invite the bright glow of the moonlight. My fortress of forty teddy bears would surround me, and I would cuddle with her, drifting to sleep.

Sirens and flashing lights paraded around us. Adam stood on the street, paramedics and police officers questioning him in attempt to understand what had happened mere moments before. A stretcher was brought out of our house, onto the street, covered. Adam, Chokri, and I stood watching. "Memo," Adam began, using the nickname (pronounced Meemo) that he had given me as a baby, "They're going to take her to the hospital. That's where people get better." Returning his stare, glancing back at the covered stretcher, "No," I replied. "I saw her die. She's not coming back, Adam."

A door closed behind Chokri and me. Bouncing blonde hair led us up a set of stairs as we followed our neighbour into her small townhouse. I took each barefooted step, aware yet unsure. I had never been in her house before, but she had always been so nice to us. At one point in time, she dated a well-known football player for the Edmonton Eskimos—a testament to her beauty. Bearing gifts of Nerf footballs, he would play with us in the yard, tossing the foam ovals in the air as we leapt and bound to catch them. But those days were long behind us now. I continued to climb each unfamiliar step, looking around me, adjusting to the foreign environment. A door was open. I glanced in. The sight of a small blonde boy, one of her sons, asleep and naked atop his sheets made me pause. Embarrassment washed over me for a moment as I continued to follow her. She took us into her bedroom.

A beautiful, sweet energy flowed from her, but her positive energy betrayed her frightened countenance and her erratic, scattered behaviour. She stripped the blood-soaked nightgown from my small body, replacing it with one of her T-shirts. With such an earnest attempt to mask how flustered she was, she gave us magazines.

"Why don't you guys lie down? I'm going to talk to the police," she said as she handed us the small stack of magazines. "And I'll go talk to your brother," she added. "And everything will be fine, okay? Everything is going to be fine." She left the room, and stillness surrounded Chokri and me. We cuddled, saying nothing of what had just happened.

In the early hours of June 22, 1988, as we lay cuddling in our neighbour's bed, Chokri made me laugh. With bravery, he made jokes that made me giggle as we flipped through the magazines before we finally drifted into the safety of sleep. The next time I would open my eyes, I would be at my aunt's house.

Chapter Two

Age 7: A Mother's Intuition

There was a second of peace as I opened my eyes. It was a lost moment in translation—one in which you can't remember where you are or what you're doing. Slowly, my body began to stir as I adjusted to my surroundings—I was on a mattress on the floor—stranded on an island of metal coils and foam, floating in a sea of dusty beige carpeting; the horizon was nothing more than bare white walls. *Where was I? What was going on?* I felt the soft outline of Freddy, a teddy bear that my mother had made for me. The feel of his soft fabric shook me into awareness. It all flooded back. Clutching him as tears came out in violent sobs, it seemed as though the pleasure of ignorance lasted only a second before I was thrown back into reality, and the emptiness I saw all around me only mimicked the emptiness in my heart. I felt alone.

Evidenced by the bare apartment they had lived in; my aunt and uncle hadn't been in Edmonton very long. A small galley-style kitchen opened to a miniature dining area, leading to a scarcely furnished living room where only a couch, armchair, and television resided. Though my Aunt Fatima's apartment was barren, she kept it clean and very tidy, just as my mother would have.

With solemn steps, I walked to the balcony on the far side of the living room. The day whirred in slow motion. Exhausted and heartbroken, I looked onto the desolate street. The notion of living a life without my mother was just as foreign to me as my surroundings.

What does it mean to die? I thought. I didn't know. My mind fluttered to the sights and sounds of the flashing lights and sirens that surrounded me the night before. *I know she's dead, I know she's gone.* Even though I had said the words out loud mere hours ago, I was at a loss. What did it mean? *Does that mean that she's never coming back, or is she just gone for now?*

As the day went on, my aunt's apartment filled with people. Amid the crowd of teary eyes and hysteria, familiar faces offered my family condolences. The entrance transformed into a revolving door, ushering in groups of swollen red eyes and sorrowful frowns. I was lost in a sea of sadness, watching the lips move in sync with the buzz of cumbersome conversation. A small Tunisian woman took a step toward me, an odd odourous combination of food and spices wafting from her.

"Listen," she began, looking at me with worrisome eyes. "Mommy is going to be just fine. She just went out for a little bit, and Mommy is going to come back."

Her lies, though intended to offer comfort, were insulting. I stared at her for the brief beat of a second until Adam appeared, breaking the moment of silence.

"She was there. She saw everything," he told her. His irritation was evident.

I stepped closer to my brother.

He continued, "You can't tell her that. She saw her die."

My eyes shifted to meet the gaze of this strange woman, "My mom is dead. She's not going to come back."

The woman burst into tears, sobbing and shaking uncontrollably. My dislike for her grew. I hated liars, I hated *her,* and her scent left my nose wrinkled in disgust—but as I watched her body shake with her sobs, I realized that the truth horrifies people. I made people sad. Fatigued and overwhelmed, I left. Returning to my foam island in the sea of beige carpet, I quickly fell back to sleep.

More people had come. In between naps, I sat in the living room, listening to the delirious crowd as I held Freddy in my arms. He was my friend in a foreign land, a connection to my mother that I could touch, feel, and smell. He was with me the night before, silently lying beside me as my father entered the room. He was with me when my world had fallen apart. I considered the crowd of people who shed tears at the knowledge of my mother's death. They, like me, were heartbroken and devastated. I felt uncomfortable. Though absurd, I thought that perhaps since I was beside my mother in her final moments, that this was my fault. I felt as though there was a secret that only I knew—which, to some extent, was true. Only I knew the exact sounds, smells, and feels of that night. Only I knew what had happened in those final moments.

"Hello, Iman."

My thoughts were interrupted. I brought my attention to the friendly voice that came from a dizzying combination of orange hair, pale skin, and vibrant patterned clothing. A comforting aura emitted from this man as he introduced himself, and his girlfriend standing beside him. They smiled warmly. Her name was Elizabeth. His name was Ben.

I searched my memory, but could not recall ever meeting them before. They were so different from all of the other guests at my aunt's place who, besides the police, were made up of close family and friends mostly from Tunisia. Ben and Elizabeth were kind. When Ben spoke to me he didn't try to tell me what I had seen or where my mother was, which was what everyone else had been doing since I opened my eyes. He simply listened and asked questions about everyday things. The mood was heavy, but somehow, he brought a sense of normalcy and togetherness when it felt like the rest of my world was falling apart. He was quirky and kind-hearted and treated me as if I were a real person. Even though we had just met, I could tell already that I liked him very much.

His connection to my family was not by blood; it was Elizabeth who was friends with my aunt. When my Aunt Fatima told Ben and Elizabeth about the death of her sister they came over to meet me and my brothers. Like my mom, my Aunt Fatima attended a school focused on teaching life skills to immigrants such as English as a Second Language, resume building, and lessons in the cultural differences of Canada. It was at this school where my aunt had met Elizabeth, her teacher.

"Who you got there?" Ben asked. I looked down at the stuffed bear—the cream-coloured body, brown, hand-sewn face, and the drawn-on eyes. He was stained in a darkening red.

"This is Freddy," I clutched the stuffed bear harder. "He's covered in my mom's blood." I could see love, sadness, and concern wash over Ben's face.

In the days following my mother's death, there wasn't a moment's rest. Aunt Fatima's apartment was much too small for all us. We had all played an odd game of musical chairs, everyone rotating to find room for three extra children. Adam slept on the couch, Chokri and I slept in Ali's room, and Ali found himself sleeping in bed with his parents. We would have to eventually move into a larger townhouse, but first we would have to go back into our home. We had to clean all evidence of our mother's death, pack all the memories of our home, and throw away a life we had once had.

Taking the first steps into the house we had shared with my mother was eerie and uncomfortable. Like my aunt's apartment, it felt foreign. The home in which we had shared laughter, meals, and love, was not the same without the presence of my mother. It was cold. My mother's warmth had slipped away from the wallpapered walls, the beige carpets, the linoleum floors—this was not our home, it was merely a house. It was a museum of a past life we could no longer be a part of. The glass on the table, the cookie jar, the humming of the fridge—though so familiar a day ago, they instilled no comfort. I was yet again in a foreign land.

We walked into the kitchen. Glimpses of my mother humming, smiling, and laughing, skipped into my mind. I paused. There was a moment prior to my mother's death that skimmed to the surface of my memory. Exactly where I stood, just a month ago, she knelt, facing me eye to eye.

"Listen to me, Iman", she had grabbed my arms as her brown eyes met mine. "I want to tell you something. I think your father is going to kill me."

I had stood there, unsure of what she had meant. Cartoons, movies, even news that distant relatives had passed away had touched upon the concept of death, but only in a topical sense. Hearing her words made little sense to me. "Daddy would never kill you," I replied. "That's not true." Her face grew serious, emphasizing the importance of her words. I stood silent.

"He's either going to shoot me or he's going to stab me. I want you to be ready."

"Mommy, you're being silly."

I brushed off her words of warning. Though I had no complete concept of death, the little I had known, combined with the pensive tone of her words, left me taken aback at the suggestion.

"Daddy loves us and he would never hurt us."

"I'm just telling you, Iman. You're going to have to be a big girl," her face was uncharacteristically solemn, her eyes warm.

"I *am* a big girl."

"I know," she gave a brief pause. "And I love you very much. Don't you ever forget that."

I had not taken anything she had said with much weight. I had walked away from her words of warning without fully absorbing or understanding them. As I stood in the kitchen, a stranger in my own home, I thought to myself, *She was right.* It's odd to think that my mother knew her own death. She had known everything.

My brothers went to gather their belongings as I walked up the stairs to my mother's room with my aunt and uncle. Like the rest of the house, this room had changed since I had last been in it. The warm scent of Chanel No. 5, the flickering television screen, the playful crinkle of the duvet—they were all distant memories shrouded in the scent and sight of stale blood. I stood there, watching tears falling from Aunt Fatima's eyes as she rolled up her sleeves and washed the blood-stained bed frame and walls. My heart ached. I looked around the room. I looked at the sheer white curtain that let light in through the window. I looked at the old black and white television that once burst with light and laughter. This was not my home.

My Aunt Fatima and Uncle Tarek began going through my mother's belongings. Adam, Chokri, and I watched as they picked through the only material evidence left of my mother, planning to donate what couldn't be kept. Bearing witness to my mother's belongings being picked apart, divided into piles of what was worthy of keeping and what was not, left us in tears. It was pragmatic, of course. We could not bring everything with us. The house, after it had been cleaned, would eventually be rented out to another family. Our task was simple, but hard. To ask children to collect only small fragments of their lives, throw away all else, and move on, is not a request that is easy to make.

Soon they were finished and we made our way to the basement. My aunt looked around the room. "I'm sorry," she stammered, "But Auntie can't take this stuff with us."

We were in my haven. The room was filled with my coveted dolls, games, and teddy bears. Though I had a small army of stuffed animals tucked into bed with me every night, large bags of them were left on standby in the basement. I was saddened at the thought of leaving everything behind.

Hoping to coax me into action, Aunt Fatima made loose promises of replacing my treasures in the future. I was still hesitant to leave my treasured bounty behind, but the reality of the situation was not lost on me. I was torn as I looked upon the sea of toys. Finally, I had made my choice. In addition to some clothes, pictures of my mom, a few trinkets, and some of her jewelry, I would take a few of my favourite dolls, the two teddy bears my mother had made me—Freddy and a small stuffed tiger—and Snowball, a large white teddy bear that only months before, I had repeatedly hidden in a shopping cart until she acquiesced and agreed to buy it for me.

As the weeks went by, we eventually moved into a larger townhouse. Like the home I had once shared with my mother, the main floor consisted of a kitchen and living room, and upstairs held the bedrooms and bathroom. As we settled into our new life, I noticed the uncanny resemblances to my old life. It was as if I was transplanted into an alternate version of my previous reality. My aunt held a likeness to my mother that became more evident as I grew to miss my mother more and more; the identical townhouse smelled of the same spices and herbs my mother once filled in her own home; the house was sparkling clean, just as my mother would keep it; and we would carry our conversations in Arabic and French, just as before.

I accepted my cousin Ali's company easily. He was a few years younger than me, but his kind heart made for an easy companionship. We, along with Adam and Chokri, would sit in the living room and watch TV, basking in the joys of youth. However, the similarities of our old life and new, did not entirely work to our benefit. It was as though Uncle Tarek had shared a similar temperament as my father. Though he appeared to have a European elegance and exoticism to him, he was just as stern and strict, with a ferocious temper to match. As soon as he entered the house, a melancholy air settled around us, keeping us on our toes. It was as though we were in his castle and should not disturb him, even though we often did. At times, he would get very angry with Ali and slap him so hard that his handprint would last on my sweet cousin's face until the next day. Worse was when he would take off his belt, beating the bottoms of his son's feet with the metal buckle until it pained the boy to walk.

Nevertheless, the similarities between my new life and old were not endless. Aunt Fatima and Uncle Tarek were not as traditional as my parents had been—my aunt had worked. Of course, the burden of caring for three children that were not her own had likely applied an additional need to step out of Tunisian customs. During the school year, this contrast in lifestyle didn't pose much difficulty for me. She would go to work, and I to school.

It wasn't until the summer that this difference between her and my mother had impacted me at all. It was during the summer that I was introduced to daycare. A far cry from the motherly care I had been accustomed to, I now spent my days in the care of a stranger, surrounded by children I didn't know.

The first time I was told to nap I was unsure of what it had meant. I wasn't tired. I was used to spending full days in my mother's company, watching her clean, helping her cook, learning to read, and nestling behind her knees as she watched the television. Here, in this odd room of strangers, I was told to lay down and sleep despite my objections. I would lay silent, my body resting on a mat placed on the floor, surrounded by sleeping peers. It felt like a farce. It felt as though, for the first time, I had borne witness to what the world was really like. I was an imposter. With closed eyes, I played the foolish game I was told I had to. The loving, kind, and gentle place my mother had crafted for me was ripped away. I was no longer in the safety of the nook behind her knees, where dreams come true, where daydreams would transform into magical tales, where I would hear the soft voice of my mother as she told me stories.

The shock of the events I had witnessed did not slip away easily. Sent to see specialists, psychiatrists, social workers, policemen, and doctors—I was tired. I was torn between being told by my family to let go and being told by doctors to recount the events of that night. I had developed constant nightmares and panic attacks, which quickly became a focal point of discussion by professionals. They feared I would grow up mentally damaged, unwell, and socially inept. This was a form of attention that I had not known, and one I disliked. Hoping that the prodding of my mental well-being would come to a halt, I would pretend to be happy, but the juxtaposition of my smiling countenance with my internal sorrow and growing anger created a conflict within me. I was left even more confused. *What was happening?*

The world was changing too fast around me. Suddenly I was being punished for not doing chores that I was not aware I had. I was left in the care of a stranger for eight hours a day. I was asked endless questions about my mental state. I was looked at with sorrowful eyes and pitiful words. It seemed cruel. My aunt would laugh and smile at the hilarity of it all. The differences between her and my mother became more and more apparent. Using subtle phrases, Aunt Fatima would evoke guilt to get what she wanted. She would use her love as a form of currency in exchange for foot rubs or help cleaning the house. Though she looked like my mother, their resemblance ended there. Any physical similarities grew more discomforting as each day passed.

Within a year after my mother's death, my aunt and her family had decided to move back to Tunisia. Asking Adam if we would all like to go with them, he sternly objected. Shortly after I was born, my parents missed their own country and had moved us all back to Tunisia for a brief while. It was strict there. Unsympathetic teachers used force, hitting student's knuckles with rulers when incorrect answers were given, or when students proved disruptive to the class. Adam would come home in tears after school, his kind heart too fragile for such harsh treatment. At the prospect of returning to Tunisia, these unfavourable memories stuck in his mind. He could not be convinced to move back there. Aunt Fatima had turned her attention to me.

"Do you like living here, Iman?"

I stood still. "I like being with my brothers."

"I've always wanted to have a daughter, you know." Her voice softening, "Would you like to be my daughter, Iman?"

"I just want to be with my brothers."

Adam voiced an objection, angry at her suggestion to separate me from him and Chokri. He was devoted to keeping us together, and Chokri and I were grateful for his defense. It was decided we would not be moving to Tunisia, and we would remain here, together. Though the unsettling unknown of where we would be relocated was not lost on us. Regardless of where we would end up, I found solace in the fact that I would remain with my brothers.

Unfortunately, although Adam's adamant objections were rooted in the desire to keep us together, he was unaware that our refusal to go would in fact separate us. In the end, Aunt Fatima's decision to move back to Tunisia would leave the little family I had left scattered. Divorcing her abusive husband, our

Aunt Samira had already returned to her previous life as a flight attendant soon after my mother immigrated to Canada. We had no family left. And so, it was then the court had made the decision that from the confines of a prison cell, my well-being was now my father's responsibility. My brothers, much older than me, had attended the endless court proceedings aimed at not only determining who would claim their guardianship, but where it would leave me. Objecting to the flawed judicial system, they, along with their prospective guardians, fought to alter the court's ruling of my custody.

The car door opened. Daycare had just ended, and as usual, my Aunt Fatima was there to pick me up. I peered into the car, the sight of my suitcase and Snowball, my large white teddy bear, greeted me. It was a sign that it was time to move on, yet again. It was settled: I would venture on to another home.

I settled into the backseat.

"Where are my brothers?"

My question was met with silence. The car engine hummed. They would not be coming with me.

A familiar smell of odd spices and food hit me as I was greeted with warm sentiments, overwhelming hugs, and unwelcome kisses. The scent of an old suitcase filled with strange spices seemed to ooze from the walls. I wanted to hold my breath. Unlike my mother's home, which was filled with warm aromas of garlic and onions, this house possessed a spicy scent that violently clung to everything in sight. I had recognized the odour before recognizing her face. She was the liar, the woman who a mere six months ago told me that my mother would return. My eyes scanned the faces around me. There was the petite, olive-toned woman who smelled of food; a bigger, jovial, older man, who I assumed was her husband; their eldest daughter, who was beautiful, with dark, thick, straight black hair that cascaded down her shoulders; and two younger boys, one my age, and one older. They all smiled at me.

My father had chosen this family to raise me, to care for me—to take over the role of a mother he had taken away from me. These people were to be my new family. I looked closely at them as we all stood in the small foyer of their house, located directly between the kitchen and the living room.

We made our way upstairs. Only having three bedrooms, I would have to share a bed with their daughter. Quickly, as if eager to get me settled, they opened my bag. Instinctively, I felt protective of what little I had. The woman emptied out all my clothes, rummaging through my mother's pictures and jewelry, taking the small amount of money I had brought with me. She held my mother's photographs in her hands. "We'll hang them in the house," she said.

My days were spent playing with Hamed and Omar, the two younger boys. After school and at lunch, we would come home to watch the latest Michael Jackson and Madonna music videos on MTV. The sounds of pots and pans would echo from the kitchen as the mother prepared Tunisian feasts for dinner. Her daughter didn't mind me sleeping with her. In fact, I think she enjoyed the prospect of having a younger sister. Every night she would brush my hair and dress me, treating me like a little doll. We would slide under the covers, my teddy bears in tow, and I would close my eyes. I would be carried away into a dream world where my mother and I would be together. She would watch me play in the basement of our old home, silently smiling.

One night I was woken up with a shriek. Hands grabbed me and shook me with violence. Frightened and shocked, I burst into tears. My mind flashed to the night of my mother's death. The sheets were wet. The image of blood all around me clouded my mind. I was trapped in a nightmare.

"You peed on me!" I opened my eyes to see the daughter staring at me with disgust, "You peed the bed! You should be old enough to know better—you're seven years old!" The door burst open at the sound of the shrieks. The mother entered the room, staring at us, trying to understand what had happened. Quickly, they both begin to undress the bed, disrobe me, and clean me. "I can't sleep with this girl," the daughter announced as she changed her gown. "She's peeing on me! I have to go to school! I can't sleep with her!" Her mother nodded, the usual frown on her face, as she took my hand to lead me down the stairs.

I was positioned near the entranceway, on the border of the living room. She laid down a sleeping bag, turned off the lights, and left me to sleep. Tears began to form as I looked around. The eerie glimmer of the moonlight cast into the room through the windows, the steady green light from the oven clock glared at me, the streetlights introducing a sullen yellow glow. Why couldn't I sleep upstairs? Regardless of my incontinence, I could have easily slept on the floor of her daughter's room. Why was I being punished? Since my mother's death, the trauma of the incident had caused a series of panic attacks and a tendency to wet the bed. It wasn't my fault. I held on to my teddy bears. *Why is this happening to me?* I felt alone. And each night I would return to my designated sleeping area, the moonlight and shadows bringing me to tears until I would fall asleep, rescued by my mother in our world of dreams.

I felt like an outcast. These people were not my family. I hated them. I had grown up in a world of positivity and love, this world was anything but. The woman was bitter. There was rarely a smile on her face. She constantly complained. She and her daughter would share malicious tales of gossip involving their neighbours and friends. I missed my mother. I yearned for a chance to be in her presence again. To stand beside her as she cooked, to sleep in the crevice of her knees, to read, and practice my letters like we used to. But that chance was gone. Instead, I would sit in the living room and watch as the woman would try to teach her youngest son to read, just as my mother had. I sat beside him as he struggled. I read the words in my mind, not understanding why he didn't understand. "See Spot Run!" I hadn't meant to, but in my frustration, the words slipped out of me. His mother looked at me with disappointment.

"Iman," she said. "This is not for you. You know how to read. This is for him."

I looked at her apologetically. But it wasn't enough.

"Just go," she told me. "Go upstairs and play."

I rose from the couch, tears welling in my eyes. *I wish my mom was here,* I thought. *I wish I was reading books with my mom.*

The woman's husband was a stark contrast to her. He was pleasant and full of joy. The Imam of the mosque, he often had visitors over. One afternoon, sitting in the living room with a crowd of guests, one of his friends from the mosque waved me over. Tall and heavy set, he sweetly called to me. "Iman," he said, reaching into his pocket, "This is for you." He handed me a five-dollar bill, "You go buy some candy with that." I smiled with excitement. I had only ever received two dollars at most from my father when he gave me my allowance. Amid all the sadness and chaos in my life, I finally felt as though something good had happened to me. I clutched the bill proudly.

"What is in your hand, Iman?" I walked into the kitchen, the woman staring at the five-dollar bill in my hand. Snatching it from my grasp, she slapped me. "Where did you get this? You're a thief!" I told her the kind man had given it to me, but she continued to accuse me of thievery, telling me I was a liar. She stomped into the living room, "Did you give this to her?" The kind man looked at her, then at me. The woman waved the five-dollar bill in her hand, "I think she stole it from you."

"No, no! I gave it to her! It's hers," he laughed.

"Oh, I wasn't sure." She looked down at me, "It's a lot of money for a little kid."

She returned to the kitchen, my five dollars still in her hand. Although she said she would just hold on to it for me, I knew I would never see that five dollars again. It was gone forever, just like my mother's pictures, my mother's jewelry, and the small amount of money I had come with.

In light of my family's situation, Ben and his girlfriend, Elizabeth, were generous with their time, finances, and efforts. During our six-month stay at Aunt Fatima's, to ease the burden of taking on three children, Adam, Chokri, and I would be invited to spend the weekend with Ben and Elizabeth, indulging in restaurant meals, video rentals, and games. Since my aunt's departure to

Tunisia, they both remained in our lives. When possible, Ben would bring Adam and Chokri to visit me in my segregated world. Awkwardly, with their inevitable departure looming, we would sit in the living room while the Tunisian family left us to our own devices.

Adam and Chokri had successfully achieved the court's approval for one of my mother's friends to act as their legal guardian, and had both moved to a farm outside of the city while I was sent to live with this family.

"Why can't I go with you? What did I do?"

I questioned them in desperation. I loved my brothers so much. All I wanted to do was be with them; they were the only family I had left. *What had I done wrong? Why was I being punished?* They would respond to my cries of angst, telling me that Mildred and George, their new legal guardians, were fighting for me. Comforting me with details of the next court date and the progress of their appeal, Adam would glare at my appointed caregivers. His disapproval of my living situation was evident. He was angry.

"They're going to court all the time," Adam told me. "They're fighting for you to come live with us."

Though each time they would come to visit, my heart grew and a lightness came over me, it was bittersweet—eventually they would have to leave. Violent sobs would pour out of me as I broke down in the doorway, piercing the silence in the room. All I had wanted was to be with my family.

I realize now that the sight of my repeated pleas to be rescued by my brothers had only made it harder for this family to love me.

Chapter Three
Age 7: The Farmhouse

The sight of buildings was soon replaced by endless fields of corn and hay. This, in conjunction with the bumpy, unpaved gravel road, signaled that we were no longer in the city. Having spent the past seven years of my short life in Edmonton, leaving the city where I was born—where I grew up with my mother, and where my memories were founded—felt odd. As I inhaled the scent of cigarette smoke, I glanced at the passenger's seat, watching as the mess of a woman's blonde, feathered hair, tussled in the wind. In sync with the movements of the car, the short, unkempt black hair of the man driving beside her bobbed slightly. Though there was a knot of unsureness and anxiety in my stomach, a small smile crept onto my lips as I sat nestled between my brothers. I had been rescued.

I had known my time with the Tunisian family had come to an end when Adam came to collect my belongings. He had disliked the notion of me staying with them from the beginning, and though they thought their protests and claims of speaking on behalf of my father would calm Adam down, it simply made him angrier. Feverishly, he folded my clothing, gathered my stuffed animals, and prepared my small suitcase; leaving no time for me to reclaim the money I had come with, my mother's jewelry, or her photographs.

As we walked out the door with my small suitcase in tow, I looked back into the townhouse, happy to finally be with my family.

A burgundy red, 1987 Ford Tempo greeted us as we stepped out onto the pavement. Adam placed my luggage into the trunk as Chokri opened the side door, ushering me into the pop-can-littered back seat. An odd excitement overcame me. For six months—which felt like years to a small child—I had lived with the Tunisian family, feeling disconnected, scared, and alone. Finally, I had been rescued, and—for the first time—I felt safe.

The sound of an aluminum pop can crushing under the weight of my foot echoed as I shuffled into the car. The dark-haired man in the driver's seat turned to me, "What did you just do?"

My voice was meek and unsure.

"I crushed a can," I said. "There's a can here."

"*Oh my God!*" he exclaimed, "That was my favourite can! I can't believe you crushed it!"

Too fragile to understand sarcasm, I burst into tears.

"Iman, he's just joking! Memo, don't worry—he's just teasing you," Adam quickly reacted to my sobs.

"It's a joke, he doesn't care about the can!" Chokri piped in.

Their words failed to subdue my sobs. I hadn't meant to hurt anything, or upset anybody. I felt as though I had been a disappointment to everybody around me, anybody I encountered—especially the Tunisian family.

"Oh, no, no, no! I'm just kidding—I'm just joking!" The dark-haired man apologetically explained.

"I honestly don't care," he continued, "You can crush all of the cans!"

An awkward laugh came from the blonde woman beside him. It was evident that they had wanted the encounter to be pleasant and welcoming, but with a simple sarcastic remark, I was left shaking in tears. Slowly, my sobs subsided. I was exhausted, not only due to the emotional stress of stepping onto the pop can, but the journey itself, and finally rejoining my siblings had left me overwhelmed.

The car ride was a long one. Lasting forty-five minutes, the longer we drove, the more I grew anxious and excited. Desperately, I hoped that this move would be the last, and my curiosity toward this new home intensified. I had longed to be reunited with my brothers for what felt like eons, and though the sensation was overwhelming, an underlying skepticism nagged within me. *Where are we going? Am I going to like it?* Not knowing my new guardians, the unknown element to my new life left me guarded. Simply, I didn't want to get my hopes up. It had been a year since my mother had passed, and every moment had been dreary and hopeless.

Please, I silently whispered. *Let this be it.*

The aggressive scent of manure hit my nostrils. Looking at my surroundings, I stepped out of the car as the door opened.

"Why is it so stinky?" My nose wrinkled.

"It's manure," Adam said, pointing to the farm in the distance. "It's a dairy farm."

I looked around in awe. A lifetime ago I had been to a farm with my mother—washing sheared sheep wool and basking in the glow of the sun— but this was unlike anything I had ever seen before. The beautiful green grass and open fields I had previously associated with farm life were now shifted to a new reality of dirt, mud, and the scent of manure. This would be my new home.

Though the farm was not owned by my new guardians, they had rented an old farmhouse owned by the dairy farmer who lived nearby in a house on this same land. Evidenced by the chipped paint bordering the windows, the unwashed glass panes, and the unkempt exterior, they had rented the house for a decent price. Though it was a lofty 2,000 square feet, the farmhouse had the appearance of a shack—it looked broken-down and decayed.

As we made our way into the house, Adam and Chokri, my guides to this new home, ushered me in through the porch, toward the kitchen on the main floor. As we walked by a small bathroom, I peered in, glancing at the rust-stained porcelain sink and bathtub, quickly averting my eyes. We made a left, walking into the large kitchen. Scanning the piles of ashtrays, the yellow, sun-stained linoleum tiles, the chipped counters, and the rust laden sink, my eyes landed on the small dining table, littered with dishes, that sat in the middle of the room. Our brief tour continued, and my brothers led me to the living room, where unmatched couches coated in animal hair, piles of blankets, and a television stood atop the dirty, brown carpet.

The blonde-haired woman, Mildred, had known my mother before she had passed. Neighbours at one point in time, Mildred and my mother would indulge in afternoon teas, sharing stories of their past and present lives. Mildred had told me that prior to her death, my mother had confided in her, vocalizing her fears and suspicions that my father would take her life. Aghast at the notion, Mildred prodded my mother to leave, inviting her to take us with her and join Mildred in this same farmhouse. Nevertheless, my mother shrugged off Mildred's offer.

My mother and Mildred shared no physical similarities. My mother could only be described as a glowing goddess, radiating a warm light through her eyes with a playfully joyous smile on her lips. Mildred, on the other hand, was frail. Large, tinted glasses, rested upon the sharp bridge of her nose and sullen, sunken-in cheeks, masking the thin, wrinkled skin that surrounded her eyes; tousled, short, dirty-blonde locks framed her small, pale face, and two obtrusive buck teeth involuntarily protruded from her thin lips as though her mouth were impossible for her to close. A chin barely formed at the tip of her thin face.

She insisted that I call her "Mum" and she stripped me of my last name. Mildred had this fear that my father would somehow find me.

Her children looked nothing like her. Previously, Mildred and been married to an abusive Fijian man. His tanned complexion, though diluted, had passed down to their offspring, as well as some his of darker, exotic attributes. Ron and Melanie, their two children, were the same ages as my brothers, making their friendship inevitable. Ron, the older of the two, was tall and athletic, with styled, dirty-blonde hair, and brown eyes. Being the same age, Ron and Adam fostered a close relationship based upon a mutual favour toward girls, athletics, and the simplicity of being teenage boys. Melanie, Ron's younger sister, was the same age as Chokri. She had darker, Fijian attributes, such as her long, dark brown hair, and her brown eyes—though they were masked by her large, thick-lensed, glasses—and she was spotted with endless freckles that created the illusion of a tanned complexion. Like her mother, Melanie stood a mere 5'1".

Leaving her abusive husband, Mildred had remarried long ago to a New Brunswick-born French Canadian. George, her second husband, was a boisterous and heavy set man, with messy black hair and a matching moustache. As evidence of his lifestyle, a large potbelly hung from his gut. Our encounter in the car had left me wary of this new character—his booming, invasive presence contrasted too strongly against my timid, fragile nature.

Exhausted from my emotional and eventful afternoon, I was taken upstairs to Melanie's room, which would now partially serve as mine. My actual quarters were found across the hall, in a small room that acted as a closet. A small window brought in light and a child-size dresser furnished the small space that had barely enough room for a small blanket to be placed on the floor. The implied arrangement was that I was to have my private makeshift room to store my belongings, and share a bed with Melanie. As with the Tunisian family, yet again, I was to share a room. Though, unlike my earlier experience, Melanie showed no signs of being inconvenienced—rather, she welcomed the new arrangement.

Anxiety quickly bubbled over as I thought about my stay with the Tunisian family. This would be my new home, and I didn't want to make the same mistakes I had previously made. Sharing a bed with Melanie opened myself up to the same horrors of wetting the bed, being sent to sleep on the floor, and being isolated yet again. Aware of my concern, Melanie was quick to dissolve my angst and comforted me to sleep. I tossed and turned as knots filled my stomach. Unsurprisingly, my endless worry led to my biggest fear—I had wet the bed. A gentle nudge stirred me.

"Iman, wake up. You peed the bed."

Processing the meaning behind Melanie's soft voice, I looked around confused until I felt the wetness all around me. I burst into tears.

"It's okay! It's not a big deal," Melanie cooed. "We just need to change the sheets, throw down some towels, and get changed."

With gentleness and care, she helped me undress, removing the soiled sheets and evidence of my embarrassment. I looked at her, relieved by not only her kindness, but her open heart. Not showing any signs of my burden on her, from openly sharing her bed, to not erupting in anger at waking up in a puddle of my shame—Melanie had shown me a kindness I had not felt in a long time.

I slowly adjusted to my new home. During the first few weeks, I was a mess of constant tears. "She's your sister now," Mildred would say as she passed me off to Melanie, instructing her to comfort me through my tears. My sullen mood and erratic emotional sobs had made Mildred, and everyone for that matter, uncomfortable. I had quickly become aware of that. I was an elephant in the room, forcing the mood in the house to maintain a constant undertone of awkwardness. I was fragile, confused, and emotional. Somewhat aware of the difficulty of this new transition, during the first week, Mildred and George provided us with meals of soda and pizza, while we watched the animated movies I had chosen. Sitting in the living room, I silently snacked on chips, popcorn, and ice cream.

My late arrival to the farmhouse, and my young age, had made it difficult for me to find companionship among my siblings, old and new. Adam who was sixteen, Ron fifteen, and Chokri and Melanie, both twelve, had more in common with each other than I—a seven-year-old. I had wanted their attention, yet my youth had prevented me from fostering genuine companionship with any of them. With no one to play with, I spent my days with the family pets—Blondie, a slender, medium-sized, ginger and white dog, and Angel, the dark grey, long haired cat—venturing out to the farm, eager to explore the livestock, feral kittens, and rodents that surrounded the acreage.

Finding ways to entertain myself, my days were often spent out on the farm, watching the animals, and playing in the grass. I had loved the animals— collecting frogs from the swamp, finding mice to play with, and searching for the small kittens as they would jump and play—they had become my source of companionship. This outside farm world felt like an entirely different planet to me. It was full of adventure, friends, and kindness. I would come home from a day in the fields, and recount tales of kittens, frogs, and mice.

"You know, kittens *love* baths," George looked at me with genuine wide eyes as Mildred sat next to him on the living room couch. I thought back to our conversation weeks before. Eager to befriend the small kittens, I told the farmer of my desire to feed them. Kindly, he offered me a large, silver bucket of fresh milk. Waddling off, pail in hand, my plan was to make the dreams of these kittens come true. Excitedly, I grabbed each tiny feline, and dunked them into the bucket. Loud meows and screeches erupted from the tin pail as I put in kitten after kitten. They had not liked being wet. I questioned George, unsure of the honesty in his proclamation, "Do kittens really like baths?"

Managing to convince me, I left for the bathroom and prepared a bath. Returning to the outdoors, I scoured the farm for kittens, collecting them into my arms, and excitedly returning to the farmhouse. Standing above the bathtub, in one fluid motion, I tossed the kittens into the tub. In an instant uproar, the kittens leaped before hitting the water, gouging their claws into my arms, neck, and face. I screamed, rushing into the living area. Adam and Chokri looked at me.

"What happened? What's wrong?" they asked.

Through my sobs, I explained to them that under George's instruction, I had drawn a bath for the kittens.

"Memo," Adam said to me, "You can't do that—cats don't like water."

Looking down at the blood and deep claw marks that had penetrated my skin, I frowned to myself. *George was a liar.*

The lifestyle I had been accustomed to with my mother was quickly dwindling. Each day that passed and each new home I was sent to stay in, brought me farther away from what I had known. Slowly my life, and my identity, was becoming more and more foreign.

Life at both Aunt Fatima's and with the Tunisian family, though a far cry from the safe life I had with my mother, carried strong similarities. We spoke

Arabic, dined on Tunisian fare, and abided by the same religious rules. In this household, however, I was thrown into a Canadian lifestyle that I had not known existed—dishes were left uncared for in the sink; overfilled ashtrays were found on every countertop; the household vernacular contained more curse words than anything; the spicy, fragrant Tunisian dishes of stewed lamb, chicken, and beef were replaced with colourless casseroles, canned vegetables, and fast food.

I found myself in a state of shock.

Adam and Chokri, pubescent boys with a love of greasy foods, did not possess the same hesitation as I did when it came to mealtime at Mildred and George's. As we sat around the dining table in the kitchen, I would sit silent, pushing the mushy, colourless food around my plate.

"What is this?"

From a blend of peas, ground beef, soggy macaroni, and carrots, I pushed a canned mushroom toward the outer edges of my plate.

"It's a mushroom."

I had never had a mushroom before, let alone seen one. In my sheltered, small life, my culinary expertise was limited to the cuisine of my culture. Tunisian fare consisted of stews, sauces, pastas, and Mediterranean ingredients—a mushroom was a *very* foreign concept.

"Try it," Mildred looked at me, mild annoyance evident on her face. "You'll like it."

Reluctantly, I slowly brought the slimy fungus to my mouth, spitting it out immediately in disgust. Though I was aware they were tired of my endless questions and my constant reluctance to exude any form of enthusiasm toward their meals, I could not hide my disgust. A tension instantly fell over the room.

"You're really fucking spoiled," Mildred's voice cut into the air.

I shrunk in my seat. Her small frame and tiny face did not match her strong, piercing temperament. I soon learned after moving into the farmhouse that Mildred was one to be tiptoed around.

Fueled by anger, her nasally voice continued, "You're going to eat that mushroom, or you're not leaving the table."

Silent, yet again, I sat at the table. I watched as everyone around me ate forkful, after forkful of this foreign concoction. Soon, my siblings had all finished and went about their evening, leaving me in the darkened kitchen. Mildred, George, and my plate of mushrooms, remained. As time ticked by, I grew stronger in my stance. *I would not eat this mushroom.* My resolve would not be shaken. Outlasting my guardians, they soon left to join my siblings. The kitchen dimmed as the sun went down, darkness surrounding me. It had gotten late.

"Get your ass to bed." Again, Mildred's voice pierced the air.

She had returned, ferocious with anger. To her it appeared that I was snobby, pretentious, and under the assumption that I was simply too good to succumb to their lifestyle. But, as a seven-year-old, my reluctance to consume the same food as the rest of my new family was not rooted in any holier-than-thou sentiments. Rather, for the entire seven years of my life, I had known a better lifestyle, *I had known a better situation,* and I did not know what this new life was. In my life with my mother, my aunt, and the Tunisian family, I had been raised in clean, Arabic households. The foods I had eaten were of the same flavours and contained no pork. In this new life, I was served plates of sinful pink meat that I was told mere weeks ago would lead me into an afterlife of endless torment. As greasy dishes of bacon and ham would greet me at mealtime, I would think back to my mother's lessons of the consequences of eating this immoral meat. I didn't want to go to hell. I wanted to be reunited with my mother in heaven. I wanted to see her again. And at each meal, as I looked down at the pork chops, ham, or bacon, I feared that each bite would keep us apart forever.

Nevertheless, my refusal to eat was not met with acceptance. Rather, I was left with no other options and was sent to bed with an empty, gnawing feeling in my stomach. I was hungry. My body began to deteriorate, consuming the little fat I had on my bones for sustenance. Quickly, I became thin, weak, and easily exhausted.

As a household tradition, we were treated with pizza, chips, soda, and popcorn on Friday evenings. Surrounded by my siblings, we would watch movies, and I would indulge in cheese-covered dough, savouring the salty crispness of each potato chip, as if I was preparing for hibernation. Unfortunately, the intent of these junk-food filled evenings was not to treat us, but to keep us children entertained and out of the way. Soon after joining my new family, I had realized that on Friday evenings, our farmhouse transformed into something akin to what I would now consider a fraternity. At the sound of the doorbell, groups of family and friends would enter our household with bottles of hard liquor and cans of beer. Soon, the house was filled with thirty drunken adults—the smog of cigarette smoke clouding the air—bellowing throughout our four-bedroom home. Mildred would sit in the kitchen, cigarette in mouth, with Lamb's Navy dark rum and Coke in her glass. George, sitting beside her, would roll a joint, gleefully smoking, sharing with his peers.

Before these evenings, I had never seen a drunken stupor, let alone drugs. Though my father had drunk wine heavily, this was a large step from his mild drunkenness. In this household, as the party progressed, laughter quickly disintegrated into shouts and cries. As if by clockwork, unable to control their emotions, Mildred would burst out into tears, George would find himself in a fight, thunderous yells would boom from the kitchen, and various things would be thrown at walls or at people. But as the clock ticked on, the rambunctious crowd would settle, resuming their night of loud laughter and giggles.

Frightened by the unruly crowd of strangers, I would cower, fleeing to Melanie's room to play with my dolls, escape into words from a book, or write in my journal. As I drifted away from our festive guests, finding peace in my solitude, hours would go by before the party would end. And though no one ever thought to look for me, I would be lost—drifting off into a world of dreams, where I would be reunited with my mother.

The eerie sound of a silent house welcomed me every Saturday morning. Rising early, I would tiptoe down the stairs, ready to indulge in the childhood pastime of cereal and cartoons. Entering the kitchen, used glasses, ashtrays overfilled with cigarette butts, and remnants of food, littered every surface. The scent of stale cigarettes, alcohol, and weed cloaking everything around me, I would search for clean cutlery and a bowl. Stirs from the kitchen table would leave me frozen mid-step. As with most Saturday mornings, George would sit amid the littered table, head in hands, dead asleep. Determined not to wake him, I would quietly find my necessary dishes, wash them in the filled sink, and prepare my morning feast.

Bodies were strewn around the living room. Indulging in an Epicurean evening of drugs and alcohol, strangers often found refuge throughout the house—the couches being the most coveted spot. I knew not to awaken our guests. Creeping in, ever so silently, I would find my place a foot from the television—ensuring the volume was exceptionally low—silently laughing at the comical animations that were broadcast from the screen. Occasionally, our dog Blondie would join me, eating the fragments of pizza that remained on the boxes that covered the living room floor.

The mornings seemed endless. After cartoons were watched, and my cereal had been eaten, I would wander the farm, paying visits to my animal friends, returning only to snack on crackers and cheese or, if luck would have it, a remaining slice of pizza.

Finally, midday would arrive and, as if rising from the dead, pale-faced cadavers stirred to life. After learning from previous mistakes of attempting to awaken a sibling to help me reach a bowl for cereal—Melanie would shout and scream, Chokri would repeatedly punch the air, and once, by accident, Adam had managed to punch me in the face. I was eager to see *people*. I had often enjoyed an entire day before anyone had woken up. Eventually, Mildred and George would finally appear, green-faced and agitated. A Saturday afternoon ritual, Mildred would sit at the kitchen table—chain-smoking cigarettes and drinking coffee until she regained strength—while George locked himself in the bathroom for hours, the smell of marijuana wafting through the seams of the door.

My eighth birthday happened within the second month of my move to the farmhouse. Though it would be my second birthday without my mother, my seventh birthday happened a mere two months after her death and warranted no celebrations of grandeur. Aware my birthday was near; Mildred had told me I would be celebrating my turning-of-age with a party at McDonald's. Though I lacked friends to invite, the guest list was composed of the children of Mildred's friends, my siblings, Ben, and Elizabeth. For the first time since my mother was taken away from me, I felt special. I felt as though people finally saw *me*. Surrounded by a group of people sharing in a day dedicated to celebrating my existence made me feel as though I finally mattered. After feeling lost in a sea of sadness and insignificance, for the first time, the attention that was focused toward me was not clouded in negativity, pity, and concern, but exuded *joy*.

I missed my mother. I missed her attention, her care, her love, *her glow*. I missed the connection to another human being. I missed being valued and loved. In the year that had passed since her death, I had been thrown from home to home, left in the care of strangers, to sleep in the entranceway, or to be completely ignored. I had missed what it felt like to feel special.

My birthday always reminded me that summer was nearly done and that the school year would begin soon. I was starting fresh and was both terrified and excited to start third grade.

"Hey, Iman."

Mildred looked up at me from the kitchen table.

School had eventually started and a life of routine had settled. As usual, I woke up, prepared myself for my day at school, and walked into the kitchen.

"I don't feel very well today," her nasally voice carried a somber, sad tone. "Do you think you can make your own lunch?"

Aside from crackers and cheese, and bowls of cereal, I had never made anything for myself. My mother, Aunt Fatima, and the Tunisian woman had prepared all my meals. Mildred's request was one I could not fulfil.

"I don't know how," I timidly replied. "I've never done it before."

Though the expected reply from Mildred should be one of understanding, or even perhaps guidance, it was neither. Erupting in anger, her voice became a thunderous, shrill screech.

"What a baby you are—you don't know how to make your own goddamn lunch?!" Her voice grew louder as I cowered, shocked at her erratic response.

She rose, walking toward the cutlery drawer, slamming it shut with violent anger.

"You're a spoiled little baby—I can't believe you don't know how to do anything yourself! I'm not your fucking maid! *Your mom's dead now*, so you're going to have to get over being spoiled and learn how to take care of yourself."

Her voice echoed throughout the house.

"This isn't a goddamn hotel."

Tears sprung from my eyes. Unaware of what I had done wrong, or what I did to warrant such a terrible response, I froze—petrified.

"What the hell are you crying about?!" Mildred screeched at the sight of my tears, lunging at me.

Grabbing my arm, with ferocious aggression, her stiff palm slammed into my back.

"You wanna cry? I'll give you something to cry about!"

Without hesitation or aim, her hardened palm continually pounded against my entire body. My sobs grow louder. Consumed by shock and fear, I quickly lost control of my bladder. Throwing me to the ground, Mildred angrily stomped toward the counters, yelling profane insults, and continued to slam drawers.

"What are you guys doing?! What's happening?!" Hurriedly entering the kitchen, Melanie looked down to see my shrunken body, shaking with sobs.

"She's a spoiled little bitch," Mildred glared at me as Melanie walked toward me. "She can't even make her own lunch."

Melanie's freckled arms reached toward me, picking up my lifeless body. Bringing me upstairs, I continued to cry as she washed my tear-stained face and changed my soiled clothing. "It's okay," her soft voice cooed. We walked down the stairs, taking the lunch Mildred begrudgingly prepared for me on the table, and exited the house.

I had not fully believed nor accepted that my mother was gone. Though no one bothered to explain death to me, my belief in her was rooted in love.

During my first Mother's Day at the farmhouse, obligated to give Mildred a Mother's Day card, I had also made one for my mother. Hoping that she would receive it, or read it, I told her I missed her, that I loved her, and that I wished she were with me.

I wish you would come back, I wrote. *If you want to come back, I won't tell anyone. I hope I didn't do anything wrong. Even if you just come back and take this card, then I'll know that you're okay. But—if you don't want to see me, that's okay too.*

My negotiations with her were genuine.

"I'm just going to leave the room, Mommy," I said aloud.

Leaving the card in a box, I placed it delicately on the floor in the middle of the room. Wandering out into the farm, spending time with my farm animal friends, I was anxious to return to my room filled with hope that she had taken the card. After I was satisfied with my length of absence, I came rushing back into the house. Opening the door slowly, my eyes immediately landed on untouched the box. The card had remained. My heart sank. *Okay,* I thought to myself. *Maybe she's just somewhere else—maybe there's another place, and that's where she is. So, she can still see and hear me, but maybe I just can't see and hear her.*

Though she had left my card untouched, I continued to talk to her—aloud, or through writing her letters and cards—believing that she was receiving my messages. Regardless of whether or not she could respond, it was my devotion to her. *I will keep loving you,* I promised. *I will keep showing you how I love you, talking to you, and keeping you in my heart and in my life—even if you can't get back to me.*

Talking to my mother gave me strength. Sharing my day, my stories, and my life with her, became second nature. From the moment I was born, she had always motivated me, believed in me, and shined her light so bright on me. Her positivity radiated through her, and even after she had passed, it lingered on, resonating deep within me.

During the first Christmas I spent with Mildred and George, I thought back to spending afternoons in the kitchen with my mother; singing and dancing with her as the sun came in through the windows, the fragrant scent of spices filling the room. I had missed singing, laughing, and having fun in the company of another. After endless pleading, on Christmas morning, I unwrapped my present to find the only gift I truly wanted: a microphone. Adjusting the yellow stand that held the microphone in place, I said hello into the mouthpiece, my voice multiplied in decibels—*it worked!* Too shy to sing in front of my family, we sat around the tree as Adam and Ron rushed at the chance to entertain me. Playing music, microphone standing in front of them, Ron strummed the invisible chords to his air guitar, while Adam silently drummed in sync to the beat.

"Hello, everyone! I'm Iman!" Introducing myself to the invisible crowd, I would pause for cheers, smile and wave, then explain to the audience that I was famous and successful. Cheers would erupt louder, and my smile grew.

As usual, I would spend my days after school alone. With the farmhouse to myself, I would creep into the pantry room that held the deep freeze. Climbing up to stand atop it, I placed my microphone on the makeshift stage.

"I just want everyone to know that life is going to be okay," I continued to my audience.

"Even if you're sad, things are going to start getting better. And if you just stay happy and positive, and just keep thinking great things, and remembering good things about yourself, and that you're nice, then life won't seem so bad! You must be a friendly person, and do what you're told! You have to be a good listener, always behave, and, *always remember that you're beautiful.*"

The list of the attributes that I would say to my invisible audience as necessary to successfully get through life were, in reality, a list of things my mother would always tell me. Though sometimes these motivational talks were given to stuffed animals, or family pets, the true audience was myself. At times, without the microphone in hand, I would stare into the mirror, repeating motivational speeches of the same message. Regardless of Mildred's pokes and prods, suggesting that my endless gazes in the mirror were a symptom of vanity, I had known the real reason. I would look into the reflective glass, and I'd look for my mother. Her brown, almond eyes, her soft, olive skin—I looked into the glass, trying to find glimpses of her in myself. I had wanted her positivity back; I had wanted her love back. Tired of being alone, being surrounded by intoxicated adults, and feeling like a burden, I used her words of light and love to bring me comfort.

During my daily baths, I would be transported back to a happier time, when my mother would bathe with me. Speaking to myself through my crowd of dolls, I would continue to motivate and spread cheer, announcing the same beautiful things my mother would often say to me as she washed my hair, bathed me, and dressed me.

These speeches became my pastime. Aside from wandering out into the fields of the farm, playing with the feral kittens and cows, I spent my days talking to myself, to my mother, and to my silent audience. I fell in love with Oprah, absorbing her kind, positive words, and began to mimic her stories and monologues on my hidden stage in the pantry. Through the fuzzy screen of our antennae'd television, I would stare, listening to Oprah's powerful sentiments. *I want to give other people the same feeling she gives me,* I thought to myself. Her words, filled with powerful affirmations, had reminded me of my mother's messages. Every time I listened to Oprah through the television screen, or spoke to Mommy through the reflection of a mirror, I would feel uplifted, strong, and happy—escaping from the true realities of my situation—just for a moment.

Chapter Four

Age 9: Circle of Trees

Unsure as to the reason why, a little over a year after beginning my new life at the farmhouse, we packed our belongings and settled into a new home. The move was abrupt. With only a few months until the school year would end, my siblings and I—with no official confirmation—believed the ill-timed relocation was because of an eviction. I lived the life of a nomad. In the two years that my mother had passed, this would be the fourth time I had gathered what little I owned into my small suitcase, leaving all traces of my existence behind, vanishing like a ghost. Nevertheless, though I would miss my world of cows, kittens, and adventure, I felt no attachment to the dirty, unkempt farmhouse.

Our new home was beautiful. We drove up a long private driveway atop a hill that encompassed several acres, and there stood a tremendous house of wooden planks and white trimmed windows, surrounded by trees and greenery. As we unloaded our boxes from the car, entering the large, four-level-split home, I walked into the sitting area that extended from the entranceway landing. I looked around, grateful for the clean, spacious interior. Unlike our previous home, this house had been maintained—a fresh-smelling scent wafted throughout the empty halls, and clear water ran from the faucets. Wandering throughout the empty house, I entered the basement where a patio door extended the television and living area to the outdoors, opening into the oversized front yard. The backyard was huge and had an open grassy area where we would soon build a large garden, and an overwhelming bouquet of various pine, spruce, and fir trees littered the surrounding acreage. Instantly, I knew this home would be better than the last—the view of the seemingly endless forest, the unsullied interior, and the abundant space left us all in awe. I suppose the intent of our new home, aside from our suspicions of eviction, was to begin a new chapter for our new family. With ample room, we could finally establish ourselves as a family of seven, as opposed to our previous lifestyle of crowding into a home that was meant for the average family of four.

Ron and Adam quickly claimed the large bonus room on the lower level as their private quarters, not caring about the washer and dryer that occupied a small portion of the space. Though there was an additional bedroom on the same level, it was used as storage, and Chokri was given a room on the top floor, where Mildred and George occupied the master bedroom. Melanie and I, once again shared a room—though this time, Ben had gifted us with bunk beds, allowing us a small amount of privacy in our confined, cohabited space.

Within the first few weeks of settling in, we had all begun to feel as though we were a family. We were proud of our new home and eager to treat this new chapter in our lives as a blank slate; sitting around the same kitchen table in our new dining room, we would share meals together—though I still found the cuisine intolerable and refused to eat—and Saturday evenings we would all lounge in the basement living room, watching movies and eating pizza as a family. It was a new beginning, and things, for a moment, seemed as though they were finally going to be okay.

Unfortunately, starting a new school just months before summer vacation was not as easy of a transition as moving to the house on the hill. Like the school we had just left, I would yet again be the *new kid*—a role I loathed vehemently. In the crowded halls of Caucasian country kids, I was shy, nervous, easily overwhelmed and, aside from my brothers, the singular ethnic minority within the entire school. Suffice to say, I was a clear target for bullies. Skinny, frail, and erupting in cold sores, prospective friendships were scarce. It seemed as though, yet again, I would be alone. Even after school, after being dropped off by the school bus, I would enter an empty home.

Ron and Adam, approaching the legal age of eighteen, would be off in their own world of adulthood; Chokri would be at a friend's house; and Melanie, though occasionally spending late-afternoons at home with me, would often be off, frittering away her free time in the company of her friends or with her new boyfriend. Just as at the farmhouse, I spent my time speaking to my mother in the mirror, performing speeches to invisible audiences, and wandering throughout the acreage.

It was during my explorative solitary walks that I stumbled upon a magnificent, magical clearing of trees. Venturing out into the forest one afternoon—with a knapsack of crackers and peanut butter sandwiches, and my entourage of teddy bears and our dog, Blondie—the endless horizon of pine trees opened into a vacant circular space. In awe of the peaceful, mystical glade, I set my teddy bears down, laid out my knapsack, and positioned myself in the centre, laying down to look up at the blue sky patterned with scattered tufts of white clouds. The trees would waver at the breeze of the wind, leaving unsynchronized rustles throughout the forest. I had found my sanctuary—a place to be at peace.

I detested the indoors. I had found no comfort or grace being confined within the white walls of our home. Though things had seemed as if they were better, our lives unfolded into the regular state of things. It became apparent that the house, though beautiful and spacious, had its own distinct flaws. Alas, the hill our house stood upon was a breeding ground for ants. There was an infestation. It was impossible to leave a glass of juice on the counter to quickly run to the restroom, without returning to find a swarm of insects surrounding both the outside and inside of the glass. Our frugal fumigation attempts and earnest efforts to fill up any cracks and holes that may have acted as doorways for these unwanted pests produced no successful results. Quickly, it became frustrating and unbearable. The ants, however, were not the only challenge our new home brought upon us. The base of the hill also housed a railway track. Every passing train filled our house with obnoxiously loud screeches and echoes, and the weight of the train against the tracks would force our house to shake. During the first weeks in our new home, I would jolt awake in a panic of anxiety and shock at the rattling of the house, feeling as though I was being shaken into consciousness. A symptom of my

Post-Traumatic Stress Disorder (PTSD), my mind would instinctively rush to the night of my mother's death until I became aware of my surroundings, calming down once I realized it was just the train.

Although the attempts to establish a familial foundation in our new home were genuine, they quickly faltered. Weekend evenings still saw Mildred pouring herself a generous glass of Lamb's Navy Rum and Coke, George indulging in a few too many beers, and a troupe of intoxicated strangers bursting out into loud laughter in between pulls from their cheap cigarettes. Though old habits die hard, Mildred and George had managed to develop a new routine. Now Friday evenings, after work, a bar acted as the new setting in which they fulfilled their need to bask in the glory of intoxication. Ignorant to the needs of their children, they would insist Melanie play chef for the evening. After she had looked endlessly through empty cupboards, finding only the occasional package of spaghetti noodles or a box of off-brand Kraft Dinner, I would be presented with what could only be described as macaroni soup; Melanie had not drained the water from the macaroni before adding the powdered cheese. Though given very few options and doing the best with what she had, it was evident that Melanie not only did not know how to cook, but found no interest in trying. Naturally, I refused to eat, falling asleep with a familiar deep knot in my stomach. Hunger was a sensation that I had grown accustomed to.

Depending on the evening, I would either be fast asleep or awake to hear the drunken attempts to open the front door that followed the loud thuds of car doors closing. Mildred and George would stumble into the house, inebriated, and without a shred of responsibility. Not only had they regularly driven while intoxicated, Mildred and George had also taken separate cars to and from the bar. It was during the return of one of Mildred and George's Friday evening trips to the bar that Mildred had been pulled over, resulting in a DUI and her license being revoked for twelve months.

Immediately a sullen, morose mood swept over the entire house. Living in the country without the ability to drive had left Mildred completely dependent on others. With no public transportation, she had no choice but to be driven around by George, or, if she was lucky, a neighbouring friend. In light of this dramatic lifestyle change, Mildred's temperament became more erratic as her emotional state was quickly dwindling. Similarly, George's disappointment in his new role as a chauffeur was not lost on any of us.

With Mildred's one mistake, our excitement and enthusiasm for our new lives unraveled into a mess of uneasiness, tension, and melancholy. However, the dizzying emotional mood swings of our household had causes beyond Mildred's DUI. Aside from suffering from alcoholism, Mildred and George were not of sound mental health, and victim to medically diagnosed depression. In Mildred's case, her erratic moods stemmed from not only alcoholism and depression, but Hormone Replacement Therapy. After undergoing a hysterectomy at the age of 23, in combination with her antidepressants, Mildred was prescribed a cocktail of estrogen and testosterone to replace the hormones her body could no longer produce. Understandably, receiving a DUI, limiting her mobility, and stripping her from her essential independence, did not aid her mental health.

Both Mildred and George, on their own respective concoctions of antidepressants, alcohol, hormones, and marijuana, were not of sound mind. Though they still partook in their extravagant Friday evenings at the bar and weekly parties in our home, they spent most of their time sullenly creeping around the house. George, as usual, would lock himself in his bedroom or in the bathroom as the scent of marijuana wafted through closed doors. Mildred, if she had not chosen to go to work that day, feigning she could not find a ride, would follow suit—locking herself in the bedroom all day, obsessively knitting, or tending to the large garden in the backyard. Our guardians became increasingly unreliable and unaware of their duties.

One day not long after Mildred had been stripped of her license, the school bus had dropped us off, and Chokri, Mel, and I walked up the slight incline of the hill, toward the house. Opening the front door, we shuffled in, removing our coats and boots. Hungry, I headed into the kitchen. Friday was drawing near, which meant food in the house would be running low. I opened the fridge door and stared into the white abyss. Aside from the half-eaten jar of ranch chip dip, empty two-litre bottle of stale cola, old bread, and a stick of butter, it was empty. I closed the doors, only to open them a few seconds later, as if food would magically appear. It didn't.

By now it had become accepted knowledge among my siblings that food was no longer a common commodity. No longer were we sharing as many meals at dinner time. Rather, we would all be left to fend for ourselves. Adam and Ron, old enough to work part-time, were not subject to the same culinary hardships as Chokri, Melanie, and me. Like Mildred and George, they would eat out. The rest of us, on the other hand, were left to dine on the remnants found in the empty kitchen.

Grabbing the loaf of bread and dip, I placed my findings on the counter to open the bag and inspect two of the four slices of bread that remained. Pinching a small portion of one of the slices that had turned green, I removed the mold and threw it to the side. Opening the jar of chip dip, I grabbed a knife.

"Is the phone broken?" Chokri held the receiver in his hand, his head turned to look at me. Grabbing the phone, Melanie held it to her ear—there was no dial tone.

"I think so," she replied.

Slathering a thin layer of dip onto my slice of bread, I folded my sandwich, carrying it in my hand to avoid returning to a pile of ants. Reaching for the receiver, I also held it against my ear. Returning it to Chokri, I shrugged.

"Well," Chokri hung the receiver back onto the base, "We should call someone to fix this."

Bursting into laughter at Chokri's joke, I walked to the kitchen table, finishing my sandwich. Though unspoken, we all knew that we would not be able to discuss the phone or the lack of food with the adults of our household. An innocent question would be met with the same rage as an accusatory confrontation. Leaving our questions about the phone and our concerns about food unheard, we accepted the situation at hand and carried on with our afternoons.

Though our household was in some sort of unspoken financial crisis, Mildred and George found no reason to hold back on their party-filled weekends. A stark contrast to the empty fridge, the electricity being periodically shut off, or the unpaid house phone, our house would suddenly overflow with snacks, alcohol, and cigarettes. As with the farmhouse, the dramatic, emotional cycle of the evening had become customary: laughter would turn into screams, a dish would break, and tears would pour from Mildred's eyes, coming full circle, back to an evening of debauchery.

"Iman," Mildred's voice bellowed through the halls, into the small sanctuary of the basement. My siblings had all gone out for the evening, leaving me alone in the house of drunken horrors.

"C'mere and talk to us," she yelled.

"Why?"

"Because I bloody well said so, that's why!" She had lost her patience. "Now get 'yur ass over here!"

My whole body tensed up, my stomach turning into knots as I slowly crawled up the stairs. Though I was looking down at the ground, I could feel everyone's eyes piercing into me.

"Yes?" I looked at Mildred.

"C'mere and sit on my lap," George's dirty hand patted his thigh, a grin formed on his mouth, exposing the dried, white saliva that had gathered on the corners of his lips.

Though his request was not uncommon, regardless of how many times he insisted I sit on his lap, it left me unsettled. Even our nightly goodnight hug and kiss, which Mildred insisted I give to each of them, would leave me nauseous. Nevertheless, avoiding further embarrassment, I inched closer toward him—finding my place on his lap.

"Iman is *always* off by herself, and she thinks she's *too good* for us," Mildred glowered at me from the other side of the table, her voice dripped with bitterness, "Don't you, Iman?"

Though she had always tried to hide her negative feelings toward me, when inebriated, her true feelings poured as freely as her rum.

"I don't think I'm too good for you," I whispered in response. I felt dizzy with embarrassment and anxiety. George's arms held me closer to him.

"Oh, really?" Mildred's eyes hardened, starring straight into mine, "Then why are you always hiding and off by yourself, writing secrets in your little diary?"

The table erupted in laughter. George's body shook, his belly pressing into my back.

"That must be where she writes about her boyfriends," a guest had chimed, spilling beer down his chin as he laughed.

"I don't have a boyfriend."

"Well," Mildred jumped out of her seat and began walking toward my bedroom, "Why don't we find out?"

I screamed out, pushing myself off George's lap as Mildred disappeared down the hall. Quickly grabbing my arm, George twisted it behind my back.

"Where d'you think yer goin'?"

He looked down at me as I fell to the ground, yelping in pain.

"Get back up here," he patted his vacant lap.

She returned with my diary, opening it hurriedly, excited to entertain her guests, and assumedly, embarrass me. She began to read from the open page.

"I don't like living here because I miss my mom, and I don't have any friends. Adam and Chokri are never home, and I have to stay here all by myself. The food is really bad, and it's always dirty—"

Mildred's eyes looked up from the page and bore into mine, *"My mommy would never let me be here because she liked everything very clean. I want my mommy to come back, so I can go home."*

The room erupted in laughter, once again. My body froze as my eyes widened.

"See? I told you she thought she was better than us!" Mildred barked.

"Maybe I should let you starve since you hate the food so much. You should be *grateful* that you're *here* and not in some group home being beaten."

She threw the diary down the hall, a thud followed the sound of papers rustling. "Get your ass to bed," she screamed. "You ungrateful little bitch. I don't want to see your fucking face again tonight."

I burst into tears, prying myself away from George's grasp, hurriedly running down to hall toward my bedroom. My diary lay on the floor, crumpled and bent. Reaching down, I took it into my arms, clutching it tightly as I continued on to my room. I sank into my bed. Tears violently pouring down my face as I earnestly tried to smooth out the crumpled pages. Clearly, my hiding place was not crafty enough. I began to remove the sheets from my bed, examining my mattress further. *I don't trust it here anymore,* I thought to myself. Looking to the closet, searching for a secret space. *Nothing.* Resignation filled me as I stared down at my mattress once again. I would need to find a better spot tomorrow.

I awoke the next morning with puffy eyes and a stillness all around me. It was early and the house was quiet. *Perfect,* I thought. Crawling under my bed, I reached between the wooden slats and placed the diary between the wooden boards and the box spring. Though it was not a permanent solution, it would have to do for now. Quickly and quietly, I slowly opened my bedroom door. I held my breath. A moment had passed and not a sound was made. I swiftly dressed myself and gathered my knapsack, carefully placing Freddy, the small tiger, and another teddy bear in the bag. Opening the door once more, I rose to my toes, delicately taking slow steps toward the kitchen. Loading crackers and a slice of last night's pizza into my bag, I walked toward the upstairs patio door with the same caution. I peered over the landing. *I hope you're all dead,* I thought as I looked down at the idle, passed-out bodies that filled the family room. I turned away, leaving the house, toward my circle of trees.

Privacy in our household, for me at least, was scarce. Aside from my trips to the sanctuary of the outdoors, and though I was often left alone and neglected in the house, I had no place to call my own. It wasn't until Chokri finally moved into the second bedroom on the lower floor across from Adam and Ron's bedroom, that I was finally, after two years, given a room of my own. I quickly took over the now-vacant room next door and Mel was left in the room we once shared across the hall from Mildred and George. Growing older, Melanie had long deserved the same minuscule luxury that any fourteen-year-old girl possessed, a luxury she forfeited the moment I came into her life. And though I was happy for Melanie and her chance to finally claim her own space, I was more enthusiastic to claim mine and escape into my own little world—a world where I could shut out Mildred and George and I could be by myself. My long-held pastime of speeches to stuffed teddy bears and speaking to my mom in the mirror could now be done in the privacy of my own room. No longer would I have to lock myself in the bathroom, only to be interrupted by the loud bangs of Mel's fists against the wooden door. Finally, I would have my own personal escape from the somber mood that fluttered throughout the house, without having to leave.

Nevertheless, this small gift of privacy, though an incredible gain, had made me somewhat lonelier. Though I was happier to have two places of peace—the forest and my room—being nine still left me without a household companion, and not as much freedom as I would have hoped. Aside from gazing into the mirror to see my mother, talking to her, and telling her about my life, I had no one. Our initial intentions to establish a family were far out of reach—now, it felt as though we were all roommates that happened to be sharing the same house.

Oddly, though the torment and bullying had yet to cease, I felt more loved at school. Every morning, my teacher would offer his students hugs, just in case anyone needed one. Of course, being bullied and isolated, I would approach him with open arms and a smile, soaking in and savouring the comforting nature of the human touch. Since my mother had died, aside from being forced to sit on George's lap, or the regular good night hug and kiss Mildred demanded I give them both, human connection was something that, like food, became a novelty.

But I found school more bearable for more reasons than just a friendly teacher—I had finally made a friend. Henry, a boy as shy as I was, had taken an evident liking to me. His cute, shy demeanour around me had sparked a natural friendship that was solely based on his childhood crush. Being so young, the complex emotions of intimate feelings were lost on us. Regardless of its foundation, I was happy to have found a friend in Henry. At recess, I had someone to play with, I had someone who wanted to hang out with me, and someone who I shared a genuine connection with. He was very chivalrous and kind. During a school trip to Drumheller to visit the various bones and fossils of dinosaurs, Henry had carried my small carry-on suitcase onto the bus for me. Though it may seem insignificant, the simple act had made me feel special, and most importantly, loved. Since my mother had passed, I had not found a friend, or someone I could be my sincere self around, until now. My new friend, my favourite teacher, my forest sanctuary, and my own room—they had somehow made my life seem a little more bearable. Though minuscule, these small treasures shone glimmers of light in a life that was otherwise filled with depression, neglect, malnourishment, and emotional pain. I thought it wise to savour the small niceties of life: simple things, such as crackers and peanut butter, watching Oprah in the basement, playing in the forest, or the occasional treat of being able to hang out with my brothers. Being nine in a house of teenagers and adults made it hard to connect and join in the pastimes of those around me, but regardless of the gap in age, with diligent effort, I tried to include myself in their lives.

Adam and Chokri had developed a new hobby: bb-guns. In the backyard, stepping past our large garden, they would aim their guns at various rodents, squirrels, and small woodland creatures.

"Can I play?" I asked repeatedly. Though I did not care for the actual game itself, I desperately wanted to be included. Leaping at the opportunity to play with someone other than my stuffed animals, I begged harder. Eventually, I had worn them down. After numerous replies that I was far too young to play with the bead-filled rifle, they conceded. With a beaming grin, I stood there, happy as could be. The gun went off and Chokri let out a gleeful yelp. I turned in the direction his gun was aimed. He had shot a gopher. In my pleas to join them, I had not truly known or understood what game my brothers had been playing. A cold stillness came over me. *Animals were my friends.* Handing the gun to me, Chokri placed the rifle in my arms. The gopher was still alive, and this was the perfect opportunity to show me how to shoot. The gun went off as I pulled the trigger. The gopher became still. Suddenly, the weight of the gun became too heavy to bear. I looked down at the contraption in my hands and back up toward the gopher. Bursting into tears, I ran off to flee from my shame and guilt. Adam and Chokri remained. Understandably, playing with me was more of a handful than a delight. My sensitivity would always lead me to tears.

Though our lives were separating and we grew more distant, there were small familial rituals that still held strong. As family mealtimes became scarcer, the only consistent gathering left was movie night. Adam, Ron, Mel, and Chokri, joined Mildred, George, and me as we sat around the television in the basement. Just as we had done at the farmhouse, we would dine on soda, pizza, and popcorn, as the flickering light of the screen would project colourful blasts against the white walls, and Mildred would sit cozily in her armchair as she knit.

George had left us early one evening, which wasn't much of a surprise. His mood, as with Mildred's, made their sudden retreats to the privacy of their room quite common. Ignoring his absence, we continued feasting on our smorgasbord of greasy fare.

"Be right back," Melanie rose from her space on the floor and made her way up the stairs, toward her room. Aside from the sounds of the television and the occasional giggle from the basement, the house was quiet. At the sound of Melanie's hurried footsteps returning, I turned my head to face her.

"Uh, guys," we all brought our attention to her as she took a brief pause, as if searching for the appropriate words, "The weirdest thing just happened."

She took another pause, "I just saw George wear Mom's bra."

Giggles escaped us as we tried to visualize the absurdity of her statement. George was a large man and, over the past few months, though we had no food in the house, had been growing larger. Mildred, on the other hand, was petite. The image of George fitting himself into one of Mildred's small, A-cup brassieres, was laughable. Mildred giggled along with us, producing no words of explanation or thought on the matter. As the laughter slowly subsided, Melanie resumed her position on the floor, and we all turned our attention back to the television.

Chapter Five

Age 10: Plucked

The creases in Mildred's brow grew deeper as she stormed around our home, urgently stuffing our belongings into large black garbage bags. Adam and Ron buzzed throughout the halls, gathering whatever they could, while teenage boys darted in and out, loading our furniture and bags into the car. Chaos was all around us. Chokri and Mel were assigned to collect garbage and our unwanted possessions, and Mildred, a feverish entanglement of stress and rage, not only demanded that I clean my room but informed me that I was unable to take everything with me.

As I looked around my messy room, my heart sank. Aside from being tasked with cleaning, which was a chore I loathed, I was faced with the same horror I had experienced in the basement of my mother's home. I began to cry. Though I owned so little, I had valued all my measly possessions, and the idea of being forced to leave *my stuff*, yet again, was devastating. I didn't want to move. I didn't want to leave my stuff behind. I didn't want to leave my circle of trees. I hated change. I was tired of moving, re-establishing myself, and getting into a new routine. I was tired of being new. But, nevertheless, I knew that my sulks were of no use, and with Mildred's lack of sympathy and erratic temperament, she was a force to be reckoned with.

With the constant financial difficulties our family was experiencing, it was of no surprise that it was time for us to move. The lack of electricity, heat, telephone, or even food, had finally proven to be too much for Mildred and

George, and utilizing the limited logic and sense of responsibility they had, they had decided we needed to relocate to a home that fit our budget. Though I was saddened at the thought of leaving my forest sanctuary and animal friends, I once again yielded to the ebb and flow of life. Allowing my curiosity to pique and my sense of imagination to take hold, I thought of what our new home would look like, and where it was. *Would there be animals to play with? Is there a forest? Will I get my own room?* My mind buzzed as we loaded the remaining garbage bags into the car, and drove away from the beloved house on the hill.

It was a bungalow. Substantially smaller, this house was an evident downgrade from the house on the hill. Eager to claim our rooms, Mel, Chokri, and I rushed out of the car and into our new home. Wandering through the small house, we made an inventory of the space. A small living room was positioned to the right of the entrance, followed by the master bedroom, and an enclosed dining area that stood perpendicular to the room, and opposite a tiny enclosed kitchen. Beside the dining room, down the hallway, two small bedrooms stood. A moment of fear overtook me. *Was I sharing a room again?* Chokri called out in excitement from the front of the house. Following his voice, I walked toward the entrance, into the mudroom. Chokri stood in a small room that appeared to be an add-on that extended from the entryway. I peered in. A single lightbulb fell from a hook that attached to the ceiling. The cord extended downwards, toward an outlet that was located outside of the room. "This is my room," Chokri piped. Though it was aesthetically lacking, it seemed rather exciting to have a room with so much privacy.

I walked toward the backdoor, eager to explore the yard. Stepping out into the warm summer sun, I looked around the property. It was no doubt smaller than the house on the hill in terms of acreage. Though there were trees, they lacked the robust shape and size of those in my sanctuary. But what the property lacked in trees, it made up for in swamps. My eyes scanned the property, determining what areas were desirable to play in. My head turned at the sound of the back door opening. Adam and Ron, carrying garbage bags and cots, walked toward a seemingly broken-down shack that stood in the yard. "Is that your room?" I called out.

Abandoning my search for acceptable play areas, I followed Adam and Ron into the shack. Similar to the addition made at the front of the house that would now act as Chokri's bedroom, the owners had also made an attempt to create an additional livable space in the backyard. The shack was a chicken coop that had been partially sectioned off. Attached to the chicken coop, a narrow room that went back roughly fifteen feet, was a separate open area of exposed drywall, hanging light bulbs, power cords that led outside, and an unfinished kitchen that was nothing more than a counter. I looked around the dirty space, feeling wary of the creepy atmosphere. My stomach curdled at the thought of having to sleep there.

As we settled into our new home, my hopefulness quickly fluttered away. I had lost my peaceful space, and my siblings, growing older, were slipping away from me. Adam and Ron, now nineteen and eighteen, respectively, had already graduated high school, and had found interests that were far beyond my reach. Their chicken coop room was littered with beer cans and cigarette butts, and their walls were plastered with posters of local strippers from their evenings out, and magazine centerfolds of exotic models. Chokri was often out, entertaining himself the same way any fifteen-year-old boy would. And though Melanie spent time with me, I was aware that it was due to mere obligation. This new home was lonelier.

Though the outdoor space was smaller, I began to explore and familiarize myself with my new surroundings. Wandering out into the swamps, I would play with mice, fish, and tadpoles. I collected frogs, playing with them as I journeyed through the property. As before, my companions were our household pets. Blondie was now long gone, but in her place, we had Kilo, a large black Newfoundland lab mix, and Jake, a small white terrier. Our cat, Colours, a calico, erred on the side of promiscuity, and to my benefit, would frequently find herself with a new batch of kittens. Mildred and George had also unintentionally gifted me with baby yellow chicks that I cared for in the chicken coop. As a part of my daily routine, I would feed the chicks, and check the heat lamps that we installed in the coop.

Not too long after settling into our new home, any trace of optimism that we had brought with us was quickly extinguished. Mildred had been fired from her job. Though she lacked the ability to openly admit or discuss events with us (as evidenced by our previous inquiries regarding our phone not working or our electricity being cut off), a quiet murmur filled our house at the news of Mildred's unemployment. In an effort to support George's addiction to marijuana, and their mutual addiction to alcohol, she had stolen money from petty cash at her office and, after being caught, she was immediately removed from her position. This incident, however, proved far worse than imaginable. Mildred was not only fired, but as a bookkeeper, was no longer bondable and could no longer be employed. Her inability to work, in combination with her license being revoked and lack of independence, had sent Mildred deeper into depression and, in turn, the household fell under a cloud of melancholy.

As the end of summer approached, I prepared myself for the regular role I played as the newest cast member at yet another school. As before, petty school kids would tease and bully me due to my ethnic ambiguity. Though my skin was not dark, my large lips, round almond eyes, ill-cut curly locks, and skinny, frail demeanour, had left me a common target. Surrounded by classmates in new, trendy clothing, I was a black sheep layered in signs of poverty. Melanie's oversize hand-me-downs draped my withering body, emphasizing my malnourished frame. Thankfully, bullying and teasing, common in schools far and wide, does not prevent friendships from eventually fostering. Despite the hateful chants and calls from others that fed my self-loathing and insecurities, I had finally found myself a group of friends—one of them being closer than the others. As our friendship quickly blossomed, Jessica and I would not only spend our recess and lunchtimes together, but began to have regular sleepovers. She had come from a family of five, with a brother and a sister, and, unlike me, she lived in a large house, had new clothing, and an endless number of toys and playthings.

Between sleepovers at Jessica's, or at Ben and Elizabeth's, I had spent very little time at home on the weekends. For this I was grateful. The cumbersome mood in our household had left me drearier and more depressed than I had ever been. Though we moved to a more affordable home, we still had very little food, and often had no electricity or phone. Out of necessity, I developed small skills in the kitchen—frying eggs and making sandwiches—to sustain myself. Mildred, too far into her spiral of medication and depression, spent her days sitting on the couch, a rum and Coke by her side, knitting endlessly. George was now the only provider in our household, and when not at work as a carpenter, he would spend his evenings in his room, as the familiar scent of marijuana slithered through the cracks of the door. I didn't mind his self-imposed isolation. My sentiments toward him had not changed. A stiff chill would go up my spine at his touch, his gaze, and even the sound of his voice.

My child instincts were, unfortunately, accurate. Unbeknownst to me, as I was fast asleep, George had entered Melanie's room in the middle of the night. He was drunk. Melanie woke up and stared at him as he sat on her bed.

"I really like you, you know? More than a daughter." He looked down at her hand and added, "I like your red nail polish a lot."

Wide-eyed and angry, Mel slapped and kicked him away. He stood up from her bed shocked and hurt by her reaction.

"I am sorry I feel this way," George mumbled as he stumbled out of her bedroom.

"Iman, wake up," Melanie's voice lulled me into consciousness. I slowly stirred, recognizing her voice, and realizing that it was unusual. Every morning, Mildred, with her screech, would open my door and yell, "Iman, it's time to get up!" I turned to Mel as Kilo, Jake, Colours, and her troupe of kittens, jumped off my bed from their night's sleep, "Where's Mum?"

"She had to go to the hospital because George tried to kill himself last night," Mel's voice was somewhat cold and factual.

"Oh, wow," I slowly registered her words. Sure, I had known what *killing yourself* meant, but there was a lack of connection.

The house was quiet. Adam and Ron were nowhere to be found. Chokri was getting ready for school. An odd tension fell over the silent house.

Melanie helped me with my morning routine—washing my face, making sure I brushed my teeth, making me cereal, and preparing my lunch. Chokri and I headed for the bus but Mel decided to stay home from school and go back to bed.

I walked into the house and was met with subtle signs of life; the sound of the TV in the living room, a glass on the kitchen counter, and the odour of both marijuana and a freshly lit cigarette. I walked past the living room to find Mildred, sitting in her usual position on the sofa, with a rum and Coke on the coffee table in front of her, and knitting needles in her hand. I quickly glanced at her as I walked toward my room, passing the closed door of the master bedroom. Whether he was just looking for attention, or licking his self-inflicted wounds, George had spent the next few days locked inside of his room. The awkward heaviness of the events that had just transpired was felt by all of us, but, in line with our household procedures, no one uttered a word. When George had finally conceded, leaving his protective shell, we whispered to each other, uttering small quips and mentions of his presence.

As the days went on, our lives resumed their regular pace. It was as if the incident had not happened, suggesting that our household policy of not openly discussing the events in our lives proved favourable. Of course, Melanie had changed. She had become more closed off, unable to voice her frustration. Quickly, whether it was to escape from the realities of her life, or to have someone to protect her, she became immersed in her relationship with her boyfriend. Spending the majority, if not all of her free time with him, he became a regular face in our household, sleeping over almost every night.

Regardless of George's suicide attempt, or Mildred's unemployment, their party lifestyle remained. Like in the farmhouse, and the house on the hill, despite our lack of food, or cut off phone or electricity, they seemed to always have money for alcohol, cigarettes, and weed. With Melanie attaching herself more to her boyfriend, I had become lonelier than I was before. It was as if we were all boarders in a house, or windblown ships passing each other.

Depression soon started taking over me, and I became somewhat of a recluse. I felt separated from my siblings, as well as our guardians, and, because of what he had done, I had grown afraid of George more than I already was.

In this isolation and loneliness, when George had started to show a liking toward me and tried to be my friend, I was receptive. Though I was still wary of him, the thought of finding companionship in my household was welcoming. On a Saturday afternoon, as I was sitting in the living room, George appeared with a flat of twenty-four canned beers. Sitting next to me, he opened a beer, and began to drink.

"Hey, do you want a beer?" his arm extended with a beer in his hand, as he offered it to me. I was shocked. Being only ten, it was a question I had never heard, nor knew how to respond to. I looked at the beer in his hand, feeling shy and as if a spotlight was shining on only me.

"Okay," reaching forward, I grabbed the beer, and pulled the tab. Although it was non-alcoholic beer, a mere 0.05%, I had felt a rush of excitement and energy. Bringing it to my lips, I took a sip and an odd, bitter taste filled my mouth. Regardless of the unpleasant flavour, I took another sip, wanting to appear cool. It had been so lonely in the house, and the company of George was all I had. I began to belch alongside of him as we opened can after can, laughing at the sounds we made. Eventually, after drinking for the entire afternoon, joyfully learning to chug, belch, and find the appeal of the malty flavour, I had become mildly intoxicated.

Learning to drink, and hanging out with George, had made me feel as though I was a part of something, a part of the household. Seeing them drink and smoke had left an impression on me, and I became enthused at the idea of being grown up like them. Stealing a few unnoticeable cigarettes when Mildred and George weren't paying attention, I began to sneak away into the backyard, desperate to learn how to smoke. Hiding behind the chicken coop house, cigarette in one hand, lighter in the other, I attempted to mimic the motions I had seen so often. Placing the cigarette to my lips, I lit the end, and as I inhaled, the cigarette smoke hit my lungs and I began to cough feverishly. The burning, hot air, left a film of toxic flavour that I spit out in disgust. But, like beer, I would have to grow accustomed to the flavour. I returned to the house, nauseated and dizzy. I would have to try again until I got it right.

My self-education in smoking became more promising as time went on. Taking puffs of the cigarettes, I would hold the smoke in my mouth for a brief second, only to blow it out right away. Studying Mildred and George as they coolly inhaled each drag, I could not understand the appeal, or even the act, but took to watching them more carefully until I was able to smoke correctly. During my weekend sleepovers at Jessica's house, I would arrive with a handful of stolen cigarettes, and together, she and I would find a secret spot on her property, and practice together, and when our stolen supply of tobacco had run dry, we would roll up dead grass in paper, and smoke that too. I was proud that I knew how to drink beer and was growing more adept at smoking cigarettes. We were cool. After studying the basics of American Sign Language, we developed a private mode of communication through codes; we played with Ouija boards, talked to spirits, and spent hours trying to summon Bloody Mary in the bathroom mirror. Jessica and I, together, felt as though we were levels above the other fourth graders in our class.

It was comforting to have a friend. Aside from George's company, I had felt so alone. Melanie and her boyfriend, Robert, had become somewhat of a packaged deal, and not only did I dislike Robert, I had missed spending time with my sister alone. Robert, though attractive, seemed somewhat mentally unwell. He would tease me, then try and offer a branch of friendship, only to quickly snatch it away. Like George, although I did not find Robert favourable, my loneliness and desire to spend time with my sister left me excited and leaping at any opportunity of companionship. I had known that I was somewhat of a burden to Melanie. I was her younger sister, and in the three years I had been a part of her family, she had been given the role as my caregiver.

Robert's family life was similarly dysfunctional. His mother had left him, and his father was an alcoholic who was never around. Melanie, blinded by the bright lights of love and affection, had not seen what I had—a very strange and damaged boy. We had walked to his home once, Mel, Robert, and me. He had known I loved the outdoors, playing with the small wood-land rodents, and catching frogs.

"Do you want to see a cool trick I can do with the frog?" he smirked at me as we approached his house. Making a frog jump was unimpressive—it was a skill they had mastered on their own—but I nodded my head, interested. Reaching into a discarded barrel that was filled with water, he pulled out a small frog and held it in his hands.

"Hold on," he scoured his surroundings. Finding a string of wire, he began to strip off the black plastic coating with his teeth, and once finished, wrapped the exposed wire around the frog's legs. A nauseous feeling came over me as Robert walked toward an outlet, inserting the exposed wire on the other end. The frog started to twitch, it's legs and whole body, extending as far as it could. He removed the wire from the outlet, and the frog, as if only experiencing temporary rigor mortis, relaxed into its natural size. My eyes closed as I looked away when Robert reinserted the wire into the outlet once again; I felt the same sorrow as when I killed the gopher with my brother's BB gun. Repeatedly, Robert laughed as he removed and reinserted the wire, throwing the frog into a frenzy. *How could anyone enjoy hurting animals?*

I had preferred to be by myself than to be with such a sadistic boy. Though I loved Mel, Robert was a creature I had no interest befriending. Whenever possible, I would escape into the backyard, and even though this house and its land much smaller than the house on the hill, lacked the same adventure and vast landscape to explore, I would play in the swamps and create imaginary worlds in the trees. I accumulated various escapes from the reality I lived in. I fabricated the imaginary worlds of *The Babysitter's Club* and *Winnie the Pooh*, pretending I was Christopher Robin, or Kristy; realized myself as a detective, hitman, or spy, keeping note of my next victim's move; and, sometimes, I would simply sit in the living room, losing myself in the most appealing television show the four channels our small antennae'd TV had to offer.

As I watched cartoons in the living room one afternoon, Robert had appeared. Standing beside me, his blue eyes glared at the screen. Without skipping a beat, he assumed his role as a tormentor, mocking not only the colourful, singing bears on the screen, but me as well. I had tried to ignore his brutish taunts, but consequently, my efforts drove him to undertake a new strategy. My eyes fixated on his hand as it moved, reaching into his pocket. Unhooking the chain that attached his wallet to his light blue jeans, a small grin appeared on his face as he menacingly began to swing the steel rope in my direction. I was aware that he would not actually hit me, but still, I was afraid. Understandably, the feeling of being jeered at is not pleasant, and I— after school days of being teased for my skinny legs, my curly hair, and my ethnic background, after being pitied and whispered about after my mother had died—loathed negative attention.

Eventually, after my flinches and requests for him to stop proved to gain me no sympathy, I left.

Running to the backyard, I found asylum in Adam and Ron's room in the chicken coop, and lay on Adam's cot. Glancing at the posters of scantily clad models that veiled the unfinished drywall, my eyes scanned the room. There was a sinister air around me. The dark, dirty shack, though an excellent place to find refuge, was not a place I had wanted to be. It was frightening.

A few minutes had passed when I had heard Melanie calling out my name. Her voice teemed frustration.

"Robert, how could you do this?" The faint sound of Melanie's voice echoed into the chicken coop, "You can't be so mean to her. She's sensitive."

A male voice mumbled.

"You can't tease her like that, Robert! And now I've lost her—and I was supposed to be watching her! I'm going to be in so much trouble."

Despite hearing Melanie's repeatedly calling my name, I remained in the safety of the chicken coop shack. As her calls subsided, and she gave up, I stared at the walls, thinking of the life I could have had. I missed my mother. I longed, so desperately, for her unconditional love, her affection, and her attention. Here I was, stuck in a life I had not deserved. *What did I do wrong?* My friends, they had large houses, they had food, they had loving parents, and I, I had *this*—a sister that only cared out of obligation; brothers, who I had tried so desperately to be reunited with, only to be left to fend for myself; and guardians that couldn't even put food on the table.

My fifth-grade class was tasked with fundraising for a school trip by sell-ing small boxes of chocolate-covered almonds. Enthused by the notion of having and making money, the fundraiser sparked a sense of entrepreneurship within me. Coming home from school, I enthusiastically told Mildred and George of my new business venture. Aware of my lack of privacy, and fearful that either Mildred or George would take the almonds, or worse, the money, from me, I hid both under my bed in a seemingly secure location. A mere two dollars each, they purchased a couple of boxes of almonds, but, being set with a goal of raising one hundred dollars, I became savvy. Targeting the one opportunity I had to raise the money I required, during their weekend parties I would go into the living room and ask our drunken guests if they would like to buy a box of almonds for two dollars. In a mere two weeks, I had success-fully sold and raised my target, though, foolishly, I loudly boasted about the large amount of money I had earned.

"Listen," sitting in the living room, I turned my head as Mildred spoke. "We're going to need your money that you sold the almonds for."

A lump formed in my throat as my face became flushed.

"No," my eyes became watery as I held back my tears. "I worked for that, you can't have it."

"We're going to give it back; it's not a big deal. We just need the money."

I looked at her, recognizing that I was in no position to win this battle. I was just a child, and she, she was a whirlwind of rage and authority. Reluc-tantly, I went to my room, crawling under my bed to retrieve the money. Even though I had made such an effort to hide it, it was of no use.

I understood I would never see that money again, just as I had lost my mother's pictures and the small amount of money I had brought with me to the Tunisian woman's house. But this was not my money. Its true owner was the school, and after two weeks had passed, it was time that I return it to them. To no avail, I had asked both Mildred and George several times to return the money they had taken, explaining to them that it wasn't mine, and that I had to return it.

"How did you do?" I looked up at my teacher, my face ruddy with embar-rassment. A moment skipped by, "Where are the almonds?"

"Well, I sold them all."

"Okay, great!" a smile quickly formed on her lips, "We just need to have the money."

"Well," a familiar lump formed in my throat, "My parents took the money from me."

Another moment skipped by, and I could tell she was unsure of the truthfulness to my words. I didn't know which was worse—being in trouble with the school, or with my family—and though I didn't want to get my family in trouble, I had not wanted to face the consequences of an action that wasn't mine.

"Iman, are you lying?"

"N-no—I…they took it from me," my words came out with such hesitation, as if signaling that I wasn't in fact telling the truth; and, as I suspected, regardless of my honestly, my teacher had not believed me. I felt the eyes of my peers piercing into my back as she told me that she would be calling my home. Immediately, classmates had begun to taunt me. I had felt like an outcast, yet again. The class buzzed with conversations of how many almonds they sold, and how much money they raised, and I, without money or almonds, sat alone.

I hated Mildred. I hated my life, my family, and my school. The embarrassment I had felt was unimaginable, and it was solely the fault of my guardians. My one desire was to leave them, to grow up and become an adult, not having to live under their roof, or succumb to their rules. Fantasies of running off, smoking cigarettes, getting tattoos, and being free, saturated my mind.

The cold Albertan winter had come too soon, as it often does. Falling leaves were quickly replaced with ice and sleet that danced in the whirling winds; the world around me was veiled in a thick blanket of snow. The temperature had dropped a significant amount, and though I only experienced the true harshness of the winter during my walks to the school bus, during recess, or while tending to the chickens in the coop, my brothers had no escape from the harshness of winter. Mornings I would wake up to find a cot in the back-door entranceway, or in the living room, with a bundle of blankets wrapped around Adam and Ron. The chicken coop had no heat, and the small space heaters Mildred and George had provided for them were far from sufficient to battle the excruciating cold.

Chokri had the same problem. The add-on that acted as his room—which was more of a drywall solarium than anything else—though appealing at first, was not only small and dumpy, with a clothing rack and cot as the only furnishings, but it was also without heat. The cold left Chokri's nights sleepless. The space heater, as with the ones provided for Adam and Ron, held no weight in contrast with the freezing temperature of the outdoors. It was not in my capacity to fully understand why his room had no heat or electricity, I was simply told that it *just didn't*. I had felt bad for Chokri, and seeing him in such agony broke my heart. In the mornings, we would find him shaking on his cot, curled up in the fetal position to conserve his body heat, and at times, when the cold was too unbearable, he would find refuge in the living room.

By nature, Chokri vocalized his rightful displeasure with the uninhabitable conditions he was forced to live in. It was not humane to allow a child, let alone an animal, undergo such insufferable and intolerable circumstances. At his remarks, Mildred and George, in their usual fashion, would blame him for being ungrateful, yelling at him for voicing any objection to the situation they had left him in. But he was relentless, and as his objections grew more persistent, our guardians grew angrier. Though I'm sure they were aware of their faults as caregivers, their inability to take accountability or responsibility for our well-being had left them on the defense; and Chokri's protests were met with Mildred's barks, and eventually, her authority.

Chokri's complaints, likely a regular reminder to Mildred and George of their shortcomings as guardians, had driven them to kick him out. When he told me of the news—that he would finish off the school year at his friend's house before moving to live with Ben and Elizabeth I, unlike him, was devastated. Living with Ben and Elizabeth was my lifelong dream and just like that, Chokri would be going there without me. He was almost sixteen years old and could decide for himself where he wanted to live. I still had six more years before I could be released from my own prison. Legally, Ben and Elizabeth couldn't take me along with Chokri. I would miss my brother dearly. Though he was often with his friends and rarely home, the thought of him no longer being with me was an excruciating thought. I had already lost Adam and Ron to the joys of adulthood, and Melanie to the affections of Robert, and now, losing Chokri, would mean I was even more alone. However, my devastation was not solely rooted in my sentiments of abandonment. I was jealous. It was a frequent threat of Mildred's that she would send me to live with Ben and Elizabeth. I would feign despair at her threats, but unbeknownst to her, it was what I truly wanted.

Ben and Elizabeth had been so kind to us—they had taken us in on weekends, spoiling us with dinners, movies, and affection. They had given Melanie and me bunk beds so we could have some semblance of privacy and comfort; they had paid for my brothers and me to visit our family in Toronto; and, most of all, they had shown me kindness, care, and concern when I felt no one else did. It was as though they had taken a vow to watch over us since our first meeting the day after my mother had been killed. They spent time with us and checked in on us, bought us school supplies, and offered us a change of scenery with fun sleepovers. These strangers had become more of our family than our blood relatives who moved far away and barely checked in on us. I didn't quite understand what made Ben and Elizabeth so devoted to us and why they never turned their backs on us, but I was more grateful to them than to anyone else in my life. I wanted nothing more than to go home with them and never return to the horrible life I had with Mildred and George.

I had kept my longing to live with them to myself, aware that if I had revealed my true desires to Mildred, she would take them away from me. And now, after everything, I was left to stay in the horrid hells of this home, and Chokri was given the opportunity to live a life I had always wanted.

Chokri would occasionally come to visit. He had gotten new clothing, had a room with heat and electricity that he got to paint whatever colour he wanted, and had gotten his first job, at McDonald's. He looked happy, and was doing well, and for this I was overjoyed. When I wasn't at Jessica's house for a sleepover, I would spend a weekend or two a month in Edmonton with

Ben and Elizabeth. On Saturday mornings, they would take me to Chokri's work and I would look at him, teeming with pride as my big brother served us from the opposite side of the counter. The contrast between the Chokri that spent nights huddled under blankets in a heatless room, and the man that served us, was significant. It was as though Chokri had found a new sense of confidence through his new surroundings. Unlike his life with Mildred and George, here he felt loved, valuable, and was given attention.

But, as all good things end, on Sunday afternoons Ben and Elizabeth would drive me back, and I would return to the dismal realities of my life. Though I was alone, I still had the company of my animal friends. I would continue to play with the chickens in the coop, wade in the swamps, and surround myself with our pets. Every night, as I settled into bed, I was followed by Kilo, Jake, Colours, and her troupe of kittens. I had made my own family, and when I was home, they rarely left my side.

Being in the country, our pets were not indoor animals; they were left to wander when they pleased. As a part of our morning routine, after waking me for school, Mildred would let Jake and Kilo out to defecate, run, and play. When they would return for breakfast, I would be ready to leave for school, give them each a hug goodbye, and we would part ways. One morning, however, they didn't return. With slight concern, but paying little mind, we continued with our days—Mel and I to school, George to work, and Mildred to knit on the couch. When returning home, clambering in from the cold, Mel and I shed our winter jackets and asked Mildred if they had returned. They had not. It was very unusual. Regardless of being outdoor dogs, they had always returned for breakfast. Not returning for the whole day, not even for food, was not only uncharacteristic, but worrisome. As the day continued, and the winter sun set, we grew increasingly unsettled until Kilo returned alone.

A sad, mopey look spread across Kilo's large black face. Though he hadn't eaten all day, and it was evident that he was hungry, he refused to eat. The sky had transformed into a gradient of navy blue. *Where was Jake?* As a small white terrier, his survival through a cold Albertan winter night was unlikely. Redressing in our tattered winter jackets, George, Mildred, Melanie, and I all wandered out into the forest, flashlights in tow, searching for Jake. After a seemingly endless search, to no avail, we returned—my eyes swollen with tears.

When Robert appeared, the next day, he had informed us that he had seen Jake. A car had swerved on the road, hitting him, and now my treasured terrier's corpse was lying dead on the side of the road. The thought of Jake no longer cuddling up next to me on my bed as I slept brought me to tears. I ran to my room, crying. Robert had left to retrieve Jake's body, and quickly returned with the canine corpse, stiffly frozen, in a plastic bag. We decided to bury him in our yard properly, but the ground, frozen solid, would not soften at our request. And so, my darling terrier was left in the backyard in a frozen plastic bag, forgotten.

I had lost another friend, another companion. The small world around me was getting lonelier and lonelier. The vacant space on my bed was a constant reminder. But, as I had trained myself to, I carried on, yielding to life's unfavourable currents—the same currents that had brought me here, that took my mother away from me, that left me broken. As I did in the farmhouse, and at the house on the hill, to ease the sorrows of my heart, I performed my motivational speeches to invisible audiences, talked to my mother in the mirror, and create a sub-reality of my own through the sanctuary of the outdoors.

I lived a lonesome life, and though I managed to entertain myself with what little I had, I detested being home. I tried to spend as much time as I could anywhere else—either playing outside, visiting Chokri in Edmonton, or sleeping over at Jessica's. Our house was a filthy, deteriorating wreck, the interior was littered with used dishes, animal hair, and reeked of cigarettes. It was a beacon of poverty, and not only did I despise being within it, I was ashamed to have anyone see the impecunious reality of my life. Unfortunately, at one point, rather than spending the weekend at Jessica's, she had instead decided to come over to our house for the day. Paying no mind, we had not noticed that Kilo had taken it upon himself to treat one of her new sneakers as a plaything. Only when it was time for Jessica's departure did we return to the entranceway to gather Jessica's belongings. Immediately, we discovered that Kilo had eaten, and destroyed, one of her sneakers, leaving Jessica with only one shoe. As she left, shoeless, an excruciating wave of embarrassment and shame came over me. Though her parents—surely aware of my family's impoverishment—had brushed off the incident as if it were no big deal, I was aware that in normal circumstances the responsible course of action would be for our family to offer some form of compensation for the damaged shoes, but I knew that an act of such class was far beyond my family's means.

Thankfully, regardless of my family's low-class demeanour, Jessica's parents still welcomed me into their home and as their daughter's friend. They were kind enough to pick me up and drop me off every weekend I had spent at their place, which was not a small task, living in the country.

I had once asked Mildred if she and George would drive me to Jessica's, and the prospect of the forty-minute drive there and back did not sit well with their indolence. I was furious. Over the years, I had grown more tempestuous. My Post-Traumatic Stress Disorder left me irrationally angry, exploding in tantrums of sorrowful rage and depression. Retreating to my room, eyes swollen and sight blurred by tears, I sat against my closed door; my breath staggered as I gasped for air between each violent sob. I hated Mildred. In that moment, a fiery rage consumed me. I had been filled with so much anger and confusion since my mother's death that I had not been granted the opportunity to vocalize my emotions. Whether it was displaced or not, I targeted my anger toward Mildred. I had never liked her. From the moment, they had pulled up in their burgundy Ford those three years ago, I had only grown more disdainful toward my guardians.

Reaching under my bed, locating my hidden diary, I pulled it from between the wooden slats, and open the tattered pages. Speaking the words aloud to myself, I transcribed my rage onto the sheets of paper. *I fucking hate her,* I wrote in a messy scrawl. *I fucking hate living here. I hate her, she's a horrible person, and I hope she fucking dies.* Then, suddenly, I heard a painful moan echo into my room from the dining room; the sound of Melanie's bedroom door opening and her footsteps rushing past my room quickly followed. "Mum, what's wrong—is…is everything okay?!" Melanie's voice was panicked.

Clutching her chest, Mildred's voice was panicked, "I need to go to the hospital."

Looking down at my journal, reading the words I had just written, I paused. For a moment, I questioned the possibility of my hateful energy being the cause of Mildred's sudden attack. *Good,* I thought to myself, *I hope she dies.* I felt a mix of amazement, guilt, and satisfaction at the prospect that I had done this to her—she deserved it; I hated her. Another moan echoed from the dining room. I abandoned my journal, leaving my self-loathing aside, for just a moment, and left my room. Entering the dining room, I looked at Mildred's pale, sunken face in pain, her hand clutching her chest. Unlike other times, when Mildred had feigned illness, it was evident that she was in dire need of medical attention.

"What's wrong?" I asked.

Melanie looked up at me, "Mum's sick, she needs to go to the hospital—something's wrong with her chest."

At the sound of her moans, George quickly appeared to take Mildred to the hospital. She had suffered from a gallbladder attack, and that same evening, her gallbladder was removed, and—to add to her dizzying cocktail of prescriptions—she was given medication that induced bile production, allowing her to digest grease and fats, which were the core foundations of our diet.

With Chokri gone, Mildred and George had one less mouth to feed. Adam and Ron, now working adults, had money of their own, and would eat whatever they wanted, whenever they wanted. Oddly, with the burden of children to feed lessening, only Mel and I being left, our financial hardships had not decreased, and food, as always, was scarce. We had still maintained a large vegetable garden, which we harvested at the end of every summer, and now we also had the added benefit of regular stock fresh eggs from the chicken coop. What I had not been aware of was the ulterior motive behind Mildred and George's initial purchase of the chicks. I had treated the chickens as friends, and caring for them, though being a part of my chores, was a playful act to me. I understood that they had given us eggs, but their true purpose was essentially lost on me.

I had made the mistake of going outside into the backyard one day at the exact moment George, with an axe in his hand, held down one of my chickens, and in one swift movement, severed its head. A violent scream left me and the blood streaked chicken, though decapitated, haphazardly ran around the backyard and began to run toward me. Roars of laughter came from Mildred and George as, despite my leaps in the opposite direction, the headless chicken continued to follow me. My screams finally came to a halt when the chicken collapsed, lifeless.

Mildred had taken the chicken inside to the kitchen and called for me, ordering me to assist her in preparing the fowl that was once my friend. The overwhelming odour had left me nauseated as I stood beside her, watching in disgust as she showed me how to pluck the feathers of the chicken. When satisfied with what we could pluck, she reached for a lighter, singeing off the remaining feathers we were not able to remove. My stomach curdled. I thought back to standing in the kitchen with my mother, helping her prepare the Tunisian dishes I had loved so much; I remembered her sweet, loving words of encouragement and understanding when I told her the notion of touching raw meat disgusted me. And here I was now, standing beside Mildred, being forced to clean the unwanted organs from a chicken that I had raised for six months and had called my friend.

My mother, not only wouldn't have made me endure such a terrible task, but would have understood my refusal to eat the chicken. Mildred, of course, did not. As I sat in my chair, glaring at the chicken, Mildred's stern voice spoke, "Eat the chicken." I glared at her from the tops of my eyes.

"I don't want to eat the chicken," I said.

"Eat the fucking chicken, you spoiled bitch!" her voice grew angrier. But, regardless of her demands, I stood my ground and refused.

It wasn't long before we had to move again. We were told that we were going to move to Maplewood Court—a trailer park about thirty or forty minutes away from where we lived. Though I had never been to one, I had heard about trailer parks in some of the movies that I'd seen. In every instance that I had heard of them, they were described as horrible places to live, a hub for the poor, brimming with filth. It seemed as if our whole world had come crashing down in such a short time. With Chokri living at Ben and Elizabeth's, Adam and Ron never home, it was just Melanie and me left. Everything about the house with the chicken coop had become a cloud of desperation, isolation, and sadness. Mildred had lost whatever sense of self she had left, and George had declined further into a serious state of depression. They hardly spoke to each other let alone to us girls. Melanie was so busy with her boyfriend Robert and it felt like I was always alone. Worst of all, I wasn't even able to finish the fifth grade with my friends, and was forced to move with only three months left in the school year. I hated moving, changing schools, and being the new girl over and over again, I was so desperate to stay at my school with my friends.

Consequently, the only thing that had made it easier to leave was the newfound hatred from my peers, and as quickly as my friendship with Jessica blossomed, it wilted away. After I had told her that I would be moving, she had altered the history of our friendship, telling our classmates that I was evil, I had believed in the devil, and had tried to convert her to my demonic religion. This, of course, was a lie—but schoolchildren, easy to sway, took her fallacious tales as true. I had been ostracized, left to eat lunches alone as the whispers of Jessica's betrayal followed me. I couldn't believe she had turned on me—we were best friends, we were inseparable, and I couldn't imagine my life without her. I couldn't understand how the simple fact that I was moving could make her hate me with such intensity, leading her to betray me with such ease. What I soon realized was that adults and children alike hated change. And, although I wasn't excited to move, in the recent weeks, I had come to hate where I was. I wasn't looking forward to a new school or a new house—any sense of optimism, hope, or faith I once had left me long ago—I was only left to wonder how much worse life could get.

Chapter Six

Age 10: Tin Castles

My final days at the chicken coop house were riddled with despair and agony. I cried every day. I began tearing up all the pictures of Jessica and me, burning all our letters, and destroying the little book I had carefully written the code to our secret language in. I hated everything and wanted to remember nothing. I couldn't wait to leave this whole place behind me. It had become increasingly evident to me, in my short ten years on this planet, that I was destined to be alone, to feel empty, and to painfully question my existence. And finally, on a weekend in late April, we had at long last made our departure, and arrived at our new home.

It was unlike anything I had ever seen. Nestled between two other identical trailers stood a long, narrow, singlewide trailer home, topped with a flat roof and white, vertical aluminum siding. It was a very strange-looking home, with a big backyard. The surrounding area was crowded with trailers. All around and everywhere I looked, it was a sea of long, narrow, little white tin homes that I assumed were filled with poor people, just like us. Charged with anger and a lack of excitement, I helped gather our belongings from the car and entered the aluminum house. As we entered a small porch, I peered into the dark house, walking farther to see the dark brown carpets and off-white, nicotine-stained walls that had begun to turn yellow. To the immediate right was a hallway, which led to two bedrooms and the bathroom that Melanie and I would share. To the left of the front door, a large living room, family room and the eat-in kitchen all opened into each other and, at the very back of the house, behind the kitchen, was Mildred and George's bedroom and small bathroom.

The new place felt awkward without my brothers, and I missed them dearly. Chokri continued his new, lavish life in Edmonton, and Adam—as a graduation gift from Ben and Elizabeth—had left for Africa for a month to visit our Tunisian family. Only Ron remained; sleeping on the couch in our living room until he figured out what he wanted to do now that he had finished school. Without my brothers, my forest sanctuary, or even my free-dom to escape into the forest and perform my motivational talks and skits or to simply walk around our land at a moment's call, I was lonely—and, worst of all, I was left without the company of my beloved pets, the only friends I had left. An obvious lie, Mildred and George had tried—with no real conviction—to convince Melanie and me that our furry companions had run away, fleeing to the swampy fields. However, as I looked around our new, small home, I knew that they had simply left our pets behind.

Although our trailer wasn't big, or much to look at, it would be home for now, and I would have to make the most of this new place if I were going to survive this new adventure. With no time to settle in, I had hardly unpacked my things when it was time to start my new school. I had been dreading it for weeks, and that day had finally come. I spent the weekend unpacking my things, organizing my room as best I could, and trying to ease my wor-ries about my first day of school. Because of our age difference, Melanie was already in high school, and I was left to navigate my first day at my new school alone.

My school was on the other side of the trailer park, a mere ten-minute walk from our trailer. Doing my best to hold my head up high, and not look as frightened as I felt, I walked into the school and quickly found my class. The teacher showed me to my desk and I took out my books. As my heart was pounding through my chest, I prayed that no one else could hear the sounds it was making. The morning went by quickly and uneventfully. A couple of girls greeted me with a simple hello and seemed somewhat friendly, but I still felt like a deer in headlights. Trying not to stare, I had noticed a girl in my class with a large, disfiguration on the right side of her face. I later found out that she had been shot in the head by her stepfather. Though she had tried to shield herself at the sight of the gun, putting her hands up to protect her face, the bullet went through her hand, blowing off half of her jaw and cheek. I felt sorry for her pain and oddly comforted by the fact that for the first time since my mom died, I felt as though someone else knew what it was like to feel broken. This poor girl survived her own murder, and her broken pieces were visible on the outside. I was grateful that I could keep my brokenness hidden deep within my body, where no one would have to see me falling apart.

At recess, I wandered around the basketball courts, aimlessly watching the other kids play. Going behind the schoolyard shed, I had lit a cigarette I had stolen from Mildred in my bag. Seeing a couple of the older kids smoking nearby, they approached me with curiosity, saying hello. A ten-year-old smoking behind an elementary school shed was not a common sight, and though they were only a year older than me, my devil may care attitude, and stolen cigarette supply, made me the coolest of the younger kids.

Unfortunately, the afternoon brought a terror I didn't think I'd have to face on my first day: swimming lessons. There were few things that I hated more than being almost naked in front of a group of strangers. I hated my body, I hated how skinny I was, I hated that I could see all my ribs, I hated that my legs looked likes sticks; I hated that I kept getting my curls chopped off with bad haircuts since my mom died; but, most of all, I hated that everyone always stared at me, commenting on how skinny I was. By then, I had come to hate food, and all the disgusting things I was continuously served daily. Making my way into the locker-room, I armed myself with a million excuses I could try to tell the teacher and, hopefully, avoid my discomfort. But, regardless of my efforts, I was forced to participate in swimming class. As I entered the locker room, I was shaking with anxiety. Slinking into a private changing room, I slowly pulled out my bathing suit and started to take off my clothes.

"Hey what's your name?"

A voice called to me from the change-room next to mine. Unsure if she was speaking to me, I remained silent. She persisted, "Hello—new girl, what's your name?"

"Um, m-my name is Iman," I stammered.

"What? Your name is Gemma?" She yelled over.

"No—my name is IMAN!" I yelled back.

"Oh, good! I thought you said Gemma," she replied. "That is my name."

With my swimsuit on, I exited the dressing room. A girl with long, dirty blonde hair, blue eyes, and gorgeous dimples stood in front of me; with a huge grin on her chubby face, she emitted a roaring laugh that shook her whole body. She seemed to like the fact that we didn't have the same name, and as with my friendship with Jessica, our relationship blossomed quickly. Our never-ending chatter made swimming lessons much less horrible—in fact, Gemma had the ability to make everything less horrible. Soon enough, I wasn't just the new girl anymore—I had a friend, and life got much less lonely.

Gemma and I would hang out almost every day after school and, on the weekends, I would sleep at her house. Living only a few streets away from me, her five-bedroom trailer was not only twice the size of ours, but also looked much nicer. Though Gemma's father—a truck driver—was never home, her mother, Phyllis, was the sweetest woman I had ever met. With her gentleness, kind heart, and constant concern, she reminded me so much of my own mother. I loved being at their house. We got to eat anything we wanted, and watch movies all night long, and, best of all, no one ever bothered us. Gemma and I would chat and laugh for hours and hours on end, with everything in the whole world to talk about, the notion of ever becoming bored of each other seemed impossible. Gemma had become like a sister to me, and I felt as though I was truly a part of her family. I had spent so much time at her trailer, I not only had my own set of pajamas that I left there, but a cot in Gemma's room for our sleepovers.

When July finally arrived, Adam had returned from his month vacation to Tunisia and, joining Ron, had come to stay with us in the living room until he had developed a plan. They had both discussed their options and

ideas of what the future may hold, debating the pros and cons of getting
their own places, or perhaps moving away. I had grown accustomed to my
new life in the trailer park. With no acreage to explore, and no woodland
creatures to befriend, I dreaded being at home with Mildred and George.
It became routine for me to spend weekends at Gemma's house, and if I
wasn't in trouble, I spent as much time as I could in the company of my
new friend.

Following tradition, Mildred's family had an annual reunion that had always
fallen on the second weekend of August. Unfortunately for me, this had
meant that my birthday would always be spent at a hall among the crowd
of Mildred's country kin, and aside from my eighth birthday at McDonald's,
my birthday had simply become an afterthought. I loathed attending the
reunion. After saying hello, having dinner, and enduring Mildred's mother's
introduction of me as "the foster child that had made Mildred go broke,"
I would escape the crowds of Mildred's drunken kin, wandering off to the
cemetery beside the hall.

It had become a birthday tradition of my own. Nobody caring where I
went, or that I had been missing for hours, I would escape to the soothing
sights of endless rows of tombstones and angels. My mother would come to
mind as I sat in the grass, the August sun beaming against my skin. Though
her body had been flown back to Africa after her death, I had always thought,
while amid a sea of the dead in rural Alberta, that she was somehow here too.
Walking from stone to stone, I would read the epitaphs, think about the lives
these people had lived, admire the artistry of the stones, and think of angels.
Though it seemed morbid and sinister, I would find peace in the graveyard—I
felt as though I had a sense of understanding that connected me to the decaying corpses beneath me. I had liked the dead and I found company among
the rested souls. It was as though my love for my mother, and knowing that
she had become one of these people, had brought me closer to the realm of
those who perished.

I returned as I saw Ron and Adam pull up to the hall. Happily, they said hello and announced to everyone that they had decided—they would both be moving to Victoria, British Columbia, and they would be leaving tonight. "Yeah," they chimed, "We're going to drive there now—it's going to be amazing!"

Upon hearing the news, I rushed to Adam's side. Tears welling in my eyes, I burst into sobs. "Don't cry, Memo," Adam sweetly cooed. "We'll be back, and I promise I'll call you as soon as we get there. I love you, Memo!" I hugged him tightly.

Running back to the sanctuary of the cemetery, caskets below me, I sat on the grass and shook with sobs. *How could he leave me? How could he leave me in this house with Mildred and George?* I had done everything in my power to be with my brothers, and now, with Chokri in Edmonton, and Adam moving to British Columbia, I had no one. I had gone from having four siblings to one, and even then, Mel had her boyfriend Robert, and was hard to be found. Feelings of abandonment and pain welled up within me—though I knew it had nothing to do with me, and they were simply growing up and moving on with their lives—I felt betrayed. It wasn't fair. It wasn't fair that I was left alone. It wasn't fair that I couldn't leave too. It wasn't fair that I was stuck with Mildred and George. It wasn't fair that my mother had died. Nothing was fair. My life wasn't fair. I closed my eyes, the warmth of the August sun cooling as it set, and wiped the tears as they cascaded down my cheeks.

Chapter Seven
Age 11: Shattered

With the absence of my brothers, Mildred and George were unchanged and remained entranced in their same depressive state. Oddly, downgrading to the trailer home, and only being responsible for two dependents, had not made it easier for Mildred and George to manage their household, try to regain mental stability, or even take responsibility for their financial duties as caretakers. Melanie was forced to work, paying the bills they had so carelessly ignored. She had gotten a job in the city, at a fast food restaurant—and when that wasn't enough, she had gained additional employment in the city at a bingo hall. Without a car, or Mildred able to take on the role of chauffeur, Melanie took to hitchhiking. Though getting into the cars of strangers was a common sight, and for this reason, not deemed dangerous—I worried for her. Despite my growing maturity, and my increasing independence, I had missed my sister, and between floating in the emotional bliss of her relationship, her two jobs in the city, and my own newfound social life, we had grown distant. But, when she and I were home at the same time—a rarity—we would spend time together like we used to. Aside from those pleasant occasions where I would sit with Mel, watching TV, talking about our lives, and exchanging jokes and giggles, my hatred for my home had become overwhelming.

Still indulging in their weekly, drug-filled parties, Mildred and George's mental instabilities had begun to affect even their most treasured pastime.

During their parties, their fights were becoming increasingly violent and loud—there was more yelling, more crying, and a darkening cloud of sadness and depression loomed above us all. I made an earnest attempt to spend as little time as possible in the trailer, finding ways to escape the sights and sounds of Mildred and George's loud drunken fighting, Mildred's erratic bursts of sobs, or, when she was not crying, her barbarous shrieks. It was like living in some sort of warped twilight zone: a bunch of strangers under one roof who could hardly stand each other. And Mildred, growing more unstable, had not only become unbearable, but increasingly violent. When she hit Melanie, I was immediately alarmed. Melanie had always been safe from Mildred's rage and had this uncanny ability to get away with a lot, but recently, her cloak of safety had withered away. Storming into a wild fury, as if on a warpath, Mildred, with no reason or warning, would yell and scream at Melanie. It was as though Mildred was having a mental breakdown.

In adjusting to my life at the trailer park, I had learned to make do without my forest sanctuary, the escape of the outdoors, the friendliness of the farm animals, or the camaraderie of our house pets. There was no longer an escape, and as the summer months left my days empty, I often sat in front of my mirror with a hairbrush or something in my hand and gave talks and speeches to my "audience." I also used the mirror to talk to my mom a lot. I felt like she could hear me if I looked into my own eyes.

Hungry for a family, I turned to the friendships of my fellow classmates and neighbours as my retreat from the hellish atmosphere of my home. Despite their obvious character flaws and poor influence, I found companionship in the children around the trailer park who were like me—the other kids who were left uncared for; who were rejected from the world; who had nothing to care about. Wandering around the trailer park, between laughs and squeals, Gemma and I would watch kids vandalize cars or throw eggs at houses for the simple, purposeless sake of wreaking havoc. We had become a band of misfits, she and I. And, if the weather was too dreary, we would find refuge in our friend Cheryl's trailer, wasting away our day.

When I first entered Cheryl's trailer, it was as though I had turned back the hands of time and had once again taken my first step into the farmhouse—except this was worse. I averted my eyes from the soiled dishes that covered every surface, and the blankets and bags of laundry that crowded the floors, as I cleared the piles of clutter from the tattered and stained floral couches to find a seat. Inhaling the musty scent of dirty laundry, stale cigarettes, and the wafting odour of marijuana, I looked to the floor—with the crumbs of food and ash stains that were embedded into the low pile carpet, the bags of clothes, the piles of dirty dishes, and the overflowing ashtrays that were crowded with cigarette butts, the house had looked abandoned. Though I had always thought our houses were a disgusting and dizzying mess, the contrast of my current surroundings suggested that our houses had been relatively fine—aesthetically. But, as I grew accustomed to the disheveled trailer, I realized that, regardless of its filthy state, it was still better than being at my home.

Cheryl had a single mother who worked out of town, and, because of this, she was often not home. For extended periods of time, Cheryl, her younger sister, and Gary, who played the role of Cheryl's roommate and boyfriend, were left alone to care for themselves. They had seemed like an odd match, Gary and Cheryl—she had a large frame, with long, blonde hair, and a domineering persona, while he was skinny and seemingly frail. Every day I would watch as Cheryl would bark, ordering around her younger sister, who was only her junior by two years, and Gary, who was her senior by the same amount. I had recognized certain traits of Mildred in her—they were both boisterous, loud, and aggressive.

Gary had a somewhat lucrative career in the illicit sale of marijuana and in their trailer a large, onyx garbage bag always sat on the floor, brimming over with green leaves. It was shocking. Though I had known what marijuana was because of my guardian's weekend parties, and George's addiction, I had never seen it in such large amounts. But, in tune with my efforts to establish myself among my peers, it wasn't long before I had become a participating member of the circle, watching as joints took their clockwise journey around the living room and nervously accepting the tightly wrapped smoke that Gary extended from his left hand. My heart skipped a beat. I was anxious. Aside from the fact that this would be my first time experimenting with a drug, I felt an immense amount of pressure. I had tried so hard to blend into this world, to find companionship, and to connect with those around me. And, when faced in a circle of peers who had mastered the art of this recreational pastime, I was afraid that my inexperience and youth would deem me uncool. Employing the skills I had developed from learning how to smoke cigarettes so diligently in the past year, I slowly inhaled the smoke into my open lungs, but, unlike cigarettes, I waited a moment before exhaling. Bursting into a fit of coughs as I released the smoke from my lungs, the room erupted into laughter at my lack of finesse. Passing the joint to Gemma, I watched as she placed the wet tip of the joint between her lips and inhaled deeply; the end glowed a vibrant red with each inhale. Holding the air in her lungs, and effortlessly blowing it out, she passed the joint to Cheryl without coughing. My eyelids grew heavy and my body became simultaneously weightless and burdening. Gary's hand extended to me, yet again. Inhaling the next few passes of the joint sparingly, a sense of comical euphoria blossomed within me. I melted into the couch, forming into one, solid, inanimate being, sinking farther and farther into the unsightly floral patterns. Four pairs of eyes glazed over as we lost ourselves to the television screen, mesmerized by the glow—it was as though we were helpless, and simultaneously in our own respective worlds of thoughts and feelings. As I sat, slouched over, I reached into my pocket and pulled out a stolen cigarette. Smoking cigarette, after cigarette, along with everyone in the room—I finally belonged.

As the rustle of the trees and soft winds of September finally approached, for the first time since my mother had passed, I felt a sense of confidence in the school year to come. My friendship with Gemma, alongside my budding reputation and camaraderie among the older kids in the trailer park had granted me a sense of empowerment and strength. I was no longer alone, and my summer days of smoking endless cigarettes and indulging in the recreational experimentation with marijuana had been well spent. Despite being eleven, I had felt mature, powerful, and in control. It was an odd sensation, one that I had not been exposed to my entire life. No longer was I the meek, cowardly girl who ran into the forest to seclude herself, making friends with fish, toads, and mice—now, I was a girl who had *friends*. I was the girl who hung out with older kids, smoked cigarettes, and did drugs. I had become a success.

Our band of two quickly became five, as Gemma and I grew closer to three of our classmates as the school year started. Nicole, who lived across from Gemma, was tall, blonde, and small framed. She had grown up in the trailer park, in a chaotic, dysfunctional household that was in constant disarray. Her countenance sorrowful, her eyes always averted, her stance meek and shy—she, like me, as evidenced by her worn, faded clothing, had been trained to make do with what she was given. She was often tasked with the duty of caring for her younger siblings. Maggie, unlike Nicole, was warm, bubbly, and friendly. Long brown hair fell from the crown of her head, framing her chubby-cheeked face. But, out of all three of our newfound friends, Andrea had stood out the most not only in confidence and innate leadership, but in looks. I stared at her, examining her creamy, chocolate brown skin, and the rich, black curls that cascaded down her shoulders. I found comfort in not only seeing someone like myself, but in the thought that she too would know the same hurt and ostracism I had felt for being an ethnic minority.

As youthful relationships often do, our friendships quickly flourished. Soon, we were inseparable, sitting together in class, exchanging notes, glances, and eye rolls at our assignments, or the seemingly foolish comments of fellow classmates. When the school day had finished, we were found with Slurpees in hand, sitting on the edge of the meagre basketball court, exchanging malicious tales, gossip, and other mild amusements. Though it may have seemed childish, or insignificant to some, I treasured this small group of friends. I felt as though I was a part of *something*—a community, a support system that I had desperately longed for since my mother died. The five of us became invincible and unbreakable. Though Gemma was clearly the most affluent of the five of us—with a huge double-wide trailer, a mother who could stay home by choice, a wardrobe of the newest clothes, a vast collection of CDs, and an endless supply of makeup and junk food—she had her own familial burdens that some of us shared. When our friendship had begun, I often wondered why a family so seemingly perfect would live in Maplewood Court Trailer Park—the same disparaging, hellhole, that a very unlucky girl like me, was subject to. Only after spending regular weekend sleepovers and after school evenings, had I become aware of the turbulence her family had suffered. Though they had financial stability, and the means to indulge in the material goods I longed for, Gemma's father, like Mildred and George, was a severe alcoholic, leaving her mother a victim to the drunken outbursts that had always resulted in thundering fists. It was as though, through the misfortune of the lives we had no choice but to endure, Gemma and I, along with Andrea, Nicole, and Maggie, were connected.

A few lots down from mine, Maggie lived in a trailer that, though not different from mine, contained a family that was. Even though her family did not appear rich, and likely had the same financial woes as we did—Maggie's sunny disposition, and the wide smiles of her siblings had made it evident that they had come from a household filled with love and affection. Her parents worked hard. Her mother was employed, and her father, like Gemma's, was a truck driver. To my luck, because we lived so close, my free time was divided between both Maggie's trailer and Gemma's. Spending our afternoons making peanut butter and syrup sandwiches, on fresh, white bread, I was happy to have found myself another refuge from my home. Her family never seemed to mind having me over, and regardless of the financial struggles, would happily serve me dinner, allowing me to share in the endless love and laughter. Generously, they had even invited me to go camping with them during a family trip in the summer. In the warming glow of the campfire, as we roasted marshmallows, and snuggled up to the sparking logs with blankets and hot chocolate, I felt entirely at home.

Like Maggie and me, Andrea lived in a three-bedroom, two-bathroom trailer—though hers was farther away. She was biracial: her father was a small, white haired, elderly Caucasian man, and her mother was a large African woman, with a matching boisterous voice. They made an odd couple. Her father, like many men in Maplewood Court, favoured alcohol, and her mother had spent her days either visiting their relatives that lived in the trailer park, or at the local bingo hall. Andrea's older brother, Jeremy, had reminded me of my own siblings that had now gone away. His complexion was similar, and, like any teenage boy, his social life was teeming. It was obvious that Andrea's family was rarely home and, because of this, we had all spent the majority of our time in her trailer, which was in a constant state of dishevelment. Surrounded by overflowing ashtrays, empty beer cans that left the countertops invisible, and soiled laundry and blankets that were heaped in piles all over the floors and couches, we would smoke cigarettes, pass joints, and detail our familial grievances and annoyances. Although I was the only orphan, they too had hatred toward their caregivers.

At the young age of eleven, our misguided childhoods propelled us into mischief that extended far past our years. We were filled with angst and rage, suffering our own forms of loneliness and neglect. Our shared circumstances brought us together and desperation for happiness had kept us friends, providing a sense of comfort and belonging that none of us felt at home.

As the Albertan winter made its entrance, it was impossible for us to continue our regular evenings of chain-smoking. With everyone's parents spending their evenings at home, hoping to avoid the violently cold weather, I was left without refuge and retreated to my own trailer. Mildred and George, fighting endlessly each day, left Melanie and me to our own devices. And, though I would have enjoyed my time with her, Mel, in frequent fights with Robert, was in her own state of emotional turmoil. Though I had never liked him, he had become different since we lived at the chicken coop house—in fact, he had started getting even stranger as time went on.

His pretty boy demeanour was now transformed by what I only assumed could be drugs. He was jumpier, more aggressive and, because of this, I was glad that he and my sister hardly left their bedroom as I would have rather been on my own.

Coming home from school, I would lock myself in my room and hope that no one noticed me, only leaving to forage the kitchen for crackers, cheese, or juice, when I was sure no one was around. Looking out my bedroom window, which faced the street, I would tap the glass barrier at the sight of one of my friends, exchanging a wave, or through an open window, trading snippets of gossip. My window had become a portal, allowing me to communicate with my friends when Mildred and George forbid me from going out, which became increasingly often. It was as though Mildred would do anything for me not to be happy. I would be grounded without cause, trapped in the aluminum prison with my neglectful captors, as though she was jealous of my friendships, my happiness. Stripping away any goodness that I had left, Mildred, in her cloud of depression, had tried earnestly to drag me down into the dark, dismal hole of misery she had been so accustomed to.

"Hurry up, wake up!" Frantically pulling the blankets off me, Melanie burst into my room and shook me awake. "We have to go!"

My eyes jolted open, as I met Melanie's gaze—her eyes filled with fear. A familiar panic washed over me—my body stiffened, my mind raced, my heart began to pound violently, but time stood still. My mind shifted to the sight of my father in the moonlight, knife in his hand as the room slowly washed over in the same shade of crimson I had so earnestly tried to forget. *What was happening?* Adrenaline rushed through me, and with quick instinct, I leapt to my feet, scurrying the floor of my room, reaching for clothes.

"We don't have time for you to change, Iman!" Melanie ripped my garments out of my hands and began to stuff them in a bag, "We need to leave *now!*"

"Mel," I stammered, "What's going on?!"

"Mum cheated on George," she quickly rushed her words, trying to explain as fast as she could. "And he just found out, and is losing his shit. He's throwing things, and breaking windows, and we have to go to Auntie Donna's *now!*"

I paused, allowing myself to take a breath. Realizing my surroundings, as the pounding of my heart subsided, I finally registered the sounds of Mildred and George's screams.

"Iman!" Her voice was sharp, "Now! Hurry up!"

Her face was drained of colour as she rushed me to put on my shoes. Grabbing a blanket and the half-packed bag, she dragged me to the entrance-way of the trailer. I could hear Mildred's deep, horror filled sobs as George threw glass after glass. Pulling my arm out the door, forcing me into the cold, dark street, the sound of a window smashing echoed in the night air as we ran across the trailer park to the refuge of Mildred's sister's home.

Greeting us in the late hours of the night, Auntie Donna ushered us into her trailer, "Come in, girls," she said warmly. "It's okay—don't you worry about anything, okay?"

Leading us into the living room, she brought us blankets and pillows, tucking us into our makeshift beds, and wished us a good sleep. Though I feigned sleep, I remained wide awake, my head buzzing with questions. What would this mean? Not only did I not fully comprehend what it meant that Mildred had cheated on George, but I didn't understand what this would mean, regarding where we would end up. Would we move? Would we have to leave this life I've finally built for myself? I stirred, questioning my future and flashing back to my past. This was all too familiar. Short of flashing lights and shrieking sirens, I had been here before. I had been ushered into a home, welcomed with pity shrouded in warmth, tucked into a bed that was not my own, and told that everything would be alright.

The winter sun streamed in through the living room window, bringing light through my closed lids. It had taken a moment for me to adjust to my surroundings until the quiet murmurs of Auntie Donna and her three daughters had brought me back to reality. As the three girls prepared for their school day, and after Auntie Donna had spoken to Mildred, Melanie and I—still slightly unsettled from the previous night's events—made small talk as we changed out of our pajamas, and prepared for our return home.

Upon arriving at our trailer, Melanie and I exchanged glances as we opened the door, unsure of what to expect. Pausing at the door, we stood still, waiting for a sound of life. Silence.

Walking into the house, we took off our shoes without saying a word.

"Mum?" Melanie called out. No one replied.

We slowly walked into the living room, making our way into the kitchen. Though there were no signs of Mildred or George, the evidence from their fight last night was all around us.

As Melanie began to pick up the shards of glass from the broken dishes and shattered window, I bent down and started to help her.

"Be careful," she said quietly, "Don't cut yourself."

The trailer fell silent, only the small sounds of broken glass made a noise.

"Just go get ready for school, Iman," crouched down on the floor, her back turned to me, Melanie continued to collect the shards of glass. She didn't even look at me.

"Okay."

I could see that this was not a good time to argue that I was exhausted, scared, and didn't want to go to school. I knew that I had no choice, and Melanie was doing the best she could. Entering the bathroom, I closed the door and looked into the mirror. I looked down at my shaking hands; the image of Melanie's small frame crumpled on the kitchen floor, cleaning a mess that was not hers, was branded into my memory.

When I came home from school, Mildred was sitting in her chair in the living room knitting with a cigarette hanging out of her mouth.

"Hi," unsure of what to say, I paused. Her eyes remained on the spool of yarn, darting up at me for a brief second, before returning to the yarn.

"How was school?"

"It was good. I have lots of homework," I slowly made my way toward my bedroom.

"George moved out." I paused for a heartbeat at the words she told me. Her voice was empty, as if she didn't care.

"Okay."

I continued toward my room and closed the door, dropping my bag on the floor and sitting on the bed. I was unsure of what to feel. *Was this good? Should I be happy? Or should I be worried?* I sat in silence, absorbing the situation at hand, until the loud echoes of Melanie and Robert fighting in the next room interrupted my thoughts.

Between Melanie having a boyfriend and working two jobs, Mildred spending days at a time away from home, and George's absence—it had been a few weeks since we had seen him—the house had felt like it was abandoned. It was as though, if I died, no one would have noticed, let alone cared. It had become dreary, and isolating—more so than it had ever been. But, I had taken advantage of my solitude and newfound privacy. When I was at home alone, I would listen to music and cook myself dinner while dancing and singing to Madonna, or Michael Jackson—just like I had watched my mother do all those years ago. I had acquired a good grasp of cooking, and my culinary skills were becoming impressive as I added spaghetti, chili, and baked goods to the list of dishes I could prepare. Although my interest in cooking had started out of necessity, I had developed a joy in creating dishes, and wondering if my mother would be proud of what I could do. The savoury bouquet of garlic and onion sautéing in olive oil transported me back to my mother's kitchen where I would sit on the counter and watch her fill our house and bellies with love.

I had grown accustomed to having the house to myself, and though at first it felt like I was abandoned, I had grown to enjoy it. It was a much more favourable option as opposed to spending time with Mildred, Melanie, and Robert, or, before his departure, George.

Entering the trailer after school one early afternoon, I came to a full stop at the sight of a strange man with messy, brown hair, a large nose that was covered in textured bumps, and red with broken blood vessels, sitting on the living room couch. His body slumped on the couch, half-asleep, as he stared at the TV. The lingering scent of alcohol surrounded him like an aura, and a lit cigarette hung from his lips.

"Who are you?" with as much attitude as I could muster, I asked him in a loud, unwavering voice. He jumped at my question, noticing me for the first time.

"Oh shit," His cigarette fell from his mouth and he caught it with his hands, "You scared me, kid. I'm John. Your mom's boyfriend." A big dopey smile spread across his face.

I could feel my blood beginning to boil as I turned around, storming toward my room. My face grew hot. *What the fuck was Mildred doing bringing a strange creepy man to our house?* I thought to myself as I slammed my bedroom door shut. *And where the fuck was she while this jerk sat in our living room acting as though he owned the place?*

Though George was not the most gentlemanly of men, at least we had grown accustomed to his presence—at least he kept to himself, locked in his room, smoking weed. I had no interest in being an audience to a parade of strange, unsettling men, as Mildred adjusted to life without George. I had no interest being in that house, *period.* Grabbing my bag, I walked through the snow-filled streets in a fury, and headed to Cheryl's trailer. Entering her chaotic home, I immediately relaxed—melting into her floral couch, as I often did, I lit a cigarette after smoking a joint, and stared at the glowing television. After a few hours had gone by, I left, creeping into my house as quietly as possible, and falling onto my bed. My mind wandered to fantasies of running away and escaping, and, as I drifted off to sleep, I thought of elaborate schemes that would possibly bring my freedom.

I often had the same dream of my mother. We were in the desert and all you can see is sand for miles and miles and miles. My mother is up ahead in the distance, she sees me, and I her. But, as I push my feet through the sand, trying so desperately to run to her, I'm unable to reach her; my feet are incapable of navigating through the slippery, shifting terrain, and the miles between us never subside, regardless of my efforts, or how fast I run. And though I'm saddened that I can't reach her, that I can't touch her, or see her face—I know she sees me, and we're both shrouded in happiness because we're finally in the same place.

Taking residence in our trailer, John quickly became a regular face in our household. A mild-mannered, bubbly drunk, he was less invasive than I originally had thought. Spending his days sitting on the couch, watching television, chain-smoking, and drinking beer, it was as if he fit into our household perfectly. Nevertheless, it was odd. Though I had realized John was not creepy, but rather somewhat of a simpleton, it was an unsettling transition. Mildred—acting as though nothing was out of the ordinary, and not attempting to explain not only *who* he was, or why he was sleeping in her room—made the situation worse. But, it was not in Mildred's character to talk to us about anything, as I had quickly learned years ago. If she was unable to explain why we had no electricity, phone, heat, or food—how would she muster up the ability to discuss a familial change such as this?

"Mel, Iman—I need you guys to come here for a chat," she called to us on evening.

We entered the living room to find Mildred alone. A knot welled up inside of my stomach. Mildred had not been one for many words, and for her to ask us to talk about something was very odd. Bracing myself, I held my breath and exchanged a nervous glance with Melanie.

"We have no money for Christmas," Mildred said as she sat on the sofa.

The knot in my stomach unraveled in relief.

"We can't have presents, and I don't think we can have a turkey, either," she continued.

Although Melanie and I didn't need a formal announcement from Mildred informing us of the financial straits we'd been living in for years, we shrugged our shoulders, and offered Mildred a few meagre words of under-standing, nodding along until there was an appropriate pause in the con-versation for us to leave and go back to our rooms. I couldn't remember the last time we had a family dinner, nor could I remember her being concerned about our nutritional sustenance. For the past few weeks, she had hardly been home—often out with John, and not returning for the evening. I looked at her, as she sat there, looking up at us, as if she was asking for sympathy, as though she was going above and beyond her motherly duties—as though she hadn't just failed in her role as mother and caregiver.

As the week before Christmas arrived, not only had John's presence come to a halt, but Mildred informed us that George had wanted to stop by and see us. With our parcels from the food bank already unpacked, we had a modest number of gifts under the small tree, along with some food in the cupboards, and a big turkey in the freezer that was donated. Though it wasn't much, there was a hopeful cheer that had not been felt in the house for months.

"Hey! How are you?" A large smile spanned across George's face as Mildred opened the front door. In suit with the wild gusts of cold wind that had burst in through the open door, George entered, boisterous as ever. Placing the two large bags he had in his hands to the side, he leapt forward, giving both Melanie and me an overwhelming hug. Wrapping our arms around him, we were both surprised at how happy we were to see him. It was unusual to see him so happy, but it was nice to see him and have his childishly odd sense of humour break the tension and gloom he had left behind.

As we all sat in the living room, George handed us each a present. Mildred sat across from him in the chair, George, Mel, and I sat on the couch.

"You girls wait until Christmas to open your gifts," he said, looking at Mel and me. Turning to Mildred, he smiled, "You can open yours now, Mildred."

A blush crept upon Mildred's cheeks, and her furrowed brow eased at the idea that George had not only bought her something, but wanted her to open it in front of us. Excitement filled the room as we all sat in anticipation. Fumbling with the bow and ill-wrapped paper, she held a shoe box in her hands, looked up at George, and smiled. Excitedly, she peeled the lid off the box and, in an instant, her face went stone cold. As her eyes glanced into the box, she burst into sobs.

"A *dildo?*" She cried, "You bought me a fucking dildo?"

Throwing the box down on the floor, she grabbed the wrapping paper that remained by her side and violently threw it at George as she leapt off the couch, "What the hell is wrong with you, George?"

Her words shot out like venom.

"What? You don't like it?" He looked at her with a smile from ear to ear, "I thought you would be getting lonely without me."

Alarmed by Mildred and George's interaction, Melanie and I got up from the couch, panicked. Grabbing my arm, she rushed me to her room and closed the door, only to sit in still silence as we tried to decipher the muffled yells, but all we could hear was Mildred's cries and George's indiscernible mumbles. Suddenly, the sound of the front door closing was followed by the loud slam of Mildred's bedroom door, and the echoes of her sobs as she cried herself to sleep.

On Christmas morning, Melanie, Mildred, and I awoke early and did our best to be cheerful despite our recent setbacks, and happily celebrated Christmas without George. With only two gifts under the tree that weren't from the Edmonton Food Bank, Mildred continually apologized for our sad Christmas.

"It's fine, Mum," Melanie reassured her, "This is perfect."

After chiming in, I opened one of the few gifts that sat in front of me. I stared down at a curling iron, and my heart immediately sank. It was as though the universe was mocking me. *Why on earth would I have use for a curling iron when I had to suffer daily with the fact that I had curly hair?* It was the least thoughtful gift I had ever received. What a joke Christmas was. I was continuously amazed at life: Just when you thought it couldn't get any worse, you get a completely useless gift for Christmas while all your friends were getting everything they had wished for all year.

By New Year's Eve, George had returned, and had resumed his role in the household. During their last interaction, a mere two weeks ago, it seemed as though he had made things worse, but eventually he and Mildred made up. Resuming where they left off—ignoring the brief separation, the adultery, the inappropriate Christmas gift—they, in true Mildred and George spirit, had a party for New Year's Eve. Surrounded by a drunken crowd of Mildred and George's friends, Melanie and Robert had decided to join in, dancing throughout the whole night. A rare and pleasant occurrence, music, food, and laughter filled our small trailer home, and for the first time in a while, it had felt as though we truly had a home. And though it was odd that Mildred and George were hugging and kissing as though they had never broken up, as if the duct-taped kitchen window that stood for all to see, didn't exist, the room was filled with too much happiness and joy to care. The radio was blasting all night, and as everyone started dancing and cheering when The Proclaimers started singing, "I'm Gonna Be (500 Miles)" Melanie called me over from the couch, insisting I get off the couch and dance with her and Robert. And, as we counted down the New Year at the top of our lungs, the drunken crowd hugged and kissed each other.

Though the countdown was done, the party had continued. The smog of cigarette smoke, the scent of marijuana, the laughs, cheers, and wild yells—it had been a marvelous evening.

"Iman! Come here for a second," Robert called to me from the bedroom, "I have to tell you something."

I looked at him, caught off guard. *What would he have to tell me?* I asked myself.

As I stood in front of him, and he sat on the bed, his hands lunged toward me. Grabbing my face, he pressed his lips to mine, and held them there. My heart skipped a beat. He stopped and just looked at me. I stood, frozen in time for just a moment, until I regained control of my motor skills. Unsure of what to say, I walked out of the room, entered mine, and closed the door. I didn't understand what had just happened. Did I just have my first kiss? Was it for New Year's Eve the way everyone was kissing? A mix of embarrassment, worry, and happiness all flooded within me—a boy had never really given me that kind of attention before and I didn't know what to make of it. I didn't think it was right to tell anyone because I was afraid to ruin all the fun we had been having for the past few days. After all, it was the happiest we had all been in a very long, long time. I decided to keep it as my very own secret.

Robert never paid attention to me again after that kiss. Mel and Robert had started fighting more and more and I could hear them argue late into the night through our shared bedroom wall. His behaviour, more violent and erratic than before, was caused by his addiction to prescription drugs, and because of this, my sister had been trying to break up with him for weeks, and unfortunately was trapped by his abuse.

One spring morning Melanie decided to end things with Robert—once and for all. She told him to pack his things and that she wanted him gone by the time she came home that evening. Robert, in a crazed and erratic state, only half dressed with pants on but no shoes or shirt, covered himself in a blanket and chased Melanie's school bus down the street. She stared back at him and cringed, hoping no one would know that she knew him. A few days later, Robert appeared at the trailer and begged Melanie to just talk to him in his car. She was in the trailer with her cousin and told her that she would go out into the car but if it moved so much as an inch, to call the police immediately. Moments after Melanie got into Robert's vehicle, he drove away prompting her cousin to yell for Mildred who then called the police. Robert finally dropped Melanie off at home just after sunrise. That was the last we would ever see of him.

As the sixth grade was coming to an end, I was not only thrilled that I would be leaving elementary school, but Ben and Elizabeth invited me to spend part of the summer at their place—they had since moved away from Edmonton to Glenwood, a little town north of Noble Plains, just five hours north of Edmonton. I was both shocked and ecstatic that Mildred and George had said yes—I hadn't seen Ben or Elizabeth for a while, and the thought of escaping my life to live in happiness with Ben and Elizabeth filled me with such joy. With the school year ending in a few weeks, and me spending the month of August away, Gemma and I had begun to make as many plans as possible for July. We planned sleepovers, and discussed things we could do to spend as much time as possible together before I left.

When the final school bell rang, though I was excited, Gemma had left for Manitoba during the first two weeks of summer vacation, and with my best friend gone, I was slightly saddened. Though I still spent time with Andrea, Nicole, and Maggie, the dynamic had changed with Gemma's absence. Andrea had become bossy and demanding, and though Maggie and Nicole just laughed off her behaviour, I began to feel out of place.

Andrea had invited me over one afternoon and, thrilled to have an excuse to leave the house, I quickly got ready, alerted George and Mildred of my plans, and made my way across the trailer park. When I arrived, Andrea greeted me, a large smile spanning from cheek to cheek, and invited me in. As we entered her room, toward the back of the trailer, my stomach churned at the sight of Maggie and Nicole. Though it was not odd that they were there, it was strange that she had not mentioned that they would be joining us. They both greeted me enthusiastically and everyone started talking and laughing like usual, but I felt strange for the first time around the three of them. I instinctively knew I no longer wanted to be there. Lighting a cigarette, I sat on one of the small, child-size blue chairs that furnished the room.

"Can I have one?" Nicole looked at me. I nodded, and reaching into my bag, presented her with an unlit cigarette.

We sat in an awkward silence as the two of us smoked and Andrea made small talk with Maggie. I had the sense that they were mad at me for something but I couldn't for the life of me figure out why.

"You know, Iman," Nicole blew her cigarette smoke in my direction "We don't really like you anymore."

"What are you talking about?" I looked at her in defiance, slightly surprised, but simultaneously registering her words.

"We just don't like you anymore," she took another drag from the cigarette I had given to her as she rose from the bed, and put it out in the ashtray in front of me. "You're weird and annoying," she continued, "We can't be friends with a loser like you."

I stood up immediately, sensing things were going to escalate by the way she walked so confidently toward me. Maggie and Andrea stood up and hung back behind her a couple of feet. As I looked at them and their pathetic smirks, I knew I had been betrayed, and I knew that they would have not dared try this if Gemma had been there.

Walking to her stereo, Andrea played the song, "Momma Said Knock You Out" by LL Cool J.

I tensed up. Not only had they planned this, they had also deliberated on choosing the best song that would play while they forcefully shut me out.

Lunging at me and grabbing my shirt, Nicole tried to pull my head down toward her knee as she violently jerked it toward my face. I resisted, preventing her from pulling me down any farther, and pushed her until she had no choice but to let go of me. Again, she tried—grabbing at me and trying, with all her might, to pull me down to the ground, but surprising us both, I was stronger than her. I could see the insecurity in her face as she let go, swinging her left fist, and punching me directly in the forehead. Recoiling in pain, she stepped back—I stood, stunned. My head throbbed as she shook out her fist from the pain. Clearly this wasn't going as planned for anyone in attendance. Andrea and Maggie had looks of both confusion and embarrassment on their faces. Rushing out of the room, I went into the washroom in the next room, staring at the mirror. Right between my eyes, a large mound had formed and almost instantly, had begun to turn into the colour of a dark plum. A feverish anger welled up inside of me. Not only had they embarrassed me, planned an attack on me, and created this welling bruise in the middle of my forehead, I would have to explain this protrusion to Mildred and George. I stood, facing the mirror, staring back into my eyes. My hands shook with anger.

Storming back into the room, I pushed Nicole backward onto Andrea's bed.

"Look at what you did to my fucking face, you bitch!"

A terrified look flashed on her face. Preying on her fear, I grabbed the same blue chair I had sat upon, moments before, and threw it at her, "What the fuck am I going to say to my parents, huh?"

Surprised by my temper, Maggie and Andrea had quickly changed their tune, "W-we're not mad anymore, Iman."

"Y-yeah, I'm sorry!" Retreating into her cowardly form, Nicole had begun to stammer, "I d-don't know why I did it. I'm sorry."

Fueled with rage, I didn't care for their pathetic apologies, or attempts to retract their actions. Repeatedly pushing her until she fell on the floor, I ignored Nicole's pitiful apologies.

"You'll fucking pay for this," looking at each of them in their fearful eyes, I stormed out of the trailer holding back tears, lighting a cigarette.

Although I had hoped her neglect would work to my benefit, Mildred had noticed the mound on my forehead instantly. "What the hell happened to you?!"

"Oh." Steadying my breath, I tried to sound as calm as possible, "It's so embarrassing. Andrea opened a cupboard, and it hit me in the face."

Satisfying her curiosity, Mildred accepted my answer, and halted her questioning.

Every passing mirror and reflective surface confronted me with evidence of my rejection and, refusing to leave the house until it was gone, I silently stewed in the solitude of my room. I didn't belong here—I didn't belong in this trailer park, and I certainly didn't belong with Mildred or George. My enthusiasm to escape to Ben and Elizabeth's quickly increased tenfold, more so than I thought possible. I had nothing here, and no one here. I frantically tried to search my mind in the hopes that I could determine what I had done to force Nicole, Andrea, and Maggie to not only ostracize me, but to try and hurt me. I came up with no answers, but the longer I searched, the stronger my hatred for them grew. *Next year*, I thought, *we will be in a new school, with new friends.* And as I was hidden away, waiting for the last shred of evidence of their betrayal to fade away, I planned not only how I would make them suffer, but vowed that I would hurt Nicole far worse than she had hurt me. She had fucked with the wrong bitch.

Chapter Eight

Age 12: Fields of Gold

Though it was just a 1988 Oldsmobile Delta, it felt like I was being ushered into a limousine. The long, two-toned green vehicle radiated regality and affluence, and as I shuffled into the backseat, the emerald green velour that rubbed against my palms felt like rich, buttery velvet. I was thrilled. To my slight dismay, Chokri did not greet me as I approached the car, and, I soon found out that he no longer lived with Ben and Elizabeth. When they had moved to Glenwood, Chokri decided to remain in Edmonton, and now lived with his childhood friend. Admittedly, though it would have been a pleasure to spend the summer with my older brother, a sliver of excitement fluttered within me at the thought of having Ben and Elizabeth all to myself.

Filling the five-hour drive with reading my books, resting my head against the window for brief naps, and gazing into the endless rows of corn, bundles of hay, and the clear blue sky, I imagined I was being whisked away to my new life with Ben and Elizabeth—that I would never have to see Mildred and George again. Despite the long journey, Ben had made it fun, inducing a whirlwind of daydreams and laughter. As we talked, and sang along to the songs that played on the radio, his bright red hair tousled in the wind. And, as always, his silly, upbeat personality matched his aesthetic. He had not changed in the years since my mother's death. Still dressed in colourful outfits of neon harem pants and patterned shirts, his garb matched perfectly with his red beard, and large glasses—he even wore wooden clogs and carried a man-purse before it was deemed fashionable.

Elizabeth complemented Ben's style effortlessly. Draped in oversize black dresses and flowing purple jackets, her dress suited not only her, but Ben's eclectic wardrobe. A classic beauty with long, black hair that hinted at a slight shade of purple in the sunlight, her large eyes looked Egyptian, sparkling a beautiful brown that mirrored her warm, olive-toned skin. With a smile that could light up an entire room, her flawlessly applied makeup and eccentric jewelry—large baubles of gold and stone perfectly framed her long, narrow neck—only accentuated her natural beauty. The smell of her perfume, her manicured nails, the collection of rings that dripped gold from her fingers—Elizabeth was a perfect contrast to Mildred. Though my mother was never so extravagant, her smell had made me feel at home, and Elizabeth, with her big smile and her tight, enveloping hugs, had made me feel safe in a way that I had not felt since my mother had been taken away from me.

We stopped at a restaurant along the way to have lunch and I felt like I was in heaven. Food was a novelty at home with Mildred and George, and dining at a restaurant in their care was an impossible dream. I looked at the menu, overwhelmed—Ben had said I could have anything I wanted. Since I had lived with Mildred and George, I was in a constant state of hunger, and the hunger pains had become nothing more than the sound of a breeze in the distance. But when confronted with such choices and the possibil-ity of indulging in an actual meal, my mind became a whirlwind of entrees and decisions. I was hungry. Too hungry. Scanning the menu, repeatedly, I finally landed on a decision: steak and fries. Moments later, when the server approached our table, my eyes widened as they set my plate in front of me. Ravenously, I gorged myself, becoming full quickly—my appetite, though robust, was smaller than the steak. I looked down at my dish, fries littered around the remaining carcass. I had expected to be scolded, to be told I was ungrateful, as I would have been by Mildred. Instead, I was offered dessert. No one yelled at me for not finishing my dinner, or questioned my gratitude for the meal. Something about Ben and Elizabeth was just all-around hap-pier and more peaceful, and I felt happier than I had been in a long time, just being in their company. The trailer park and all my troubles were so far behind me.

Once we left the city, the scenery changed from concrete and buildings to farmland and never-ending fields. The smell of sweet summer air filled the car and the sunshine felt like warm gold on my skin. As we drove by fields of bright yellow canola, Ben turned his head, looking at me from the front seat, "You see all that yellow? I painted it for you."

A smile formed across my face. I looked outside in awe at the buttery yellow fields, "Really? You painted that all just for me?"

"You bet I did! I had to wake up pretty early too!"

I finally figured out that he was joking and the car erupted in laughter. That canola was the most beautiful painting I had ever seen.

Finally, around dinnertime, we arrived in Glenwood. A large white bungalow, with forest green shutters around every window, sat on a large lot that also housed Ben and Elizabeth's latest business venture—The Highland Inn. I looked at the row of sixteen rooms that lined up just steps away from the house as we all clambered out of the green Oldsmobile, gathering our belongings. Walking into the house, a fuzzy orange cat came rushing out the door. A smile quickly spread across my face as I saw the cat leap past me. I had missed my pets so terribly since Mildred and George had left them behind.

I turned my attention to Ben as he pointed around the house, giving me a tour. The front of the house, separated by a curtain, was sectioned off—acting as the front desk of the hotel. Two shelves, holding common motel necessities, such as candy, chips, and toiletries, lined the front walls. I had never seen anything like that before, especially in a house, and was so intrigued with this new adventure. In the private portion of the house, the kitchen and dining room opened into each other, and the counters were filled with breads, rolls, cakes, and a large wicker basket of fruit. My mouth started to water. I hadn't seen so much food out in the open, for all to eat, since I was still with my mother.

Cream leather sofas and two oversized arm chairs—one dark green and the other brown—furnished the living room that was positioned next to the kitchen. Asian-inspired art hung from the walls and decadent vases and trinkets decorated the tables; a phenomenal sculpture of grapes made from expertly polished amethysts sat on a beautiful bronze stand; and the enormous television was tucked away into a closet at the far end of the room. I was surrounded by beauty and luxury—two things that my life had been lacking.

"Now don't eat too much dinner or you won't have any room for dessert!" Ben smiled at me as we sat at the dining room table in front of a large feast. Eating was just so different than what I was used to. Mildred and George were always nagging at me and complaining about everything I did. They never tried to serve me food I liked or even took the time to ask what kind of things I wanted to eat. Happily, I took Ben's advice, managing to finish my meal with two large helpings of banana cream pie. In one day, I felt like I had eaten more than I had the entire week before. I loved all the food we had eaten and having dessert was such a rare occasion at Mildred and George's that I could have devoured the entire pie. I could certainly get used to laughing and eating all day. Is this what everyone else was doing who wasn't orphaned? *Clearly*, I thought to myself, *I was missing out.*

After dinner, Elizabeth showed me to a lovely bright white room that was right next to theirs, furnished with two single beds and a tall dresser. Beaming, I quietly unpacked my things. As I unpacked, I thought about what it would be like to live with Ben and Elizabeth. Why would Chokri ever leave such an amazing home? If I had a chance to live with them, I would never want to leave—we would laugh, cook, eat, and be a happy family. Nestling into bed, my mind wandered into a dream world of laughter, food, peace, and happiness.

I awoke in the morning shrouded in warmth and joy. Enthusiastically, I rose out of the single bed, dressed myself, and was greeted to a large plate of pancakes with fresh berries and whipped cream when I entered the kitchen. My eyes widened not only at the sight, but at the fact that Ben had woken up early to prepare us such a wonderful breakfast. An endless variety of juices, syrups, cinnamon, and icing sugar was set on the table. And, once again, I ate until I felt like I would explode.

After breakfast, Elizabeth showed me around their property. Having never seen a motel before, I was not only excited, but filled with curiosity. As we walked from room to room, I noted their identical furnishings—two double beds, a desk, chair, television, and washroom. At the end of the row of rooms was a laundry room and linen closet. I peered into the busy laundry room, staring at the piles of sheets and towels that seemed to tower as high as the ceiling. Kindly, Elizabeth asked if I could help her, and I happily assisted her in switching the loads from the washer into the dryer, loading up the washing machine, and folding the newly dried sheets. Though it was a menial job, I felt proud to be tasked with a chore that helped and to be a part of Elizabeth's everyday errand.

As the week went by, Ben and Elizabeth showed me all around town, taking me to the library where I borrowed several books to keep me entertained during my vacation. We went into Peace Brooke, which was a town just eight kilometers away and got delicious milkshakes from a fast food place called The Pink Flamingo. As we toured the area, Ben showed me where he grew up on a nearby farm, which was pretty much just an old tiny shack. He told me how he and his three brothers had to share a two room shack with their parents. I stared at the small shack in awe—it made our trailer look like a mansion, and was hardly standing up on its own. Soon after, we went to visit his parents who had a huge plot of land with a big house and cavalry of horses. I was over the moon with how big and open and free their property was, thinking back to when I had lived at the house on the hill, amid the open forests and my private sanctuary. I had forgotten how much I missed the country and how peaceful my heart felt to be outdoors.

The motel was prosperous, each room filling swiftly after being vacated. Since they were understaffed and business was thriving, Elizabeth was forced to clean some of the rooms to maintain their regular traffic and motel standards.

I asked if I could help too, explaining that at the trailer I was the one who was tasked with cleaning. With a smile on her face, she welcomed my help, and showed me how to make beds with hospital corners, tucking them in at the bottoms perfectly. We laughed together while loading and folding the laundry, restocking the cleaning cart, and bringing all the freshly laundered linens to the rooms. I felt so accomplished and so proud of all that we had done.

On one of my trips to the laundry room, Elizabeth informed me that as part of their services they laundered the clothing of their guests upon their request. Since the guests were mostly men who worked on the various nearby oil rigs, the guest laundry was often caked with layers of hardened mud. My head fell forward as I opened one of the laundry bags—all I could see was dried mud. The pants, saturated with the wet dirt, had almost solidified. Nevertheless, with a jovial grin on my face and a task in front of me, I shook them outside, as best as I could, and threw them in the washing machine with the guest's other clothes. I had wanted to make Elizabeth proud, and ensure that I had done my small role as best as I could. Timing everything to make sure I could fulfill my duty efficiently and effectively, I switched the loads at the sound of the loud buzzer, folding the laundered clothing as soon as it was ready, and kept up with the loads that waited to be washed. When I was done, I packed the nice clean clothes into a bag and made my way to the guest's room and knocked on the door.

"Well hello, little lady!" The door opened and a large man looked down at me with a smile on his face. Surely, he was shocked to see me, a small-framed child, delivering his clothing.

"Umm…hi!" I proudly presented the bag of laundry that I had just done on my own, holding it in his reach. "Your laundry is clean!"

"Already?" He happily reached for his possessions, a look of astonishment on his face, "I just brought it in a couple of hours ago!"

"Yup! I made sure to time everything so I could get it done quick for you."

The man reached into his pocket and pulled out some change and handed it to me. I looked down in my hand and saw two dollars in quarters. I squealed thank you and ran all the way back to Ben and Elizabeth's. It felt good to get praised for something and I was smiling from ear to ear. Telling them of my good fortune, I could barely contain my excitement—I had made my own money. Feeling pride and a rush of delight, I asked if I could do the laundry of anyone else who asked and Elizabeth said yes. Ben, giving me a jar, told me to start collecting my earnings to see how much money I could accumulate over the next two weeks.

Unlike the money I had collected from selling the chocolate almonds, I proudly placed the jar atop the dresser. Dreamily, I wondered how many loads of laundry I would have to finish to fill it. I beamed at the thought of filling the jar, having something of my own and, most of all, starting my very first business venture. As Ben joked that I was now an entrepreneur, I laughed, determined to do as many loads of laundry as I could before I was condemned to return to my impoverished life at the trailer park, where no one had money, Mildred and George would complain, and Mel worked two jobs to keep the lights on. Smiling, I looked at the empty jar as if it were filled with gold.

In the evenings, I would walk to the tree-lined park that was ten minutes down the road. Reminding me of my forest sanctuary and the splendor of the outdoors, I sat in the serene silence, listening to the frogs croaking in the small swamp nearby. I loved being alone among the trees again. Everything felt so tranquil. As I sat in the dimming sunlight, the sounds of nature all around me, I imagined that I lived in Glenwood—that I had been rescued from my horrible life. Things just didn't seem so bad when I was with Ben and Elizabeth. In fact, they were almost perfect. They had treated me like a real person; they looked me in the eyes when they talked; they asked me questions, really listening to the answers. In their presence, I felt loved. I felt as though what I wanted *actually* mattered. When I was with them, I didn't hate my life, I didn't hate myself, and I never thought about escaping or dying—I just felt happy. Every moment was filled with laughter. Every day was filled with food. Every second, I felt safe and needed. I wanted them to be proud

of me, and I vowed to work as hard as I could to help them before I would
have to depart.

As my twelfth birthday approached, Elizabeth asked me what kind of cake I
wanted. I was in shock. For the past four years, my birthdays had been spent
in the solitary fields of tombstones and buried corpses. The question of what
type of celebratory dessert I desired was one that had never been asked. No
one had bothered because, simply, no one had cared. Oddly enough, Garfield
the cartoon cat, was the first thing that popped into my head. A momentous
occasion, Ben and Elizabeth invited some friends over to celebrate. After a
large dinner around the table, the glorious sight of a cake appeared from the
corner of my eyes. Placing it in front of me, twelve small waxed candles lit,
Ben joined in the chorus as our guests sang the age-old "Happy Birthday."
I closed my eyes, savouring the moment, inhaling deeply, and as my breath
escaped my puckered lips, I wished to be happy. One of Ben's friends, who
brought a guitar with him, began to strum the chords of an unknown song,
singing along to the melody as we cut into the Garfield-themed dessert. I
sparkled with delight as I looked around the room—it was one of the best
birthdays I had ever had, and I was grateful to hang among the living and, for
just this moment, be so spoiled.

Ben and Elizabeth had a friend with a twelve-year-old daughter, Katy. She
had lived in Edmonton, with her single mother who had raised Katy alone.
During my last week in Glenwood, her mother had gone on a trip, and Ben
and Elizabeth, enthused at the idea of my fostering friendship with a girl my
own age, had invited her to stay with us.

Katy was born in the Ukraine and, after Chernobyl, she and her mother
had moved to Canada. She had a petite frame, and soft brown hair that
lightly curled around her face. I had thought she was rather serious for a
child, and imagined that she, like myself, had her own troubles that awaited
her in Edmonton. She told me stories about living in Ukraine, having to line
up just to get bread. She said that the bread would be covered in mold and

after they had stood for hours to get it that they would just be so happy to have walked away with something, picking off the mold and eating what was left. I sympathized with her. Living with Mildred and George, though not comparable to her life in the Ukraine, had granted me plenty of moments where I too would have to pick the mold from the little bread we had left in our empty kitchen just to make a butter and sugar sandwich.

I told Katy about the great job I had doing laundry and asked if she wanted to help me. Though she had said yes, her excitement did not mirror mine. Nevertheless, we worked every day to get the laundry done. Sometimes my entrepreneurial knack would take hold of me, and if I saw one of the men walking out to the parking lot I would ask if he wanted me to do his laundry while he was out. My approach had earned me more customers than I had anticipated and, at the end of every day, I would put all my money in the treasured jar that greeted me every morning. And whenever Katy helped me, I would split my money with her. She didn't seem too excited and I guessed, since her mold picking days were long behind her, it had made sense. She mostly just wanted to sit and read her book, which, to be frank, was not a bother to me—I really was only sharing the work to be nice. I was quite glad to have all the money for myself. After all, I did become an entrepreneur before she even arrived.

Chapter Nine

Age 12: Overexposed

Igot a call from Mildred one evening. Though I was slightly taken aback that she contacted me since I thought she would not have cared that I was gone, her call made sense when she informed me that we would be moving again, and since I was in Glenwood, I would not be there to pack my belongings. My face grew hot—I couldn't believe that we would have to move while I was on vacation. Immediately, my skin began to crawl at the image of Mildred going through my belongings, relishing the discovery of my treasured hiding spots, and unveiling all of my hidden possessions. *Idiots*, I thought. *Couldn't they just pay the fucking rent for once?* I asked to speak to Melanie, becoming increasingly frantic as I thought of Mildred's frail hands pawing through my various effects.

"Hello?" Melanie's voice came through the receiver.

"Mel," I lowered my voice. "I need you to go into my room and pack my journal, smokes, lighters, and weed."

Telling her my various hiding spots, I begged her to promise me she wouldn't disclose the sensitive information I had just given her. As I hung up the phone, a wave of relief came over me. *Thank God, she was home.* I walked into my room, sitting on the clean sheets. The thought of moving again had created a nauseating sensation in the pit of my stomach, and the orb of happiness that had surrounded me these past few weeks burst with one phone call.

Before I knew it, it was time to go back home. A couple of nights before we left I started having panic attacks and nightmares that my father was at my window with a butcher's knife, trying to break into my room. I woke up crying, shrouded in darkness, a thin film of cold sweat resting against my skin. Katy, unperturbed, slept silently in the bed across the room. Already staggering to breathe, I began to heave deeply as silent sobs erupted from my lips. Lying in bed, my head against a dampened pillow as tears rushed from the corners of my eyes, I prayed to God that something would happen that would make me stay with Ben and Elizabeth. I didn't want to go back to the nightmare that I was living with Mildred and George.

When the morning came, my tears had not yet subsided—I couldn't stop crying. Ben and Elizabeth, gentle in their words and touch, tried to console me. Though they had earnestly tried to alleviate the sobs that came pouring out of me, all I could do was cry. I told them I didn't want to go back and that I would miss them. My heart ached at the thought of leaving the dream I had just been living in for the past month. I so desperately wanted to ask them if I could stay, if they could take me in, if I could just be with them—but, I couldn't bring myself to ask. The thought of them saying no, dismissing my hopes and dreams, was too much to bear. If they had said no, what would I have left to dream about? What would I have left in my life? Imagining my life with them had become my saving grace when I wanted so much to escape the negativity and abuse of where I was.

With reluctance and despair, I packed my things, emptying my money jar for the last time. I had made almost forty dollars from hard work and the tips of kind strangers and, though I was heartbroken, knowing that I would have my own money had brought some small cheer and a feeling of accomplishment. I would miss so much about Glenwood. I would miss going to the park and working at the motel. I would miss all the yummy food and having dessert every day. I would miss laughing at Ben's silly jokes and how Elizabeth could make everything better with a cuddle on the couch and a movie. I wanted them to be my family so badly.

Listening in silence to the audio books we had borrowed from the library the day before, I looked out of the car window that only a month ago escorted me to paradise. *Charlotte's Web* echoed in the background as I gazed at the fields of the yellow canola Ben had painted *just for me*. If only my life was my choosing and someone in the world cared what I wanted. I promised myself that when I did finally get to choose, if I made it that far, that I would choose to be happy. I would make all my own decisions and I would never ever spend time with people like Mildred and George.

It was nightfall when Ben's car pulled into the trailer park. He had gotten directions from Mildred the night before and, with keen eyes, we kept watch for my new home. As we pulled up to the trailer, I wondered why we had to move in the first place. This new trailer was a stone's throw away from our last, and looked identical. I scanned my mind, landing on the obvious reason—Mildred and George probably didn't pay the rent. My face hardened at the thought of not only their complete lack of adult maturity, but at the notion of being in their care once again. The car engine came to a lull as Ben parked the Oldsmobile outside of the tin box and my heart grew even heavier. Letting out a large sigh, I stepped out of the car door Ben held open for me. He opened the trunk, helping me gather my belongings. As I hugged him goodbye with all the strength in my body, I silently begged him not to leave me.

I felt the sensation of tears forming in the back of my throat. His hands moved forward toward me as we released our hug, and he pushed two hundred dollars into my hands, "In case you need anything for school." I looked up at him, fighting back my tears, thanked him with a kiss on the cheek, and turned to make my leave. A few steps toward the doorway, I paused, turning back to watch him get into the car and drive away without me. In that

moment, more than any other time, I wished that I wasn't legally bound to
Mildred and George.

A table stood in front of the entrance, providing a barrier between the foyer
and the eat-in kitchen. I looked around the room. The same shade of stained
yellow coated the walls, and the dirty, brown carpet resembled our last trailer's. The living room was positioned in the front of the house, with three large
windows that presented a view of the street. Mildred rose from her seat on the
couch, approaching me for a hug; George remained seated.

"How was your vacation?" She asked me as she let me out of her embrace.

"Good," the somber tone of my voice was unmistakable. I stood still as
she paused, as if she was hesitant, and followed her eyes to the floor. She had
begun to explain why we had moved.

"The landlords were assholes," she murmured, continuing to say how
they hadn't cut her any slack. Immediately, I had known my suspicions were
correct—she and George hadn't paid the rent. Silently, I nodded. I had no
interest participating in this conversation nor did I care for Mildred's excuses.
There was always an excuse as to why things didn't work out for Mildred and
it was never anything of her doing.

"Your room is down the hall, second door on your left," she turned away,
walking toward the couch.

I carried my bags past the kitchen and the table with barely enough room
to get past the table into the hallway entrance. I could hear music coming
from the first bedroom and knew Melanie was home—a sigh of relief escaped
me. Making my way to the second bedroom, my fingers reached to the left
of the doorframe scrambling for the light switch to fill the darkened room
in light. Quickly, my eyes made an inventory of the space. My exposed mattress, sitting bare on its frame, was positioned against the back wall under a
window, there was a closet parallel to the bed, and the entire room was filled
with boxes of all my stuff. As I put my bags down and sat on the mattress,
I sighed, yet again—although, this time, my sigh was one of disappointment.

This place was atrocious, and this room, which was a mess, was two-thirds the size of my last one. Resigned to my fate, I began opening garbage bags until I found my bedding and I started to make my bed. A knock on my door gave me pause. It opened, and Melanie walked in.

"Hey, Sissy!" She opened her arms, walking toward me to give me a hug. "You're home! How was it?"

"Hey!" I smiled at the sight of Melanie. Though I had a summer of bliss, I had missed her. "Yeah, I just got here. It was amazing and went by so fast."

"What do you think of the new place?"

I looked around at all the unpacked boxes, and rolled my eyes. I held my breath, "Did you pack my room?"

"*Yes.* And you owe me big time!"

She gently punched my arm and laughed. "I have your secret stuff in my room. Let me know when you want it, okay?" She made her way toward the door, pausing for a brief second and called over her shoulder, "By the way, I smoked your cigarettes."

I laughed at her comment. It was a small price to pay to have her pack my room and avoid the possible outcome. The last thing I wanted was to come home and be confronted with Mildred's rage if she had found my secret treasures of cigarettes and marijuana. I thought back to the last month. *I hadn't smoked in weeks.* I was having so much fun at Ben and Elizabeth's that I didn't even miss the habit I had so carefully formed. But now, surrounded by boxes, a cigarette was the only thing I wanted. *How quickly things change,* I thought. Dismissing the craving, I resumed my task, dressing the bed and tucking the corners of the bedsheets underneath the mattress. Thinking back to only a few weeks ago, when Elizabeth taught me how to fold the corners of the bed so neatly, I felt so displaced. This morning I woke up in Glenwood, surrounded by love and laughter. Now, six hours later, I was in a different trailer in the same old trailer park, unpacking boxes in a home I couldn't stand being in, and left in the care of two guardians who could barely take care of themselves. The usual sadness and solitude quickly rose to the surface. I had nothing and I had no one. Reaching my hand to my pocket, I felt the outline of the neatly folded bills Ben had handed me. I pulled them out and walked to my bag, combining the money Ben had given me with the tip money I had accumulated over the summer. *At least I have this*, I thought. My eyes darted around the room, landing on the shelf in the corner of my room. I placed the bills in an envelope that was on my dresser and duct-taped the money to the underside of the corner shelf. I made a silent prayer that it would remain safe. After all, nothing in this place was sacred—not even me.

Fitfully tossing and turning, I could hardly sleep the night before my first day of the seventh grade. My mind spun with fear and nervousness, but also with excitement at the thought of finally being in junior high. Since my departure from Glenwood, Ben and Elizabeth had come to take me shopping to prepare me for my return to academia, gifting me with new clothes and school supplies that would have otherwise been un-purchased. If not for their kindness, I would be stuck with Mel's hand-me-downs for my first year as a pre-teen. Though my month in the serenity of Glenwood had seemed like an eternity ago—living in a dream of buttery pancakes, fresh laundered sheets, and showers of love and affection—returning to the trailer park had a way of cancelling out not only the luxurious escape, but time itself. It was what I imagined prison to be like: every day melting into the next and never being able to tell quite how long you'd been there or how much longer you had left—the only measurement of time was tallied notches I etched into the concrete walls of my mind.

Gemma and I met up early in the morning before school and her mom drove us to Birch Heights Junior High School in Cedar Grove, which was twenty minutes from the trailer park. Although we were as giddy as ever—teeming with energy, enthusiasm, chatter, and laughter—as we approached our destination, a nervous pit formed deep within me at the thought of Nicole, Andrea, and Maggie, attending the same school. The pain, hurt, and bitterness within me had not left. I had not forgotten what they had done to me two months ago, let alone forgiven them. The betrayal I had felt that day had resonated deep within me, growing stronger like a wild flame.

I absentmindedly grazed my fingers against my forehead on the same spot where Nicole had created the now-healed protrusion. *I'll get her back.*

New schools were a common occurrence in my life and Birch Heights Junior High would mark my eighth. I had grown accustomed to the change. Holding my head high, and taking a deep breath, I slid on the invisible shield I had protected myself with during my last seven first days. The pit in my stomach dissolved and was once again replaced with bubbling excitement, fear, and anxiety. *But*, I thought to myself, *this year is going to be different.* I looked at Gemma and a small smile crept upon my face as a sense of calm washed over me. I was now equipped with another defense: a best friend—and she and I could adapt to anything.

We walked up to a bustling crowd of teenagers, buzzing around the one-level junior high. Lost in a sea of new and returning students, Gemma and I quickstepped to keep pace, keeping our eyes locked so as not to lose the only familiar face in the crowd. The building was large, a series of small plain windows studded the front walls and four blue doors stood together as the main entrance against the monochromatic cream exterior. I couldn't believe how many people there were. I couldn't believe that this was my new school. I couldn't believe I was *finally* in junior high.

The first few days were a bit of a blur, making our way around the school and getting acquainted with all our classrooms was a rush. Unfortunately, unlike our small world of elementary school, separate schedules had forced us to be in different classes. Though I felt panicked to sit in rooms of rows of desks filled with strangers, the chime of the class bell brought Gemma and me back together, where we would reunite during breaks and lunches, allowing us to hide behind the school and smoke cigarettes. We would rush through the forested walking path just beside the school, exchanging tales and rants about our new classmates and courses, finding sanctuary in our final destination: the smoking pit. Here, amid a small congregation of fellow nicotine addicts, is where I would meet many of my new friends that year. I passed by

Andrea, Nicole, and Maggie at least once a day on the school grounds and they would just stop and stare at me. In the same ways I had trained my pet dogs growing up, I would stare back until they looked away. My eyes, not wavering not even to blink, would stay steady. The tell-tale sign of submission was looking away first, and I, filled with rage and power, would always leave the victor.

Within a couple of weeks, I had found my footing in my new surroundings; I knew where all my classes were; successfully transitioned from having a desk to a locker; and recognized the maturity I had developed in only weeks of being in the seventh grade. I had developed a routine. Gemma and I would congregate with the other kids across the street from the school at the Reddi-Mart. One morning, as we shared horror stories of teachers and homework between cigarette puffs, a classmate a grade above us reached into his pocket, and pulled out a joint, "You guys want to smoke before class?"

Gemma and I burst into laughter. The clock hadn't even struck 8:00 a.m. and here we were, presented with a joint. Gleefully, we nodded our heads.

As the joint got passed around to the few of us that were standing there, the owner of the joint began to tell us how he got the weed from a friend of his in Edmonton, reminiscing on past adventures of the previous weekend with his friend. Everyone around us was laughing, and he smiled.

"It's laced with PCP," he nodded at the joint that was in Gemma's hand as she finished taking a large drag. "You're in for a wild day," he laughed.

Gemma and I looked at each other, unsure of what to make of what he had just said. Our eyes asked the same question: *What's PCP?* We had never heard of it, and now, we were faced with what would apparently be a wild day. Our faces, however, did not show our concern. Fearful of seeming uncool, we continued to laugh and smile along with those around us. I wondered how bad it could possibly be since he offered it to us at eight in the morning before school.

Suddenly, cigarettes fell from Gemma's hand, one by one, dropping to her feet. Her face was pale, and her eyes were glazed like in a trance, and their only focus was the ground below her.

"Hey Iman," her eyes remained glued to the pavement, "Check it out. Cigarettes are growing out of my feet."

Another cigarette fell from her fingertips.

Grabbing the pack from her hand, I quickly gathered the garden of tobacco that had sprouted at her toes, and stuffed the cigarettes back into their proper place. Instantly, my nerves went wild, "Come on, Gemma. We've gotta go!"

Anxiously, I grabbed her arm and led her across the street, turning back to say thank you to our newfound friends. Though my steps were slow and calculated, Gemma seemed to know where she was going and wandered off down the hallway toward her homeroom class. I made my way to the bathroom because I suddenly felt incredibly ill. Rushing into the bathroom stall, I shut the aluminum door, and sat on the seat, trying to regain my composure. Taking a deep breath, I left the aluminum confines of the stall and walked to the sink, beginning to wash the smell of cigarettes and marijuana from my hands. I looked up. Catching a glimpse of myself in the mirror, I froze. Bloodshot eyes and a pale face stared back at me. A knot formed in my stomach. I had never seen myself this bad, and feared that everyone would see me like this.

The sound of a stall opening shook me back to reality. A tall, slender girl with long, straight, brown hair that fell past her waist stood at the sink next to me. My eyes shifted to hers in the reflection of the mirror. I recognized her; she was outside the store with us just moments before.

"Hey, are you okay?" she said as she washed her hands, staring at my reflection, "You don't look so good."

It took me a few seconds to register that she was speaking to me and everything in my body felt like it was slowing down and I felt so heavy.

"Yeah, I'm okay, I think. Just tired," a mumble escaped through my heavy, melting lips.

"My name is Kara," she turned off the sink in front of her. "I saw you earlier with those older guys at the store. They're bad news, you know?"

I stared blankly at her.

"Here, take some water and wash your face," Kara took a step closer to me and adjusted the taps of the sink in front of me. "You'll be okay. Just tell the teachers that you're sick and you can go lay down in the infirmary."

Taking her sound advice, I stood there, splashing water on my face. I mumbled my gratitude to her as she led me to my homeroom, which I hadn't realized until now, was also hers.

My feet were as heavy as lead with every step that I took. Though I desperately wanted to lie down, it took all my strength not to fall into a crumpled heap on the floor. I expelled every ounce of energy within me, trying to look normal as I focused on my desk, urging my frail body to make it to my seat. I sat there, both weightless and feeling as though my limbs weighed a thousand pounds. Within minutes of roll call, my teacher dismissed my peers to go out to their first classes of the day. As I stood up, moments after everyone else, the teacher called my name and walked over to me.

"Iman, are you okay? You look a little pale and your eyes are very red."

My worst nightmare had come true and with all my might I tried to look normal. I looked down at the ground and mumbled, "Yeah, I am fine. I just feel tired."

Towering over me, he was unconvinced; my demeanour had spoken truer words than my voice could. "Have you been drinking or doing drugs?" he asked, his voice filled with genuine concern.

I looked up at his tall frame and kind eyes, shaking my head. "I just feel sick," I lied. "I think I need to lie down."

Walking down the hall, trying to keep in stride with my teacher despite my lead-laden feet, we had finally arrived at the infirmary. As he checked me in with the nurse, she saw my flushed face and asked me if I needed to throw up. Her question went unanswered because I hadn't the strength to try. Instead, I pulled myself up onto the small bed that sat in the corner of the room, and told her I just needed to sleep for a little bit. A few inaudible words escaped her lips as she turned off the lights, closing the door behind her.

The deafening sound of my rapid heartbeat forced my eyes open. Two big skulls appeared in the middle of the dark room, racing toward my face, and I let out a terrified gasp, closing my eyes tightly, shielding them with my hands. Every attempt I made to reopen them led to the same terrifying sight. Appearing out of the dark with a malicious taunt as they darted toward me, my only escape from the skulls was to close my eyes tighter. *Please make it stop*, I silently begged. I just wanted to feel normal again. I wanted to open my eyes. I wanted to go back in time and stop myself from smoking that joint. *What the fuck was in that weed?* Whatever PCP was, I hated it with all my being. With closed eyes, I thought about Gemma, hoping she was doing far better than me.

The next time I opened my eyes it was time to catch the bus and go home. The nurse checked my temperature and blood pressure and asked me how I was doing. I didn't really feel like talking and tried to pass off my horrible drug experiment as simply feeling under the weather.

"I tried to call your parents to come and get you but the phone was disconnected," her eyes tried to search mine, as if she could penetrate my mind and figure out what was going on.

"Oh," I paused, "Yeah, our phone hasn't been working lately. I think we are getting it fixed this week." My eyes averted in fear she would be able to tell that I was lying and discover that we didn't have a phone because we never paid our phone bills. At our house, a phone was a luxury much farther down on the list of necessities than beer and weed.

When I finally arrived home, I immediately scurried into my room. I felt terrible, not only because my mind and body had been left beaten and abused or because of the fact that I had come incredibly close to getting caught doing drugs, but—most importantly—I had taken drugs from a stranger. *What kind of loser am I?* The image of my mother's angelic face flickered into my mind: *What would she think of me?*

Breaking down into a heap of tears, I threw myself onto my bed, burying my exhausted tangle of flesh and bones beneath the covers. In my hatred for

my life, I had grown careless and foolish. This was not the person I was supposed to be. This was not the life I was supposed to have. Violent sobs poured
out of me and I clutched my comforter closer, *I'll do anything to escape this
place.* My mind buzzed with thoughts as I planned elaborate getaways in my
head until sleep whisked me away to a place where nothing needed to make
sense, and I was finally safe.

I tried my best to keep a low profile after my delusional drug trip. I decided to
stop smoking weed for a while and to regain focus on my schooling. I really
wanted to get good grades, not just because I always did, but because not
doing so would have given Mildred another way to control me. My studious
nature had gifted me with perfect grades, and, if I didn't get perfect marks,
Mildred wouldn't let me out of the house. After almost five miserable years
with her and George, getting away from the tin box of alcohol abuse and
mental instability they called home was my only saving grace.

   My studious nature, however, did not extend across all classes. I had struggled with math. Ironically, it also happened to be the subject that the teacher I
hated the most taught. An angry-looking old man with big ears, a large belly,
and thinning grey hair with black tufts stood in front of the class every day.
What he lacked in hair, he had made up for in deep creases that fell from the
corners of his nostrils, down to his jaw. It was as though these permanent
frown lines showcased his disapproval of the world, etching the eternal scowl
into his flesh. Unsurprisingly, my sentiments toward him were not uncommon. None of the students liked him. He and his perverted nature were often
the butt of our jokes at lunch hour. His claim to fame was his tendency to
stand over girls, putting one hand on their shoulder and gently pushing their
blouses forward to reveal their budding cleavage. It was disgusting. Female
peers would stiffen as he approached their desks, bringing their arms up to
protect their tiny chests.

   Of course, it wasn't long before I became prey to my math teacher's
behaviours. As he came to check on my work and began to walk toward me

I felt my body tense up and freeze. The sound of his footsteps stopped and, standing behind me, he asked how I was doing with the assignment. I tried to act busy, as though I was too engaged in my books to hear him. My eyes focused on the numbers in front of me, I held my breath, hoping that he would keep walking.

A familiar feeling grew within me. I had felt this same uneasiness many times before, when George lingered too long, held me too close, or looked at me when he thought I wouldn't notice. I felt the rage that hardened in my gut fill my body. My hands started to shake. My heart pounded vehemently. And, as he placed his hand on my shoulder, I reacted instantly, slapping his wrinkly, veined hands. Jumping out of my seat, I leapt to face him in one fluid motion, "Don't fucking touch me!"

My voice was loud, teeming with anger. The room was instantly silent, aside from the few gasps of the students around me. The teacher looked completely startled, his face turning bright red, the vein in his forehead pulsing as though it would pop at any moment. "Get to the office NOW!" he boomed, taking a small step back to gain distance.

Quickly and effortlessly, I gathered my books, spun on my heel and headed toward the door, "Fuck off, pervert."

Sitting in the principal's office, the hardened rage in my stomach had begun to soften. I explained my version of the story, telling him how my math teacher had developed a reputation, how he was always ogling the girls and trying to look down their shirts. I explained that I didn't like it when strangers touched me, that he didn't need to put his hands on me to teach math. I had never had a problem with the other teachers—just the one who was trying to touch me.

I was sent to sit in detention for the rest of the day, though I wasn't sure how getting to miss my classes was considered a punishment. Walking into the bland room of cream walls and typical school posters, my eyes landed on a girl that sat at a desk, carving something into the wood. Dressed in all black, her clothing had matched her onyx hair and the heavy, dark makeup that layered the lids of her eyes. Her skin was very pale, juxtaposing the darkness she had tried to shroud herself with. But, unlike the shade of her skin, the layers

of black that covered her fell in place with the angry look on her face. I had
never seen anyone dress so differently or, for that matter, anyone my age wear
so much makeup. She was beautiful and frightening, all at once. As I gazed at
her, I instantly wished I looked like such an exotic beauty instead of a scrawny
waif with giant features and an untameable afro.

She briefly looked up at me when I walked into the room and looked back
down at her carving as I made my way to an empty seat. "What's your story?"
She asked, not once looking up from her art.

"I told my perverted math teacher to fuck off. And to stop trying to touch
my tits," I rested my head on my desk.

"What a fucking asshole!" She laughed, abandoning her etch, and looked
up at me.

I smiled.

"I'm Frances," she continued. "I just moved here last week from Edmonton
to live with my dad. This place is a shit-hole."

Her uncouth demeanour had made me laugh. "I'm Iman," I said. "I have
to live here with my foster parents because my mom's dead and my father's
in prison."

In our misery, we had found the best company and spent the rest of the
day catching the other up on all the misfortune that we had experienced during our terrible existences.

Frances and I had become friends quickly. Her father lived in the trailer park
a few blocks from mine, and soon we were hanging out every chance we
could. I would go to Frances's house as often as possible on evenings and
weekends and, though I tried to introduce her to Gemma, I got the sense
that they didn't like each other and that it was best if I hung out with each of
them separately.

I discovered that Frances used to live with her mother and sister in
Edmonton but, because she and her mother were in constant squabbles, she

was sent to live with her dad for a while. Her dad was a seemingly kind man who laughed a lot and was barely ever home. And even when he was home, he left us to our own devices and we would sit in Frances's room, listening to music. It felt as though I had found one of the best friends I had ever had in Frances. Our conversations spanned not only the *regular* things I had talked about with my friends, but our misery, unhappiness, and what it would be like if we had decided to remove ourselves from the world entirely. I had never told anyone how much I hated my life before I met Frances and, somehow, it felt natural to tell her because she hated her life too. Sharing tales of incompetent parents who were too preoccupied with drinking, drugs, and sex to worry about our happiness, I had found someone who understood what my life was like. I told her all about Mildred and George, and all the times we had moved, and how our homes were getting less and less beautiful, and more and more impoverished.

Frances's life in Edmonton was a far cry from my childhood of playing with toads, pretending to be a magical princess, or hiding in the forests. She regaled me with tales of her wild adventures in the city and the trouble she and her friends would get in during their drug and sex-fueled parties. At this, I was taken aback. I didn't know any friends who were having sex. But as Frances's stories became more wild and entertaining, I had become increasingly intrigued. It was as though she was this feral, untamed creature that lived in a completely different world, only to cross paths with someone like me. She was a mythical creature, full of whimsy and life, and I wanted to be just like her.

During our many conversations, I eventually confided in Frances, telling her of the betrayal I had suffered over the summer, when Nicole, Andrea, and Maggie had tricked me into thinking they were my friends, only to lure me over to try and beat me up. I told her how lucky I was that Nicole wasn't stronger than me and didn't get more damage done while she had the chance.

"We should beat her up at school," Frances said in a tone of confidence and assurance as she filed her nails on her bed. I sat on the floor looking through her CDs.

"What do you mean?"

"We should just beat Nicole up for punching you," Frances spoke as if this was simple logic, and I just needed to process the facts some more. "She deserves it and she started it when she hit you last year."

"Well, I don't really know how to beat anyone up. I've never done it before," I said, slightly nervous that Frances would see how less cool I was than she.

"That's okay, it's easy. You don't need to know how—I'll help you and teach you how to make a fist. It's really not hard at all."

I sat in silence. I didn't know what to say to this plan.

"I mean, you're not a pussy, are you? What if they decide to beat you up again this year? What if this time they *really* beat you up?" Frances's face was filled with concern. I hadn't really thought of the possibility and, frankly, I didn't know what I would do if it happened again.

"Think about it, Iman," she said. "You embarrassed them. They probably hate you for getting away and because Nicole wasn't strong enough to *really* kick your ass. They brought you over to kick the shit out of you and you walked away with a bump. They're probably planning ways to pay you back this year."

My heart was racing at Frances's words. Though I had tried to maintain my dominance over my former friends, it wasn't impossible for them to plan to attempt to complete their original plan. *Could they really be planning to beat me up?* I asked myself, *What had I even done to these people and why the fuck did they hate me so much?* I was in a panic. I couldn't face being humiliated again. I couldn't face being punched in the face again. I looked at Frances, trusting her conclusion, and assumed she was right. I had to stick up for myself and show them that I would not cower so easily, that they couldn't just toss me around like garbage whenever they felt like it.

It was in those moments that we had planned to take Nicole into the smoking pit beside the school and pay her back for betraying me. But, vindictive and malicious in thought, we didn't pick just *any* day to fight her, Frances said we should pick picture day. That way she would be all dressed up and have to get her picture taken with a black eye.

As picture day approached my stomach was in knots. Not only had I hated fighting, but I genuinely had no idea what I was doing. Hesitating, I began to question everything. Was I even mad at Nicole? Though I was still hurt every time I thought of how she humiliated me and how the people I thought were my friends betrayed me, I wasn't sure that I could go through with it or that I wanted to. But, somehow, when I talked to Frances about my uncertainty, her logic and reasoning was so sound that I would get fired up, ready to continue with our plan. She kept reminding me that this was the only way to let them know that they can't just pick on me; I had to stand up for myself.

When the day finally arrived, Frances and I were waiting for Nicole to arrive at school. We watched her get off the bus, slowly making our way over to her. "Hey, Nicole!" Frances called out, a grin on her face.

"Hey, Nicole! How's it going?" I chimed. She turned to look at us, her confusion evident.

"Uh, pretty good. How are you?" she stood in front of us shifting her weight, looking nervously, first at Frances, then at me, and then finally, her eyes landed on the ground.

"Iman wants to talk to you," Frances's voice sounded genuine as she smiled sweetly and led us toward the path of trees. "Let's go into the smoking pit for a few minutes."

Nicole and I followed, making small talk as we walked deeper into the path and past the smokers.

"Cigarette?" I pulled out my pack, looking at Nicole. It was almost identical to the way the first fight had started. Frances reached into her pocket, pulling out a lighter, and walked over to Nicole motioning to light her smoke. But, instead, Frances punched Nicole right in the face and the cigarette flew out of her mouth, onto the ground. Nicole let out a moan and grabbed her left cheek. I stood frozen.

"That is what you get for fucking with Iman, bitch," Frances spit her words as Nicole stood shaking and holding her face.

I'm sorry, Iman—I am!" Nicole was almost in tears. "I shouldn't have tried to fight you. I didn't even want to but, Andrea and Maggie told me I should." She stumbled over each word.

"Your turn," Frances looked at me, pointing at Nicole, "Go on! Punch her. Like I showed you." Feeling out of place, lost in a total wave of embarrassment, I wanted to disappear.

"I don't know…" my voice wavered.

Frances was getting impatient and she pushed me toward Nicole, "Iman, punch this bitch in the face!" she screamed at me.

Clenching my right hand into a tight fist, I walked up to Nicole and punched her cheek as hard as I could—the sound of our bones colliding was sickening; it felt like I had punched cement. Nicole's lip was trembling hard. Her lip was bleeding. Frances came up, without hesitation, and punched her in the face once again then grabbed her by the lapels of her jacket.

"Don't ever fuck with us again, do you understand? If I ever so much as *see* a dirty look cross your face when you *think* of us, I'll find you and kick the fucking shit out of you." Frances spat her words through clenched teeth.

Nicole, shriveling up, desperately tried to hold back the tears that were on the brink of falling down her face.

"I p-pr-promise I won't do anything or say anything. I'm sorry. I swear. I am so sorry," Nicole started walking away toward the school as Frances tauntingly wished her a great day.

"Good luck with your pictures!" She said and burst out laughing.

My adrenaline was rushing through my body. I couldn't believe what had just happened. Although I felt bad for hitting her, I also felt on top of the world for standing up to Nicole, and in celebration and victory, Frances and I had a cigarette before heading back to school.

As I sat in class that day, the guilt of what I had done came over me and I started to feel horrible for hitting Nicole. Thoughts of us as best friends, just months before, flooded my brain. I wondered where it had all gone wrong. It didn't seem to make any sense. I knew that this madness was beneath both of us. But, I had done what I had done, as she did what she had, and I justified the events with the fact that I had to stand up for myself and avoid getting an even worse beating.

I heard Frances's name being called over the intercom as I was heading to the gym to get my picture taken. A huge lump formed in my throat and fear took over my body. *Nicole must have ratted on us.* My legs began to shake as I walked down the hallway, waiting for my name to be called next. It never came.

After school, the buzz of gossiping school kids was all around me. I stood by the buses, silent, listening to the misinformed details of "some fight that happened in the morning" and how Nicole had to take school pictures with a bruised face. I found out that Frances took the entire blame for what happened after someone said they saw her with Nicole in the morning. Frances was suspended and though they asked her several times who else was with her, she never once said my name. I stopped by Frances's place after school and she told me that someone had said her name and she got called to the principal's office and admitted to hitting Nicole. Nicole, too afraid to say anything, kept her word and never opened her mouth with either of our names. Though Frances was suspended for a couple of days, she didn't seem to worry about it. As I thanked her for not ratting me out, she said she would never ever do that to her friend. I smiled. We hung out in her room, replaying the events of the morning over again, laughing at what a crazy day it was and how it all played out.

That weekend I went to hang out with Frances. Although she was grounded, she was still allowed to have friends over. We sat in her room listening to music and talking about what it would be like to live on our own. She had all kinds of fun stories from her life in Edmonton. Boyfriends, drugs, parties, and sex. She sounded far more exciting than the people in the trailer park.

Frances took out some pills from her backpack and showed them to me, "They're sleeping pills I stole from my dad." She opened her hand, showing the small canister to me, "Want to try them?"

Five hours later, I woke up in a haze. As I looked at the clock, I jolted in disbelief. I couldn't believe that we were asleep for so long. I knew I needed to get back home before Mildred and George started looking for me. Frances gave me a couple of the pills and I shoved them in my pocket, unsure as to what I would need them for. I've never had trouble sleeping. In fact, I loved sleeping, and looked forward to it as the best part of my day.

When I got home Mildred and George were out somewhere and I had the place to myself. I grabbed some leftover pizza out of the fridge and sat in the living room. As I looked into the kitchen at the fridge, the half-dozen orange pill cases on top of the fridge caught my eye. They had always been there, but having just taken the sleeping pills earlier in the day, I was now curious as to what these pills were. I knew that Mildred had to take hormone replacement medication due to her hysterectomy, and that she and George both suffered from severe depression and could hardly function even with the pills and were almost completely useless without them.

I walked over to the fridge and examined each container carefully, opening the bottles and taking a couple from each of them. Hiding them in my room—in a small bag inside my mattress where I had sliced open the side so I could stash things—I thought I might need to use the pills for something, *someday*, and added the two sleeping pills that Frances gave me to the bag, shoving it deep within my mattress. *Maybe if things got too bad here, I could just kill myself.* The thought had crossed my mind now and again, but as life continued to weigh on me and I felt more and more alone, it seemed like an appealing option. I wondered if I would get to be with my mom if I was dead. Did it matter how you died to get to heaven? *I guess you don't really know until you try.*

What I did know was that living like this was killing me slowly. I hated every minute of my life in the hellhole I was meant to call home and I would do anything to get away from the fights and drunken madness. Sometimes it felt as though I had more sense than my own guardians. Where were they?

Why didn't they look after us? Why did Mel have to work two jobs to help pay the bills, while Mildred and George were off getting drunk someplace? *I bet no one would notice if I wasn't even here.* They probably would only miss the money they got from the government for taking care of me.

Within a couple of weeks, the fight between Nicole that had gotten Frances suspended had blown over. People were talking about other things, and the black eye was old news. Our lives had also resumed to their normal state. Frances's grounding was now over, and, as usual, I spent my evenings and weekends at her trailer. One school night when I was over at Frances's, her boyfriend, Andy, and his friend Noah had come from the city to see her; at sixteen, they were old enough to drive. Andy was shorter than Noah, had dark brown skin and jet-black hair. Although she had not confirmed it, I could only assume that Andy was her boyfriend because she pounced on him immediately at his arrival, and began kissing him heavily. The other boy, around 5'10", had a medium build with dirty blonde hair that was slicked back onto his head. Though I had often acted older than my age truly was, his large blue eyes and warm smile made me shrink, and I instantly felt like a child.

We drove around the trailer park and into Cedar Grove. The weather had gotten colder with winter just around the corner, and I, swaddled in a hand-me-down jacket that was several sizes too big with bright squares of yellow, green and pink, felt overwhelmingly self-conscious. Sitting beside Noah in the backseat as Andy drove around aimlessly, it took everything in me to act as though I did not look ridiculous in my neon layers. Though Noah and I exchanged a few glances and smiles, I was far too shy to say anything pro-found or witty enough to contribute to the conversation. My heart raced. I was in unknown territory; I didn't have any friends with cars and, for that matter, had never been anywhere without my siblings, guardians, or friend's parents. Having not told anyone where I was or where I was going, I felt rebellious and carefree. I knew that I would have never been allowed to ride around in a car with boys I didn't know.

By the time I got back home, I had developed a rather large crush on Noah. Thoughts of him consumed me. Throughout the remaining week at school, Frances and I talked about the boys, and as she repeatedly claimed that Noah had liked me, my heart beat faster. And with perfect timing, Frances told me she was going to her mom's house for the weekend in Edmonton, and asked if I wanted to come, "Andy's going to come over, and Noah could totally come over too!"

My cheeks grew hot with nerves. I had never had a boyfriend before; I didn't really meet a lot of boys that I liked or that liked me. And, though a lot of my friends in the trailer park were older than me, and we had gotten along fine, Noah's age intimidated me. I thought back to my sweet friend Henry back at the house on the hill. *That was just a silly crush,* I thought. *I was just a kid back then.* Playing in the forest and talking to animals. I was so much different now. I didn't play in forests; I hadn't had an animal to take care of in such a long time. I was hardened by my circumstance. I had new hobbies: I spent my days hanging out with my friends, smoking weed, and getting into trouble. Although my nature-loving days were not that far behind me, I was a completely different person—*sadder* somehow. Life without my brothers felt so lonely. I had nothing to look forward to but my friends, and even they sometimes betrayed me. I should be so lucky as to have a boyfriend; someone who wants to hang out with me and care about me. I was lost in a world of daydreams, imagining what it would be like as I listened to Frances tell me stories about her own misadventures with love.

I came home to an empty trailer again. It wasn't unusual. Many nights I would be left alone to fend for myself. I put down my bag, took off my shoes, and headed toward my room. I was startled when I heard the phone ring in the kitchen; it was a foreign sound that I hadn't heard in weeks. As I placed the receiver to my ear, Mildred's voice greeted me through the muffled speaker. She and George were going out for dinner. *Great.* As much as I hated being around them, I wished they cared about me enough to show even a shred of concern about what I was going to have for dinner. Shrugging off my annoyance, I took this as the perfect time to ask if I could go over to Frances's mom's house in Edmonton for the coming weekend. Mildred paused to think and my breath grew still. *Please, please, please,* I silently begged.

"We'd just be at her mom's," I said coolly, not showing too much desperation in my voice. "We won't even be going out anywhere." For the most part, it was true. The boys would be coming over.

"Alright." The sound of Mildred's voice had never brought me such joy. It took all my strength to keep my composure as I finished up the call. I would be going to Edmonton. I would be seeing Noah. I would maybe have a boyfriend. I teetered with delight as I hung up the receiver, running into the living room to leap on the big chair and flop onto the couch in pure excitement. I jumped up from the couch, racing to the phone to tell Frances the good news. She quickly came over, and we called Noah, informing him of my visit. Enthusiastically, the three of us started planning our weekend, laughing at the prospect of all the fun we would have. And, after Frances had left, I went to bed beaming with joy, feeling truly happy at the idea of leaving the trailer park and heading to the city where I had been born—where I had once lived my happy life with my happy family.

Chapter Ten

Age 12: City Girls

As Frances's dad drove us into the city after school on Friday, I gazed out the window, barely holding in my delight. Since her mom worked nights, we would have the house to ourselves, and Frances and I had planned the perfect weekend.

When we arrived at the modernly furnished duplex, her mother was just getting ready to head out. She was the same height and frame as Frances, and just as pretty, though she seemed a bit nervous as she frantically walked around the house, gathering her things for work. I looked around the house. It was clean and well decorated—much nicer than the houses I had lived in for the past six years. With all the planning for the weekend, I hadn't thought of what my accommodations would look like, and this was a pleasant surprise.

Ordering us a pizza as she left, Frances's mother told us that she would be back in the morning and gave us a stern warning to be good and not to leave the house. And though Frances informed her that we would be having a couple of friends coming over, she didn't seem bothered at all. As she walked out the door, Frances and I began to figure out what we would wear. Letting me borrow a black lace top, we laughed as we got dressed and Frances did my makeup. After we finished, she went into a cupboard, pulled out some vodka and Coke, and poured us each a glass, "The boys will be here any minute." I took a large sip. "And, just so you know, Andy and I are probably going to want to be alone."

A small lump formed in my throat. I hadn't really thought too much about what it would be like when we got to the city. Foolishly, I had assumed that we would all be hanging out together. My body began to heat up with anxiety at the thought of hanging out with Noah alone.

When the doorbell rang, I swallowed the lump in my throat and Frances skipped through the house to answer the door. Armed with a few plastic bags filled with whiskey, soft drinks, and a pack of cigarettes, the boys entered the house, removing their shoes and coats. As the four of us headed toward the living room, Frances prepared two additional drinks for our new guests and refilled ours. I was nervous. I felt awkward. The only thing I could manage to do was take large sips from my glass. As the moments passed, I felt my face flush as I refilled my drink, yet again. We all sat around talking and laughing for a little while until Frances and her boyfriend went upstairs to be alone. My heart sank. A mix of nerves and embarrassment, I was far too shy to be alone in a room with this boy I had been lusting after for a week's time. Searching my mind, I was left with nothing to say; I became increasingly aware that he was four years older than me and, as a result, much *cooler*. As I sat on the couch, fidgeting with my drink, eyes darting around the room, he sensed my awkwardness and came over to me on the couch. His fingertips gently grazed my arm, moving toward my hair, "You're so pretty."

He moved his face closer to mine and began kissing my neck and face. I could smell his cologne as he pressed himself against me.

Aside from Melanie's boyfriend on New Year's Eve, I had never kissed anyone before. Even then, it was short. This—this was different. As Noah caressed my arms, he slowly inched closer and closer to me. My body froze. *What am I supposed to be doing?* I wanted to kiss him but, I didn't know how. Pressing his lips against mine, he pushed his tongue into my mouth and placed his hands on either side of my face. *Finally,* I thought. Our kiss turned into an endless mix of tongue, teeth, and lips. It felt as though it lasted an eternity. When our lips finally parted, our eyes locked, and we both burst into laughter. Though I had tried to look calm, I was jumping out of my skin. *I just had my first real kiss,* I silently screamed. The last thing I wanted was for him to know that I didn't know what I was doing or, worse yet, that this was my first kiss.

"You want to go upstairs?" His ocean blue eyes darted toward the stairs. I nodded. Although my gut clenched and I wanted to run, I knew I had nowhere to go. It was now or never, and there was no point in being humiliated for being a novice. Leading me up the stairs, we found a bedroom that had a bed in it and some clothes strewn on the floor. *Is this Frances's room?* I asked myself. It looked somewhat lived in, yet too small to be an adult's. I walked toward the bed, sitting on the edge as Noah came and sat beside me and handed me my drink. I smiled at him, taking a large swig to calm my nerves. The vodka burned. Noah lifted my shirt and started licking my back from my neck all the way down to the top of my pants. He lightly blew on where he had licked and I could feel the cool air give me goose bumps on my skin.

The muffled sounds of Frances and Andy echoed from down the hall. A mix of laughter and moans, it sounded like they were having a good time. *What am I doing?* I sat frozen on the bed, wishing that Frances would come out, and that the four of us could just hang out and talk. I wasn't prepared for this one-on-one interaction with an older boy I had just met only once before.

Suddenly Noah stood up, pulling me up with him, "Come on, let's go to the basement." He grabbed his drink with one hand and led me downstairs with the other. We walked through the living room and went down the stairs into the basement which I had never seen before.

"Let's sit over here," he walked toward the couch on the far side of the room, leaving the lights off. The stairwell light lit enough of the room to reveal shapes and furniture. I followed his lead and sat down beside him on the couch. As we drank the rest of our ill-made drinks, Noah pushed himself on top of me, kissing me hard and furiously. His hands became ravenous, clawing at my shirt, pulling it over my head, and tossing it on the floor. I hardly had time to think before he was ripping my belt off and yanking my pants off. He seemed to have lost his gentle touch from just moments before and had turned aggressive. I shut my eyes tightly, praying that this was merely a nightmare as he kissed all over my bare body.

"Wh-what are you doing?" I asked, afraid to look at him.

He ignored me and started to take off his clothes. Pressing his whole body against mine, I could feel him harden as he lay on top of me, pawing at my flesh, kissing and biting my skin.

"*Stop! Wh-what are you doing? Please stop!*" With all my strength, I frantically tried to escape from under his weight.

"Just relax. You'll be fine." His voice was stern. This was not the boy I had met last week. This wasn't even the boy I had been with all evening. His gentle, kind voice, his sweet smile—they were all gone. He pulled out a condom with one hand, holding my wrists down on top of my chest with the other. I felt like mouse in a trap, immobile and unable to free myself. He tore open the condom wrapper with his mouth and managed to put it on as I lay there, helpless.

My body felt as though it was being ripped open. I screamed, tears streaming down my face as he pressed his hands over my mouth and told me to be quiet. "You're okay," he hushed me. "You're safe."

I thrust my body with all my might, trying to escape. I was not okay. I was not safe. I screamed and thrashed until he stopped, "*I don't want to!*" I yelled as the pain tore through my abdomen.

"Okay! Okay! Relax!" He pulled the condom off and began to dress himself, "Shit, girl. What's wrong with you?" I quietly put my clothes back on and walked up the stairs, and went into the washroom to clean myself up. When I came back out, Frances and her boyfriend were sitting in the living room with Noah. Glancing at me, he smiled. I sat on the floor near the coffee table and lit a cigarette.

"*Soooo…*it looks like you guys had fun," Frances laughed. I smiled and smoked my cigarette. I could hardly breathe. Though I had no idea what just happened, I knew it wasn't *fun.* I just wanted to go home, but I knew that wasn't an option. I couldn't call Mildred and George. They were probably drunk somewhere. I couldn't call Ben and Elizabeth. I couldn't tell them what a horrible person I was, or how I'd gotten myself into this situation—they would think I was such an idiot. I had nowhere to go, and no one to turn to. So I sat, smoking my cigarette.

We sat in the living room making small talk and watching the television for another hour before the boys left. When we got to the door to walk them out, Noah went to kiss me on the mouth and I quickly moved my face to the side. I couldn't look at him to say goodbye.

After they had left, Frances went into detail about the lewd acts she and her boyfriend had done in the other room.

"Did you guys have sex?" she asked.

I shook my head, "No."

"You frigid virgin," she laughed. "No one is ever going to want you if you act like a kid."

I couldn't wait to get back home, which was very much unlike me. All I wanted was to be alone, in the sanctuary and security of my own room, and to not think about what had just happened to me in the basement moments before.

That week at school Frances told me that she talked to Noah and that he wanted to talk to me on the phone. She came over after school, calling him from my house. As her fingers dialed his number, my heart started to race. She began to talk to him, and I could feel my hands get sweaty as I sat waiting for what he could possibly have to say. His actions were so animalistic, and I imagined he wanted to say sorry for what had happened.

She handed me the phone and sat on the kitchen chair while I walked down the hall toward my room for some privacy.

"Hello?" My voice was barely a whisper. I was shaking and my stomach was in knots.

"Hey, Iman," his voice sounded apologetic and soft through the receiver. Not at all how I last remembered him. "How are you?" he continued.

"I'm fine. What's up?" I tried to remove all emotion from my voice.

"Listen," he began, "About the other night—it was great hanging out with you, and I had a lot of fun but, I just don't think I can have a girlfriend like you. You're really young and, I mean, well, you aren't exactly the prettiest girl I've ever seen…" His voice trailed off.

I paused, not believing what I was hearing. What was happening? My mind scurried to process what was happening. *Is he breaking up with me when we weren't even dating?* My face began to flush with heat as I thought back to his body pressed against mine in the basement of Frances's mother's home. *Did he just call me ugly?* I hung up the phone, storming into the kitchen to where Frances was sitting.

"What happened? Are you okay?" She was reacting to the tears that poured down my face.

"He just wanted to break up with me," I sputtered through sobs of rage and sadness.

"Yeah, I figured as much," in so few words, Frances was incredibly sure of herself. "You have to put out if you want to have a boyfriend. He told me you didn't want to have sex."

I was glad that Frances had to leave so I could be alone in my shroud of humiliation and anger. I couldn't grasp the situation. I couldn't understand what was happening. I felt betrayed. I felt humiliated. I felt ugly. I felt alone. Everything in my life was a constant stream of sorrow and pain. I sunk into my sheets, sobbing into my pillow for hours, thankful that Mildred and George were out for the evening, allowing me to wallow in my own self-pity for the rest of the night.

As I opened my bedroom window, lighting a cigarette, I thought of the chain of events that had led me to that basement. *Why did I agree to go with her in the first place? What kind of idiot was I for thinking that it was going to be fun and that Noah would actually be a nice guy?* When I thought about it, I didn't really know any nice guys outside of my brothers, except for Ben. But he was different in every way, not just for a man but for a human. My brothers were nice guys but, where were they when I needed them? Chokri was still in Edmonton with his friends and hardly came to visit; Adam and Ron had moved back from Victoria. Ron went to live in Edmonton with friends and Adam went to Glenwood with Ben and Elizabeth to start working on the oil rigs. *But why couldn't they just move back to be with me? Wasn't I enough to want to be with?*

My mind wandered. I thought about Mel's ex-boyfriend, Robert, and how crazy he turned out. I thought of George, and how creepy he acted. I felt nauseous. *Maybe all men were disgusting, or maybe I'm just a fucking loser with no luck. Why did all this bad stuff always happen to me? My sweet, amazing, vibrant mother is murdered, my father is a fucking psycho, my brothers—the only people I have left—leave me, I live in shit-hole after shit-hole, my friends turn against me and punch me in the face, and now, the only chance I had at a boy liking me, and he hurts me, and then throws me away like garbage.*

The more I cried, the worse I felt and the more self-loathing filled me. I didn't deserve this life. I didn't deserve to be here. I didn't deserve to be thrown away like garbage. Or, maybe I did. *Maybe that's all I am.* I ripped the sheet off my bed and stuffed my hand into the hole that hid all my precious secrets. *I can't take this anymore.* I grabbed the small bag of pills I had been collecting, running down the hall to get water from the kitchen. Tears falling down my cheeks, I could hardly breathe between each violent sob. *This was not the life I wanted to live.* I reached into the bag and looked down into the palm of my hand at my collection of pills, closed my eyes, and swallowed handful after handful, emptying the bag. *I don't want to be in this hellhole anymore,* I thought. *Whatever awaited me on the other side couldn't possibly be as bad as my life right now.* I opened my eyes and looked around the room. Everything was a blur through the tears. I lit cigarette after cigarette, until the room started to spin. I closed my eyes, feeling the weight of my body fall against the floor.

Chapter Eleven

Age 12: Mexican Sunsets

I was surrounded by darkness. My eyes, heavy and lethargic, peered open to see a dim light that came from down the hallway. My body ached, my head pounded, my mind was disconnected from everything around me. Wiggling my fingers, I felt a wetness encompass my fingertips and, as my senses returned, I began to register my surroundings, realizing that I was in the darkened trailer I called my home, laying in a puddle of my own vomit. I stirred, closing my eyes, trying to gain the strength to move. The madness of the evening flooded my memory and I suddenly remembered eating all the pills I had been stealing. I crawled to the kitchen table, pulling myself up with the chair. I looked at the clock. Four hours had passed since my failed attempt at suicide. *I couldn't even do that right.* Filled with self-hatred, I willed myself to action, cleaning up the remains I had purged that were soaking into the living room carpet, fearing Mildred and George would walk in and see the mess I had made.

I drew a bath and melted into the hot, soapy water, tears falling from my swollen eyes, joining the water that surrounded me. *How did everything always go so wrong?* I asked myself. The hot water scalded my flesh, purging me of the sadness and hatred I felt for myself.

I found myself at Cheryl's trailer as the weekend finally arrived. Sitting around and wasting time, I felt comfortable amid the bags of dirty laundry and the overflowing dishes. There was a girl I hadn't seen before. Although I had never met her before, I had heard plenty of stories about Danielle. The neighbourhood buzzed with tales of her wild and crazy adventures, and people often suggested that she had something mentally wrong with her and that she had to take medication for her severe anger and outbursts. She was seventeen with beautiful blonde hair that sat disheveled in a ponytail, her nose reminded me of Miss Piggy, and her curves did as well. She was full of life, causing all those around her to break into fits of laughter when she spoke, and her animated stories kept the room entertained for hours. Spending the day and evening laughing and drinking with friends was exactly what I need to cheer me up.

After a few hours, Cheryl, Gary, Danielle, and I were sitting in the living room, stoned and drunk, talking about life.

"I fucking hate this town," in the few hours I had known her, this was the first time Danielle had shown a shred of annoyance or unhappiness. "I wish I could take off and go live somewhere else—somewhere hot like Mexico." Her eyes looked up at the ceiling, as if the hot, Mexican sun was beaming above her, "Yeah, we should run away to Mexico, man."

We all laughed and I thought about what she said. It would be nice to live somewhere else. Anywhere else but here. Though I had never been to Mexico, it sounded better than a dilapidated trailer park in the middle of nowhere.

"I'd go to Mexico with you," as the words escaped my lips, I surprised myself.

"Yeah? Seriously?" Danielle sat straight up on the couch with excitement.

Suddenly realizing what I said, I had no idea if I wanted to go to Mexico. I took a pause. "I mean, yeah," I pondered the idea of venturing off into an unknown place. "I hate it here. I would rather live in prison than with my foster parents."

My truthful words sent the room into a fit of laughter. I had often thought prison would be better than my terrible life with Mildred and George. In prison, you were surrounded by people, there was a routine and, most importantly, there were proper meals.

"Well then we should fucking do it, man," the wheels in Danielle's mind began to turn. "Just, like, steal a car and take off to Mexico." A small grin formed on her face, suggesting she was satisfied with her impromptu proposal.

As we sat in the sullied living room of Cheryl's trailer, we devised a plan to steal Danielle's mother's car in the middle of the night on a school night and drive all the way to Mexico. Being only twelve years old at the time, this plan seemed quite logical and straightforward. Of course, I hadn't really thought ahead to needing a passport or money.

Over the course of the next two weeks, as Danielle and I discussed our plans, the prospect of leaving Mildred, George, and the trailer park behind me had become a prominent feature in my mind. It was like a clip from a film in a theatre, the image of driving down a long road, heading toward the sun, cigarette in my hand, replayed in my head repeatedly. Of course, before my romanticized vision of freedom could come into fruition, some details would need to be addressed. *Where in Mexico would we go? What would we do when we got there? What do we need to take with us?* At the question of how much money we would need, Danielle dismissed my concerns.

"We don't need that much money to start off with," she said with confidence, as if she had done this before. "We just need a bit, and then we'll make money along the way."

Although she didn't share how we would manage to accumulate money while we were on our journey, I imagined that since she was seventeen, she had more foresight in regard to world matters than I would at twelve.

I loved having a secret that would take me far away from all my troubles and out of foster care. My mind began to race, thinking about what I would carry in the one bag I could bring with me. I packed a few outfits, a ring I had of my mother's, and removed the money I had collected during my summer at Glenwood from under the shelf. As I held the wadded bills, I thought back to Ben slipping the two hundred dollars into my hand before he left me that evening in late August. Though he would have never thought of it—and it would have been impossible for me to know at the time—the money he gave me that night was the gift of a chance to escape. I smiled, thanking him silently, and placed the cash in my bag.

I had everything ready and soon I would be gone. I looked at the clock. Danielle said that she would need to wait until her mom was sleeping before she could steal her car to eliminate any chance that her escape would be heard.

The night of my departure had finally come. I bubbled with both excitement and nervousness. *This is it,* I thought to myself. Before I made my way to bed, I wished Mildred and George goodnight, made sure to stop by Melanie's room, giving her an enormous hug goodbye. I went to my bedroom to pretend to sleep. Following Danielle's instructions, I was supposed to wait up in my bedroom until one or two in the morning, and at the sound of rocks hitting the glass pane of my window, I would throw my bag down and climb out after it. My biggest concern was being quiet and not having Mildred and George chase me down the street. I opened the window wide and looked down at the jump I would have to make. It wasn't that high but if I fell wrong, I could be injured, left with a sprained ankle or a hurt knee. A small frown crept upon my face. *I'll have to be careful.* Taking a deep breath, prepared for the adventure ahead of me, I slumped down beneath the window and waited, listening to my Walkman to stay awake.

My eyes opened to sunlight beaming in through the window above me. I was perched against the wall, folded over my pillow with a knot forming in my neck. Fully dressed and with my makeup on, I had fallen asleep despite my best efforts. My heart pounded at the thought that I had missed my ride to Mexico, my escape from this prison. *Oh my God, Danielle! Would she be disappointed? Was she upset?* The image of her tossing rocks against my window, trying to wake me up to no avail and giving up, flashed before me. *What have I done?*

Defeated, I brought myself to my feet. With a deep sigh of resignation, I went to school, unable to forgive myself for sleeping in and missing my one chance at escape. Embarrassment flooded over me. *I ruined everything.* I was foolish for planning such a grown-up getaway. With tears on the brink of falling from the corners of my eyes throughout the entire day, it was impossible for me to concentrate. All I had wanted, all I had wished for, was to be far away from Mildred and George.

When I got home I called Danielle's house. The sound of the line ringing brought a lump to my throat. I closed my eyes, nervous. *Click.* The sound of Danielle's voice greeted me from the other end of the receiver. *She's home!* I silently exclaimed.

"I couldn't come last night," her muffled voice spoke into my ear. "My mom stayed up late and I couldn't get the car." A wave of relief came over me and I squealed with delight.

"I fell asleep last night," I confessed with a giggle in my voice.

After telling her the events of my day, we had decided we would attempt to go through with our plan once again. On Friday evening, after telling our parents that we were going to hang out with friends, we would drive off into the sunset, the tin boxes we once called home far behind us.

Making sure I didn't ask for permission to hang out with my friends too far in advance in case something else happened and I got in trouble and punished with staying at home, I waited. After school on Friday, I was hanging out with George in the living room watching TV. He seemed to be in good spirits so I casually asked him if I could go play with my friends at the basketball courts. Though it was met with hesitation, my pleading had finally gifted me with his approval. Rushing to my room, I threw my backpack out the window that had previously been my portal for escape, and casually walked out of the house, waving goodbye to George as I closed the door. I quickly walked around the side of the house, grabbed my bag, and bolted down the street as fast as I could. I ran all the way to Danielle's house. She answered the door and whispered that her friend was coming to pick us up and take us to Cedar Grove. I could smell the alcohol on her breath; she looked a little disheveled, and was slurring her speech.

I waited inside until her friend came. Her mom was home and asked us about the sleepover we were about to have. Not privy to the tale Danielle had told her mother, I smiled and nodded, making up details as I went along. Luckily, our lies didn't cause alarm and Danielle's friend arrived before her mother could do anymore prying.

The winter sun had set and we climbed into a dark car. I crawled into the backseat and Danielle rode shotgun. The driver was a pretty, bubbly girl around the same age as Danielle. Straight brown hair cascaded around her face as she turned and smiled at me; her perfume of sweet flowers filled the car. Danielle made quick introductions and turned up the music.

Unsure of our exact destination as we drove away, a twinge of guilt sparked within me for not telling anyone where I was going. I thought of Melanie. *I'm going to miss her so much.* Though I hated that I had become this person, I couldn't stand living there a moment longer. To not change my mind about running away, I began to think of all the things I wouldn't miss: I hated all the fighting, getting yelled at by Mildred, and hit for no reason; I hated being alone all the time and never having anyone to talk to; I hated how invisible I felt and how my brothers had left me; and most of all, I hated myself, and how dumb and unlucky I was in this life. I was cursed, and the only way I could break my bad luck was to try and change it myself.

The smell of marijuana filled the car as Danielle lit a joint. Soon, all our troubles seemed far away. We had only been driving for twenty minutes when Julie, our driver, exclaimed that we were almost there.

"Where are we going?" I asked nervously. We hadn't driven very far to be running away.

"Oh, we're crashing at Julie's tonight. We'll figure out what we are doing tomorrow," Danielle called back to me.

My heart sank. *I thought we were running away.* I had packed my things and said goodbye to my family. I was ready to move on and away. I was ready to start a new chapter of my life. I was ready for freedom. I was ready for *anything*, just not *this*. I couldn't go back. I couldn't just go for a sleepover and *see in the morning*. I needed to go as far as possible tonight so I could ensure a proper escape from my life. I tried to convince Danielle that we needed to go right now, but regardless of my pleas or my attempts to preach through logic and reason, she wouldn't have it. In a drunken stupor, too high and not motivated enough to do anything aside from going to Julie's, she had halted all my dreaming. Now we would just "see in the morning."

We arrived at Julie's parents' place and unloaded our things from the car. Her parents were in the living room. Julie called out to them and they said hello, but remained in their seats. Making our way upstairs, we walked into Julie's room and started to settle. Now face to face, I could see Julie better. She was pretty. "Danielle, are you okay?" she looked over at Danielle, slumped over on Julie's bed.

Too busy fantasizing about running away, Danielle's condition hadn't become apparent to me until I looked over. She was almost passed out. Severely intoxicated, she could hardly keep her eyes open, but at the same time, it was obvious that she had little interest in going to sleep.

"Dani, look at me. Did you take your medicine?" Concern flooded Julie's face.

"What medicine?" I asked faintly. Recalling the rumors I had heard months ago, I stiffened.

"She has to take several medications every day; she shouldn't be drinking with them, but she does anyways," Julie hovered over Danielle. "She has ADD, and her Ritalin doesn't mix well with drugs and alcohol."

I paused. My eyes darted to Danielle, then back to Julie.

"Are you taking us to Mexico?"

"*What? Mexico?* No way," Julie's voice was shocked, as if I had just told her pigs could fly. "I don't want any part of whatever you two are up to. Danielle just said she wanted to come stay over for the night. She always fights with her mom and comes and stays here for a night or two. I can drive you home in the morning." She went to the hall closet, collecting blankets off the shelf.

"Look," she returned, arms full of blankets. "I don't know what you're running away from, but don't you think you should go home? I mean, how old are you? Your parents must be so worried."

"I can't go home. I hate it there," I looked at her, tears filling my eyes. I willed them to return to their ducts. *Please,* I begged, *Not now.*

"Well," she paused, "We can figure it out in the morning. C'mon, we'll make you a bed on the floor."

As she laid some blankets and sleeping bags on the floor, I crawled into bed, drifting off to sleep, wondering what tomorrow would bring.

The next day I woke up to an empty room. *Danielle must have gone downstairs.* I heard voices coming from the kitchen. I went to the washroom, packed up my things and was ready for the day's adventures. I made my way downstairs. Julie, her mother, and Danielle sat around the table, eating breakfast.

"Hello, dear!" Julie's mother looked up as I entered the kitchen. "You must be Iman. How are you?" her voice was just as sweet and kind as her daughter's.

"Morning," I shyly smiled. "I'm good, thank you. Uh, thank you for letting me stay here." I looked at her warily, fearful that she would make me return home.

"Oh, *of course!* We're so happy to have you girls here," she paused, her face grew slightly serious. "Do you want me to call your parents and tell them you're okay? I think they'll be so worried about you."

I quickly glared at Julie and Danielle, feeling betrayed by their decision to tell others about my plans of escape.

"Um, no thank you," I strained to give her a small smile. "I really don't want to go back there." I took the muffin she offered me and sat down at the table to eat it.

After finishing our breakfast, we went to the mall to hang out while we decided what to do about our escape plan. We needed to find a car that Danielle could drive to Mexico. Wandering around the mall for a bit, we grabbed some lunch in the food court and stood in front of a clothing store as we chatted. After Julie had left, which was shortly after we had arrived, a small group of Danielle's friends joined us. As we stood in the group, Danielle's face dropped. She looked at me, alarmed. "Run," she muttered under her breath. Confused, I asked her what she was talking about. She said it again, this time through gritted teeth, "*Run!*"

I turned around, my feet freezing at the sight of Mildred and Adam walking toward me. My legs began to shake. I had not expected to see them, *especially Adam.* And though I was happy to see my older brother, Mildred's face was furious and the creases in her forehead burrowed into her brow. I was both humiliated and terrified of returning home.

"Get your ass over here now!" Mildred screamed across the mall.

Mortified, I immediately starting walking toward her and my brother. There was no use in running. *Where would I go?* Danielle was supposed to have a car and, at this point, it became obvious that she hadn't thought very far ahead, or perhaps had never taken our plan seriously to begin with.

"Of all the stupid things you have *ever* done, Iman…this one takes the *fucking* cake!" Marching a few steps ahead of me, Mildred fumed. Adam didn't say a word.

Adam's car door slammed, trapping me in silence. A moment skipped by. "Why did you try to run away?" Adam turned to me from the front seat. I burst into tears. "I don't know," I sobbed.

Though the car ride home was silent, the sound of my heart filled my ears. When we finally arrived home, I walked into the trailer. George was sitting at the kitchen table staring straight ahead and away from me.

"You're *grounded*!" His booming voice bounced off the stained walls, "Go to your room and stay there for the rest of the day!"

I stormed down the hallway, bursting through the closed door of my room, slamming it loudly behind me. *I fucking hate my life,* I screamed silently. Every time I thought I was catching a break, I was pushed deeper into the dirt. I hated everyone and everything. *Why did they want me so badly? They didn't even love me! Why did they like to make my life so fucking miserable?* I crawled under the covers of bed, my sobs muffled.

Hours passed and the sound of my door opening brought me back to reality. Adam entered. He had come to check on me. "Memo, are you okay?"

"*No!*" I exclaimed through sobs. "I hate it here. I hate my life, Adam. Can't I come with you?" I so desperately wanted him to take me with him, to scoop me up and rescue me from the life I had been thrown into.

"I'm sorry, Memo, I can't take care of you," he came and sat on the bed beside me. "I wish I could, but I can't right now."

I shoved my face into the pillow.

"What's wrong?" He looked at me with sad eyes, "Why don't you like it here?"

"Because I hate them, Adam," I sobbed. "They don't care about me. Nobody cares about me!" my words stuttered between each breath.

"Memo," his voice grew more concerned, yet slightly hesitant. "Don't be upset, but when you were missing I came into your room. I read your diary. Why do you want to kill yourself?"

Though anger bubbled inside of me at the thought of Adam rifling through my belongings, I was too exhausted and diminished to care. Nothing mattered anymore.

"B-because I wish I were with Mommy, away from this horrible place. *I hate them,* Adam. They're horrible people. You don't get to see it, but they are," the pressure in my head from the violent sobs, my struggle for air, and the effort to complete my sentences was too much to bear. I felt as though my head were about to explode.

As I lay in my bed, endless tears falling from my eyes, Adam stayed with me. He had a job he had to return to, and he had only come to help find me when he had been told I ran away. The next day he left, returning to Glenwood.

As punishment for my attempt to escape, I was confined to the trailer; the only time I could leave was to go to school. In addition to being homebound, my television privileges had been revoked, as well as my ability to talk on the phone or have visitors. I wasn't even allowed in the yard. I spent all my time in my room writing poetry, reading, and sleeping. When Melanie was home, which was rare, I would hang out in her room, but on her days off, she was out with friends. Just when I thought my life was as unbearable as it could get, I was forced to stay in the one place I loathed the most. This was a punishment far worse than anything I could have imagined.

Still furious, Mildred and George ignored me. It was as though I didn't exist. When I spoke to them, I was met with silence. I knew that this was an act of punishment, but I was so feverish with my hatred for them that I didn't want to speak to them anyways.

The only positive outcome of this punitive action was my newfound love for school; it was my only escape from the hellhole I was living in. Between 8:00 a.m. and 3:00 p.m. I caught up with friends, living vicariously through them. Although Gemma and I hadn't spent too much time together the past few months, we were still best friends and spent every lunch together. It seemed as though Frances disapproved of my time spent with Gemma, but I did so regardless. I had begun to grow tired of Frances. Nothing good came from hanging around with her, and when she had blamed me for not wanting to have sex after the incident with Noah in her mother's basement, my desire for her friendship quickly dwindled.

During recess one afternoon, Frances came up to me, inviting me to hang out with her that evening, along with some of her girlfriends from the city who were coming to see her. Declining due to my parentally imposed house arrest, I told her that I had been grounded and, for the time being, wasn't allowed outside of the fortress of cheap metal that I had called home.

When I returned home later that afternoon, I sat in my room thinking about what my life would be like if my mom were still alive. My mind wandered. I thought of death. There were different ways I could commit suicide outside of overdosing on prescription medication: though a knife would be messy, it would be exactly how my mom died, and that could be a good way;

leaping from a tall building was an option, however, there weren't any tall buildings to jump from, and, as luck would have it, I was afraid of heights. I wondered what would happen if I leapt off a building, and like my attempt with the pills, it failed. *What if I was crippled and I had to have Mildred and George take care of me the rest of my life?* I shuddered at the very thought of spending the rest of my life with them.

The next day of school started out like any other except Frances wasn't on the bus. I went to the smoking pit before first class and waited for her to show up in case she got a ride from her dad, as she occasionally did. When the bell rang and Frances still wasn't to be found, I headed toward the school and went to class.

The room buzzed. A tragedy had occurred the night before. I looked around the room, hearing snippets of the event. Apparently, Frances and her two girlfriends went to Cedar Grove, drove around looking for something to do, and saw a girl named Carly walking down the street. I had known Carly, just as everyone else in my school had. She was the most popular girl at our school. She was gorgeous, with thick, straight brown hair, and an athletic build. Carly was also incredibly friendly; she was nice to everyone and made them feel as if they were the most important person in the world when she spoke. Her family was wealthy, she was an avid player of every sport, and a member of every school committee there was. Everyone loved Carly. It was easy to love her because she really was so perfect and, at the same time, it was easy to hate her because she seemed to have the perfect life.

When Frances and her friends saw Carly walking, they decided to stop and see what she was doing. They approached her and began teasing and taunting her. Suddenly, they grabbed her by the hair and the three of them began to punch and kick her repeatedly until she fell to the cement sidewalk. The girls continued to kick her until she transformed into a bloody pulp on the ground. They drove off in the car when they were pleased with their results.

Carly, broken, bloodied, and bruised, had managed to stand up and walk to a friend's house nearby. As her friend's mother opened the door, Carly was barely recognizable; her face was severely damaged, her body covered in blood. After calling 911, Carly was taken to the hospital and received several stitches on her face, and had been diagnosed with not only a concussion, but several broken ribs. She had almost lost her eye and, according to the doctors, she was just three kicks to the head away from losing her life or being completely paralyzed. Frances was immediately expelled and sent back to Edmonton to live with her mother. I never saw or heard from her again.

I sat in pure shock listening to the events that had taken place the evening before. How could this be true? I just saw Frances yesterday. She told me her friends were coming, even invited me to join her. I couldn't help but wonder what would have happened had I joined them on their joyride. *Would I have been witness to this horrible crime or would I have been able to divert it?* I'd never know, though it haunted me for a long time.

Uneventful as it always was, Christmas came and went in a blink of an eye. Even when I was finally released from my punishment of house arrest, the bitter cold of the winter had made it impossible to hang outside with my friends. Melanie still worked two jobs and had to hitchhike to work in blizzards and freezing temperatures. She had become a different person in the past months and kept mostly to herself; she was always tired and not her usual happy-go-lucky self—the responsibility of paying our bills weighed heavily on her shoulders. Considering all this, Melanie had announced that she would be heading to British Columbia for the month of February with Ron since he was going to move there for school. They would stay in Vancouver together and she would have a vacation.

Devastation took hold of me at her announcement. I didn't want to be stuck at home alone with Mildred and George. What was I supposed to do? Even though I didn't see her much, I still knew she was there if I needed her. The thought of being left by another sibling was more than I could stand. I had lost my brothers, and now I was losing Mel. Knowing it was of no use, I went to her room, pleading with her to stay.

"I'll be back in a month," she replied. "I just need to get away."

It was only fair, Melanie had been working so hard and doing so much and as she told me that she needed to take a break from working and trying to take care of Mildred and George, I knew I had no rebuttal.

"They can pay their own bills," she muttered. "I'm sick of being the responsible one."

I didn't blame her for wanting to leave, I was more jealous than anything. I was aware of the validity of her words. We couldn't just lean on her all the time and expect her to be around to save the day. My sweet, loving sister was always the one who had to do the right thing: she had to take care of me as soon as I arrived all those years ago, she had to cook for me, clean up after me and hang out with me; now she was forced to pay our bills, work two jobs, and suffer on the highways in the cold, catching rides with strangers. Although I knew it would be lonely without her, I was happy for her. If anyone had deserved a vacation, an escape from this life, it was Mel. I just prayed for my sake that it would go quickly. Thankfully, February didn't differ much from any other month of the year. Pretending that Mel was at work, I would tell myself that she would be home soon. When she was away, I would sit in her room and think about her while I looked at the various knickknacks and teddy bears that decorated her shelves. Careful not to touch anything, I had been cautious so as to not make my occasional visits known. Mildred and George, like usual, kept to themselves and ignored me. George told me it was easier for them if they pretended that I wasn't there and that I needed to take care of myself. And though I wondered how their new course of action was any different from the way had been treating me for years, I resigned myself to it, remembering their mental and intellectual insufficiencies.

Chapter Twelve

Age 13: Heads Will Roll

With Melanie's return in March, life resumed and I was happy to have her back. As I walked into the trailer one afternoon, weeks after her return, I was hit with a burst of freezing cold air—the temperature didn't differ from that of the outdoors. *What went wrong this time?* I asked myself as I shuffled in through the entranceway. The sight of Melanie wrapped in her winter coat greeted me. She had turned on the oven and left the door open to warm the house as much as she could.

"What's going on?" I asked. "Why is it so cold in here?"

"We don't have any heat," her voice dripped with anger. "It got shut off because the bill hasn't been paid." I realized that her anger was not rooted in the fact that she was currently hovering over the oven in a winter jacket, but because she had been giving Mildred and George money for the bills. It was clear that they weren't spending her hard-earned paycheques the way they should have been. Leaving the kitchen, Mel walked into her room and returned with a small space heater. "Put this in your room," she said to me, her face still furious. *At least we still have electricity for now,* I thought as I walked toward my room. I plugged in the space heater, sitting next to it, absorbing the small amount of heat it emitted.

That night felt very long as we all froze beneath bundles of covers, fully dressed for the outdoors. Just when I thought I couldn't hate Mildred and

George anymore, they gave me new reasons to try. In the middle of the night Mel came into my room and woke me up.

"Get up, Iman, we have to go," she stood over me in her coat and hat, shivering and panicked.

"Wh-where are we going?" I asked dreamily, still half asleep. "What's wrong?"

"We have to move. *Right now.* We've been evicted and we need to leave right now," as she pulled the blankets off me, I could tell by her tone that she was serious and that I needed to ask questions later. The commotion down the hall encouraged me to get up and listen to my sister.

My fingers were numb, stiffened by the cold as I rummaged through my things, throwing them into garbage bags. Anger keeping me warm, I wondered why we would have to move again—in the middle of the night, no less.

George, hauling furniture into a borrowed van in the driveway, dodged Mildred as she frantically packed dishes and linens, and ran up and down the hallway. Through hazy eyes, I absorbed the scene in front of me. Even here, in the crumbling village of trailers, they had found themselves kicked out, yet again. I didn't know what had happened to make us leave our home, I didn't know where we would be living now, but I prayed it would be better than where we had been. Filling up the vehicle as much as we could, I walked out of the trailer for the last time; the sight of a sink filled with soaking dishes that had now been transformed into a solid block of ice embedded itself into my mind as I closed the door behind me and got into the van.

The days that followed our quick departure from the trailer were nothing more than a blur. Mildred and George had not yet secured a new place for us in Edmonton, and we were left to spend a few nights with family. George, along with his friends, returned to the trailer to salvage the large pieces of furniture that were too heavy to bring with us during our midnight escape. Oddly enough, I still didn't know why we were forced to flee. All I knew was that, according to Melanie, Mildred and George hadn't paid the rent, and because of this, we were given 48 hours to vacate. Their inability to be responsible had caused us to have the same problems repeatedly. It was as if

I was living in a recurring nightmare: being forced to gather what little I had in the middle of the night; opening an empty fridge and being left with a constant rumble in my stomach; facing winter nights of sub-zero temperature with no heat, swaddled in sweaters and blankets. You would think that they would learn from their mistakes, but it was like they were small children— focused on themselves and unable to really understand the consequences of their actions. My frustration with my guardians had become tiresome, and all I really wanted was to no longer be associated with their failure.

Our apartment in Edmonton was in a rundown neighbourhood with streets lined with old, beat-up cars and four-storey walk-ups. The last time I had lived in this city, aside from the year with my Aunt Fatima and the Tunisian family, was with my mother in our townhouse. Since I had left, I had lived the life of a country kid; roaming in the forests, playing in the swamps, and making friends with farm animals. Looking around this new neighbourhood, it was a far cry from the one I had lived in with my mother, and an even larger leap from the homes I had lived in with Mildred and George. The apartment was on the third floor at the back of the building, and faced an alley. A galley kitchen stood beside the front door, leaving little to no room for an entranceway. It was a narrow, small kitchen, with old, brown wooden cupboards that reminded me of the farmhouse. A tiny dining area sat beside the kitchen that had just enough room to fit our kitchen table, chairs, and our old hutch. The living room was about the same size as the last trailer but had a sliding door and a small balcony that looked out onto the graveled back alley and a parking lot filled with broken-down cars that had looked as though they had been there for centuries.

The only bathroom was the first room in the hallway that led to the three bedrooms that were side by side. My bedroom was right at the end of the hall, next to the bathroom. It was larger than my last and from the window that looked out to the side of the building, I could see the parking lot, the main street, and another neighbouring apartment building. Mildred and George's room was right next to mine on the other side, and Mel shared a wall with Mildred, George, and the living room. The carpets were beige, stained with cigarette burns and dirt.

This apartment was a dump, and I not only lacked any enthusiasm at the thought of living in this new prison, but loathed the thought of yet again going to another school. With only three months left in the seventh grade, it was an unjust punishment to force me to reroute my life, to make new friends, and find my identity in a crowd of strangers. Mildred told me I would be going to Riverdale Junior High, which was two bus rides away from our apartment. I shuddered both with excitement and fear. I had never taken public transportation before.

The night before my first day I was a mess of anxiety, nerves, thrill, and panic. After trying everything I owned on, I still couldn't decide what to wear. I even went to Mel's room and begged her to let me borrow something that didn't make me look like a hand-me-down-wearing orphan. Finally agreeing to my pleas, I went to bed with Mel's clothing folded neatly on my dresser, trying with all my might to fall asleep, talking to my mother until my alarm went off. The sound of Mildred's nasally voice calling my name stirred me back into consciousness. *This is it*, I gulped, forcing myself out from underneath my covers, and proceeding to take a shower and dress myself in Mel's clothing. Taking a deep breath, I left my room, walking into the kitchen hoping to find something to eat. Mildred, sitting at the kitchen table in her bathrobe and a cigarette in hand, was reading the paper.

"You nervous?" she asked, not looking up from the black and white print.

"A little," I stared into the empty fridge hoping to see something I could grab quickly,

"I don't even know which buses to take." Knots twisted in my stomach.

"Oh, you'll be fine, you big baby," Mildred laughed, peering over her paper. She got up from the table and walked toward me and pointed at the counter, "I made your lunch." She grabbed a paper bag that was folded over and handed it to me. I peered inside and saw a sandwich and an apple.

"Thanks," I mumbled, hardly looking forward to the meal.

"Oh, quit your moping. You'll be fine! You're such a follower, Iman. Can't you do *anything* by yourself?" Her anger started to rise. "It's just a stupid bus. I gave you your bus pass, and that's all you need."

I felt myself getting flustered as the tears started filling up my eyes. Although I was taking deep breaths and trying to be calm, I was nervous. I hated first days of school and I had already had my fair share. I didn't like being the new girl and was tired of having to start from scratch, making friends all over again.

Mildred walked to her bedroom as I began to slide on my shoes and put on my jacket. Unfortunately, the chilly weather forced me to have to wear the hideous garment, magnifying my shame and embarrassment I had tried so earnestly the night before to hide. Within moments Mildred came out of the bedroom fully dressed and started putting her shoes on. I looked at her confused.

"I'll take the bus with you, okay? Just the first one though, you'll have to take the second one by yourself."

I thanked her quietly under my breath as we made our way out of the apartment, descending the three flights of stairs to the main door. My mind flashed back to when I first moved in with Mildred, when I didn't know how to make my lunch and she had become angry and violent. Although it seemed like a small gesture for her to take the bus with me, it meant more than she would ever know. I knew she would probably throw it in my face later, reminding me of what a *baby* I was, but in the moment, I had finally felt supported, and it meant the world.

There was a bus stop right next to our apartment building and Mildred and I caught the first bus that went directly to Jasper Place Terminal, only a handful of blocks away. When we got off the bus, Mildred showed me where I would catch the next bus, and after saying a quick goodbye, returned home. I was in awe. I had never been to a bus terminal before, and it was thriving with life. There were so many different buses pulling in and out, and people were everywhere. It was certainly a far cry from my life in the trailer park. As my bus pulled up, a twinge of adrenaline and nervousness flickered within me.

I flashed my bus pass as I got onboard and found an empty seat. My eyes peered eagerly out the window, fearful that I might miss my stop, or worse, get lost. Within fifteen minutes, we approached a large school. The sign on the building confirmed that we had finally arrived at Riverdale Junior High.

The building, though only two floors on one side, seemed so long. I felt my throat tighten as I slowly made my way toward the brick building, and finally to the office to introduce myself as the *new student.* The secretary, a cheery, motherly woman, welcomed me and sorted through all my paperwork. I was directed to my homeroom and given my books and agenda. I had tried to prepare myself for the number of stares I would receive from the other kids, but regardless of my stoic exterior, inside I was shaking and sweating with nerves. I knew I couldn't show my true feelings or I would look weak and fall victim to the cruel taunts and bullying of the other kids. As I made my way from class to class, I did my best to concentrate on the lessons but found myself too excited and nervous about my new surroundings. However, as the clock neared lunchtime, I became almost frantic at the thought of eating lunch by myself. Hoping to avoid the situation entirely, I decided to go back to the office and sit in the waiting room to eat my lunch.

The same secretary who had been so kind that morning asked me if everything was alright. After I told her it was and that I just wanted to eat my lunch there, she assured me that I was just fine to sit there anytime I wanted. I opened the now crumpled paper bag that Mildred had packed as my lunch and peered inside. I pulled out the sandwich she had made and opened the two slices of bread to reveal butter and ham. I gagged at the thought of eating the strange pink meat that was between two slices of stale bread. Mildred knew I didn't eat ham. In fact, I had never eaten ham in my life. My face grew hot with rage as I thought about how stupid Mildred could be. I was sure she had made me a lunch she knew I wouldn't eat on purpose, just to spite me on my first day of school. I threw the sandwich back into the bag and took out the apple. As I took a bite, I recognized a couple of students that shared the same homeroom as me walk in and out of the office. They looked busy with a project and didn't really notice me sitting there. After I finished what was left of my apple, which I hungrily devoured, I decided to make my way to the next class in case I couldn't find it since I still didn't know where I was going.

I walked through the hallways which were growing busier with students with every moment that passed by. *Everyone here looks so different,* I silently said to myself. It was as though everyone had looked older; the girls dressed fashionably in the latest styles, in clothes that made them look like they had just stepped out of a catalogue or off a runway, and their hairstyles were sleek and beautiful; they all looked like they could have been in high school.

Immediately, I became much more aware of how dowdy I looked draped in baggy clothes that were faded from their past lives with different owners. I thought of myself dressed in the same clothes as the girls that passed me in the halls. *I couldn't do it.* I liked wearing baggy clothes, they helped hide how skinny and malnourished I had become. My bones protruded through my skin, and I hated how I looked without clothes and couldn't imagine what it would be like wearing clothes that clung to my body. I certainly didn't have a figure like the girls around me. As for my hair, it had just gone from one bad haircut to the next since my mother had died, and it seemed that no matter how many hairdressers I encountered, no one knew how to manage my wild mane. Every time I left a salon I was in tears, devastated at the latest butchery I had endured. My short, boyish hair did nothing to flatter my already androgynous frame and style. I had often been mistaken for a boy out in public, which had deeply crushed my self-esteem to depths too low for me to imagine looking like these voluptuous girls that passed me by. My only hope for popularity was to be funny.

As I walked down the busy hallway a boy walking toward me caught my eye. He looked very much like Noah. He had a medium build, blonde hair and was wearing a leather jacket. What I noticed the most, though, was that the entire right side of his face was covered in what looked like scars made by knife cuts and slashes. The scars were thick and old but I couldn't help but stare as he walked toward me. I wasn't aware that I was staring until a frantic and angry girl walked right up to me and screamed into my face, "What the fuck are you looking at, bitch? That's my man you're staring at!"

Caught completely off guard, I was brought out of my thoughts by a frantic brunette dressed in a cropped shirt and black tights. She towered over me with an evil grin on her face. "If I ever catch you flirting with my boyfriend again, I'm going to rip your fucking head off and roll it down this hallway. Do you understand?"

As much as I wanted to speak, my lips were motionless. With a simple nod of my head, I quickly walked to my next class. I could feel my whole body vibrating as the adrenaline rushed through my veins. *How could I be so stupid? Why the fuck am I acting like such a loser, staring at people in the hallway?* I was humiliated as I sat down at my desk. Everyone had seen and heard that girl yelling and screaming in my face. I was probably the laughingstock of the school.

I couldn't get home fast enough once the final bell rang at 3:15 p.m. I remembered how to get back to the bus terminal and boarded the second bus to the apartment. As I unlocked the door to our place I could no longer hold back the tears that had been bubbling behind my eyes all afternoon. I hated my new school. I hated living in this new shit-hole, and I hated that fucking bitch who humiliated me on my first day.

"What the hell's wrong with you?" George called out as I ran to my bedroom, loudly slamming the door shut. I threw my backpack in the corner of the room and flopped face-first onto my bed. Holding nothing back, I cried into my pillow as I recalled the horrors of the day. I hadn't even gone one day without getting death threats. *How would I survive at this awful school?* And, worst of all, I had no friends, which meant I had nowhere to escape to in the evenings to get away from Mildred and George. I had never felt so trapped in all my life. I felt like a rat in a cage sitting in that dingy apartment. I stayed in my bedroom all evening and only came out to use the washroom and get a drink. Mildred and George made some snide remarks at what a baby I was and how I always overreacted.

"You need to learn how to toughen up, Iman." Mildred called out to me from the living room. I stood in the kitchen staring into empty cupboards, trying to find something to eat.

"You've been spoiled by everyone and now you're not ready for the real world."

"Yeah, I need something, don't I?" I gave my reply from behind the kitchen wall, two middle fingers up in her direction.

Toughen up? How the fuck could I do that? I grabbed a handful of crackers and some jelly, making my way to my room. I wasn't sure how tough I could get in this world. Everything always seemed to be so messed up. I watched my father murder my mother. I lived with court-appointed guardians who were deranged addicts who told me I was worthless and hit me whenever I didn't agree with them. My brothers had left me alone, Melanie worked all the time and was never home, and I was hungry almost every minute of the day. If I was such a baby and not tough enough, maybe it was because I was just not cut out for this world. I wished I were dead more than anything.

I wasn't sure what real world Mildred referred to, but if it was anything like my life, I wanted no part of it. I couldn't handle any more of that world, and I refused to believe the world I lived in was real. *There must be a better way to live than in this dump of a life.*

That night, before bed, I prayed to God. I begged him to give me some friends, to let me feel like I was part of something the way I felt when I was with Gemma and Frances in the trailer park. *I'd do anything to have friends.* I didn't want to feel lonely anymore. I hated my life, I hated coming home, and school and friends were the only things that made me feel like I was human, like I mattered somehow.

The next morning, I woke up and got dressed, masking the evidence of my tears the night before with makeup. I went to the kitchen and Mildred was there again with her coffee and cigarette. She once again pointed to the brown paper bag on the counter and I could only guess that she had decided to make me a ham sandwich again. I said thank you and bolted out the door before she could ask me about my first day at school. I crossed the street to the bus stop, peering into my lunch bag. This time there was just a ham sandwich. I rolled my eyes, tossing the bag into the garbage can next to the bus stop. *Today is going to be better,* I repeated to myself. *It has to be.* I couldn't have another disaster or death threat.

The bus stop had a few people at it this morning and there was a girl who looked only slightly older than me. She was full figured with red hair and a big smile on her face. She called over to me, "Hey! How's it going?"

I awkwardly looked at her and then away as I said hello back.

"My name is Becky," her face lit up when she spoke.

"I'm Iman," I was afraid to look at her since I was reprimanded for my eye contact yesterday and wasn't sure about these city girls.

"What school do you go to?" she asked. I told her I had just started at Riverdale. She told me that she also went there and asked me if I liked it.

I paused, then replied truthfully, "I don't really fit in there."

"Why not?"

I paused again, searching for the correct words. I told her about my situation the day before, how some girl threatened to kill me and screamed at me for looking at her boyfriend. I explained that he had so many scars on his face and that I hadn't meant to be rude but I was curious.

Becky seemed to know the girl I was speaking of instantly. "Julia said that to you?" Her voice became irritated, "What a fucking bitch."

Quickly, I realized that I could be getting myself in more trouble by snitching on her like a baby. A frown crept upon my lips.

"Don't worry, Iman," Becky smiled at me. "I'll have a little chat with Julia, and if she ever tries anything to hurt you, I will kick her fucking ass, okay?" Her eyes looked at me in such a supportive, sisterly kind of way. I felt at ease for the first time in days.

Becky and I sat together on the bus and laughed all the way to school. She was so funny and gregarious and was so approachable. By the time we reached the school, I felt like we had been friends for ages. "Stick with me," she said. "I'll show you around school properly and introduce you to some people."

I felt so relieved that my prayers had come true: I had made a friend, my own guardian angel to protect me at school.

Becky and I walked down the hallway and spotted Julia coming our way.

"Hey, bitch," Becky's friendly tone was replaced with venom as she spat the words at Julia. "I hear you have a problem with the new girl."

Julia was alone and didn't look quite as brave and fierce as she did the day before. Her face went white and she had the same look of fear in her eyes as Nicole had right before Frances had punched her in the face.

"I didn't realize she was your friend, Beck, I'm so sorry. I thought she was flirting with Kevin." Julia seemed so small now.

"Well she wasn't flirting with your freak show boyfriend. She can look at people, you know?" Becky's dominance was evident.

Everyone was staring at us as they made their way to first class.

"Well, tell you what, Julia. If I ever catch you looking at Iman the wrong way again, I will rip your head off and roll it down the fucking hallway, got it?" Becky was inches away from Julia's face.

"I get it. I'm sorry." Julia could hardly keep eye contact and had her head bowed toward the floor.

"Don't tell me. Tell her." Becky's finger pointed in my direction.

"I'm really sorry, I fucked up yesterday. It won't happen again." Julia looked like she was about to cry as she apologized to me. I didn't say a word.

Becky and I walked away and she put her arm around me.

"Don't worry, kiddo, I got your back. If she ever bothers you again, you let me know, okay?"

I was smiling from ear to ear, in utter disbelief at the turn of events. *What luck I had sharing a bus stop with Becky and just happening to be there at the same time. My prayers were answered.* I felt as though I had won the lottery. Suddenly, the new city, new school, and new place, didn't seem quite so bad.

Within weeks of living in Edmonton, Mildred and George had befriended the usual suspects in the neighbourhood and, before long, our apartment was filled with local riffraff each day after school and on the weekends. Drug dealers, crackheads, hookers, and lots of neglected children occupied our home. I didn't understand what crack was exactly, but I saw pipes different than what people smoked weed out of. The smell that came out was awful too. It smelled like burning rubber and material and made me feel sick to my stomach. People would go into the bathroom with their pipes and when they came out, their faces looked different. It was as though their minds had escaped from their bodies, but they were still walking around. Our tiny apartment would be filled with these strange-looking adults with caved-in scruffy faces, missing teeth, and torn clothes. There was one man, Mack, who wasn't so bad. He was nice to me and always smiled, and acknowledged me—which is more than I can say for most of the people who came over. Mack was a small man with long straight brown hair and was covered in tattoos. He was a drug dealer, and because of his profession, he was over a lot due to George's frequent calls. Often, Mack would also bring his toddler son over, and I would play with him along with the other kids who came over when their parents wanted to party. Once the adults came over, it was like they forgot that they brought their children at all, and I felt the sorriest for the little children who were left to fend for themselves as their parents smoked from pipes, drank in excess, and ignored them.

After scavenging their parents' bags for diapers, I would gather the little ones and take them to my room to change the urine-soaked diapers that had likely needed changing hours ago. Hidden in my closet, I had a tiny black and white TV that used to be my mother's. I didn't let Mildred and George know that it worked for fear they would take it away from me when I was grounded or needing punishment. It had a small antenna on it that got three basic channels and was more than enough entertainment for me when I was holed up in my room. It still had my mother's blood caked onto the side of it because it was the little TV that she kept on her bedside table. I couldn't bring myself to wash the blood off. I would turn on the small television to keep the kids busy with whatever was playing, or by playing games with them. From the kitchen, I would bring crackers, peanut butter, and jelly into my room and make snacks for us. Sometimes, we would all just fall asleep on my bed as I sang lullabies and rubbed their backs.

The little ones brought me comfort. They made me think of when we used to have lots of animals to keep me company, and it felt good to have beings to take care of and look after. I felt less lonely when I had to take care of them, and I was glad to not have to be alone with Mildred and George. It worked out for everyone.

Since there were only three months of school left when I arrived at Riverdale, the remainder of the school year went by in a fluid flash. With so many new experiences living in the city, I was caught in a whirlwind of navigating through a new school, catching up on the curriculum I had missed, and adjusting to my new surroundings. My love for reading did not falter during my transition to city life. I took books out from the library and read during my leisure time after school, escaping into a world of literary fiction. When I discovered Shakespeare, I couldn't stop reading *Romeo and Juliet.* Although the first few times I had read it, it made little sense, as I continued to read the play over again, I would look at the footnotes and make note of all the words I didn't understand. Soon, I had created my own Shakespearean English dictionary of all the words that I had deciphered, and I would ask my language arts teacher about concepts, phrases, or words that I couldn't quite figure out. As I read his words, over and over again, little by little, I fell in love with William Shakespeare and his incredible wit and talent for writing. I would pretend that I was Juliet and, in a world of imagination and daydreams, I would wait for Romeo to rescue me from the life I so hated—even if death was our only way to escape. I understood how the pull of what might be waiting on the other side of misery could be alluring.

Chapter Thirteen

Age 13: Transported

Since the move to Edmonton, Ben and Elizabeth had come to visit several times. I treasured their company; it was a sense of normalcy in my decaying world. As we were out for dinner, I told them about my new obsession with Shakespeare and they both showed enthusiasm and pleasure as we discussed my favourite play. They told me of other plays by Shakespeare, such as *Macbeth* and *Othello,* and though I hadn't yet grown tired of the Capulets and Montagues, I was excited to read other plays.

During one of these dinners with Ben and Elizabeth, they asked if I would like to go to Toronto during the summer to visit my Aunt Fatima and Uncle Tarek, who had moved back from Tunisia. I leapt with joy at the thought. I hadn't seen them in such a long time, and not only did I miss my younger cousin, Ali, but I thought of being submersed in the sights, smells, and sounds of Arabic culture once again. Ben informed me that when I arrived, my brothers would be there too. It seemed that Adam and Chokri would be moving to Toronto and my brothers and my mother's family would all be together, like old times. I was filled with excitement at the notion of being with my family, once again, and being far away from Mildred and George.

I could hardly wait for summer to spend time with my Aunt Fatima, Uncle Tarek, Ali, his little brother, Moe, and their half-sister, Chantelle, who had moved in with them the year prior. Chantelle was born and raised in Paris. Her mother, like mine, had passed, although very recently and under different circumstances. I had been told that she had committed suicide, jumping from their apartment window. Chantelle had been visiting her father in Toronto when her mother committed suicide. She never returned to Paris. I couldn't help but be envious of Chantelle; she got to live with Fatima and Tarek, and I was left to suffer with Mildred and George. It was as though my life was fated to be in distress, regardless of how hard I tried to avoid it, or make a better life for myself. No matter what, it always ended up worse than it began. I knew that one day, when it was up to me, I would do whatever it took to be happy, and my time would never be spent in the company of drug addicts who were more preoccupied with scheming ways to buy a case of beer, than with caring about feeding their own children.

With weeks before my trip, I couldn't wait. I began to pack immediately, debating on what to bring. I had never really been anywhere before, and not knowing if it would be cold, I brought clothing for every season. I took pictures that were in frames and carefully wrapped them in my sweaters. Staring at a picture of my mother and me, when I was barely a year old, on a plane to Tunisia, I smiled. Of course, I couldn't remember anything from back then. Folding the photo in a thick sweater, I closed my suitcase. This trip to Toronto would be a bigger trip than I could have ever hoped for.

My suitcase was overwhelming in size and weight. "How much stuff did you pack, love?" Ben's face wrinkled as he heaved the heavy luggage into the trunk of his car.

"I don't know," I thought of the suitcase's contents. "I guess I didn't know what to pack, I just brought as much as I could." My mind raced for anything I may have forgotten. The only items I could think of were my mother's jewelry; I was too afraid to lose it and chose not to pack it with me. I had concluded that it would be best to leave the jewelry in my jewelry box, just in case I were to accidentally forget it someplace during my big adventure across the country.

Once we checked me and my bag in, Ben and Elizabeth took me to my gate and then gave me a quick play by play of what to expect on the plane.

They told me about how to find my seat, how long it would be, and if I needed anything at all, to simply ask the flight attendant. After boarding the plane with my stomach in knots, the flight itself was uneventful, though I was in awe of being in the air. It felt like magic to be on a vessel so powerful that it could whisk a group of people from one place to another. Imagining that I was on a flying dream machine that could take me as far away from my life as possible, I felt like the luckiest girl in the world to be leaving everything behind and finally reuniting with my family, the people who loved and cared for me and who reminded me of my mother. I had long forgotten the discomfort I felt living with my aunt and uncle so many years ago. Now, they were all I had of my mother. I thought of the food, the smells of spices, my aunt's face that was the spitting image of my mother's—I wanted it all. As I dreamed of all that was to come, I fell asleep on the plane and woke up just as we were about to land.

As I made my way off the plane, I was greeted by the familiar faces of my family. Adam, Chokri, Aunt Fatima, Uncle Tarek, Ali, Moe, Chantelle, even my Aunt Samira, her daughter Nesrine, and Malek, Nesrine's husband, had come. My smile spanned from ear to ear. It felt like such a beautiful homecoming.

I do belong somewhere after all, I thought to myself as I rushed to hug my family. I hugged Ali tightly, surprised at how much he had grown in the years that had passed. He was so much taller now and still had those beautiful big brown eyes with the longest eyelashes. He had filled out since I had last seen him and was a little chubbier than the skinny little boy I knew. He was slowly coming into his own and looked like a handsome young man. His big smile and signature laugh hadn't changed at all. I was so happy to be with my family. I had just climbed the tallest mountain in the world and I was finally home.

The journey to Aunt Fatima and Uncle Tarek's house was filled with hugs and laughter. They had such a lovely home. Though it was simple, it was large and tidy with modern furniture. The familiar scent of bleach and spices overwhelmed me; it was just like my mother's house when I was growing up.

With a simple inhale, I was transported back in time, back into a world of comfort, love, and joy. For the first time in a long while, I felt so close to who I really was.

After settling into the house that would be my home for the duration of the summer, I was finally given a chance to get to know my cousin Chantelle. Though we had been speaking on the phone, her English was slightly broken since she was born and raised in France, and I was excited to finally speak to her despite the mild language barrier. She was beautiful. Her French accent and brunette hair that fell into a perfect Parisian bob accentuated her fair skin and deep brown eyes. Her laugh sounded like mine, and was large and full of heart. We quickly became friends. My heart hurt for her and her recent loss of her mother. She, too, understood how sorrowful the world truly was, and we bonded over our broken hearts and the unjust ways of the universe around us.

I had found a confidant and friend in Chantelle. She was smart, funny, and most importantly, just as mischievous as I had been. When I confessed that I had smoked, she burst into laughter, reaching under her bed for a pack of cigarettes. My eyes widened, and I quickly joined in her laughter. Running to the park across the street, cigarettes in tow, we hid behind the slides and indulged in deep inhales of tobacco. I was dizzy with delight. With so much in common, we could hardly stop talking to catch our breath; I felt like she was my sister and I wished that I could stay with her every day.

As the summer unfolded, we spent entire days together, basking in the light of friendship and companionship. Chantelle and I would be left alone when my aunt and uncle had to go to work, and we would play at the park or lounge around the house and watch TV, then clean every bathroom and the kitchen so that everything was clean for when the adults came home.

When I told Chantelle of my life in Edmonton, she couldn't believe some of the things I shared. As I told tales of midnight escapes from one broken-down place to another and Mildred and George's alcoholism and drug addiction, and the lack of food in our home, Chantelle's eyes widened in shock.

"Tell Fatima," she insisted. "Maybe you could come stay with us!"

Though the thought of leaving my destitute life in Edmonton behind had seemed more than appealing, I couldn't bring myself to bring my living situation to Fatima's attention in fear of what might happen to me. *What if I ruined my chances and got sent to another home? What if Mildred and George got to me first and did horrible things to me before sending me somewhere?* Sometimes I could swear Mildred hated me with an unmatched passion and would do just about anything to ruin my happiness, and I wouldn't risk missing my happiness for anything. I made Chantelle promise to never tell a soul. She agreed. We kept each other's secrets and I knew we would do anything for one another.

Spending time with my brothers and cousins had reminded me of the days when we would sit in Aunt Fatima's living room watching television after my mother had passed, and I was beaming with joy at the chance to see Adam and Chokri every day. We would all go on day trips to various Toronto malls, or to the large amusement park, Canada's Wonderland, and return home to stay up late, drinking Tunisian mint tea, and chatting with the adults as they chain-smoked on the patio. I had missed being around my family, having a sense of culture, and a sense of identity. In the evenings when the adults came home from work, Aunt Fatima would make the most amazing meals, like couscous with lamb in a deliciously spicy sauce—just like my mother used to make. And after every meal, my stomach felt as though it were about to burst. It was amazing to fill up every night with such delicious cuisine. I had forgotten what it was like to eat Tunisian fare. Since I had left to live with Mildred and George, it was as though my ethnic roots had been ripped away from me. I had even forgotten how to speak Arabic. Though Aunt Fatima and Uncle Tarek kept insisting that I would still remember, it had been almost seven years since I had spoken the language of my family. Mildred and George, along with showing no courtesy toward my religious and cultural dietary restrictions, had made it apparent that speaking my mother tongue would not be tolerated when I moved in with them all those years ago.

As the summer began to slip away, my thirteenth birthday approached. Unlike so many of my birthdays in the past, I would be surrounded by family, and was enthused at the thought. Aunt Fatima had planned a special evening with all our family, making a special dinner for me and got me a wonderful cake. I was *finally* a teenager. After we all indulged in my favourite meal, spaghetti and meat sauce, we played Arabic music and belly danced in the living room. My heart was bursting with happiness. My mom would often belly dance with me and I hadn't felt so close to her since she left. All the smiles, the food, the laughter, and the love had me in a euphoric trance. My troubles were miles away and I couldn't have been happier. In those moments, I loved my life and my family with a ferocity that I hadn't felt in so long.

When the evening had finally come to an end, Chantelle and I stayed up all night talking and laughing. At the sound of Uncle Tarek coming in to check on us, we pretended to sleep until he closed the door and we could hear him walk away. We slept together every night, holding hands as we drifted away into our respective world of dreams. Chantelle wasn't just my cousin; in the short six weeks, she became everything I had missed in my life back home: a sister, a friend, a confidant that I had never had before. Maybe it was just our age, or the fact that we both knew the torture of having to say goodbye to our mothers so soon. Regardless of why, I couldn't help but love her with all my heart and wished so desperately that we could stay like this forever and live together.

As the days passed and my flight back to Edmonton crept closer, my heart hardened with sadness. I had become accustomed to never having what I desired and knowing in my heart that my fate was to continuously long for something just to never have it within my grasp. My whole life was one big longing—a desire for everything and anything other than what I was living. The grass wasn't just greener on the other side, it was made of shimmering gold, and I would never get to cash it in.

Chapter Fourteen

Age 13: To Pawn a Queen

My flight home was the opposite of the trip to Toronto. My sobs couldn't be concealed and there wasn't a flight attendant on the plane that was gifted enough to soothe my pain. Returning to Edmonton was like walking back into a burning building. *How could I possibly go back to a place where it felt like my soul was dying every day? A place where people didn't even notice me.* There were no giggles and kisses, no laughter and fits of joy, no delicious smells and eating until it hurt; no reminders of my mother's smile or tales of her adventures told by her sisters. Only my prison cell awaited me, and there was nothing I could conceive of doing to avoid it. Thoughts of how I could escape came racing back into my mind as soon as I left my family. I swore that one day, when I was in charge of my life, if I made it that far, I would never settle for anything less than unbridled joy. I would live a life I didn't need to escape from. I would laugh far more than I cried. I would find a way to fall repeatedly into happiness.

I was greeted at the airport by Ben and Elizabeth, and as Ben lugged my suitcase into the trunk of the car, I relived all my amazing adventures. I was so happy to see them and they were just as excited about my tales as I was to share them. With hugs, kisses, and a little pocket money, they unloaded me at the dreary apartment I was forced to call home. Mildred and George feigned happiness at my return, and Mildred told me she missed me. There was hardly anything that crossed her lips that I took to mean much. I wasn't going to start now.

I lugged my overstuffed bag into my bedroom and got ready to unpack. I stood in the doorway and looked around at the familiar room. It felt different somehow and I looked very carefully at my belongings. My bed, my closet, my stuffed animals were in the same order I had left them. As I noticed the stereo that Adam had given me last year was missing from its corner in my room, my eyes feverishly scanned the rest of the room. I glanced over to my dresser. It looked different somehow, as though things had been moved.

My jewelry box lid was open and turned sideways; I was positive I hadn't left it like that. I rushed to the box that held my most prized possessions and looked inside. My mother's rings and earrings were gone. My mind raced, I thought back to six weeks ago when I had packed my suitcase. *I didn't take them with me.* My heart began to beat, overwrought with panic. *What the fuck? How could this be?* I left them there to keep them safe and they've vanished. In a fury of fear and desperation, I checked everywhere in my room, ripping open drawers and rummaging through their contents.

Frantically, I ran into the living room choking on my tears. Mildred and George sat there, watching television; Mildred knitting, George with a beer in hand.

"We've been robbed!" I paused, waiting for a reaction. *Did they not hear what I had just said?*

"My stuff is gone!" I rephrased my earlier statement. "My mom's jewelry, my stereo…i-it's all…it's gone," I flailed my arms trying to gain the reaction the situation warranted. They looked up at me and didn't say anything.

"Did you hear me? We've been robbed!" I shouted in disbelief. "It was probably one of your friends. Maybe Mack, that drug dealer guy. My mom's stuff is gone. We must do something. Call the police!" Mildred and George remained motionless.

"We didn't get robbed," George kept his eyes on the TV. "We needed some money so we pawned your jewelry."

My body stiffened, paralyzed with shock.

"Wh-what? You what?" I couldn't quite register what he was saying. "You pa-pawned…you st-stole…" I couldn't collect a solid thought.

Mildred stopped her knitting and looked at me. "Look, we needed some money for beer. We were here suffering while you were off *gallivanting* on your vacation. Some of us weren't having so much fun." A snarky look shot upon her face. "Don't worry about your stupid stereo and jewelry, we'll get it back as soon as we get some money." Her voice suggested that she felt justified in her theft of my most prized possessions.

My body shook with rage and it felt as though I would burst into a million pieces. I broke down into uncontrolled sobs. *Was I being punished for having fun? For seeing my family?*

"H-how could you? Wh-why did you do this?" I ran to my bedroom, slamming the door behind me.

"IMAN, DON'T SLAM THE FUCKING DOOR!" Mildred rose from the couch, storming into my room. "It's just stuff, Iman," she snarled, "We needed the money, okay? We didn't have any food or beer! Not that you cared because you were out having fun with everyone and living the good life, *weren't you?* You're so fucking selfish—you know that? YOUR MOM IS DEAD. Her jewelry is just stuff. It won't bring her back, and it's time you realized that. I told you we will get it back when we get paid so stop your fucking crying and grow up."

My entire world came crashing down around me, exploding into a million fragments that were impossible to piece back together. *I must be in a nightmare; this can't be real.* I screamed, tears pouring out of me as I fell to the floor. I kneeled by my bed and clasped my hands as I prayed, *I'm so sorry, Mommy. I should have brought them with me. I should have protected everything. Please forgive me.* This weight was too much to bear; my heart was exploding in pain. I couldn't believe that they would do this to me. *How could this happen? Why hadn't I brought it all with me? Why was everything so fucked up in my life?*

My body shook with rage and hate. I hated them. I hated how they were and everything they represented. *How could they steal my mother's jewels…for beer? How could they dishonour her this way?* I could feel the small place that I had kept alive through all the horror and trauma that I endured since my mother's death wither away into nothingness. In that moment, I felt it die. I felt the small light that had kept me going extinguish into darkness. Nothing was left and emptiness consumed me.

I rose from the floor, walking into our tiny bathroom, locking the door behind me. I turned on the light, looking around at the mess of towels on the floor, the overstuffed upright hamper with a lid that couldn't shut because the laundry had been neglected; the bathtub ledges were decorated with half-empty bottles of shampoos and shaving creams, and there was an array of soap slivers in the soap dish that were old and forgotten; the trash from the garbage can poured onto the floor beside the toilet. Reaching for the faucet, I turned the knob, allowing the sound of running water to echo in the small room, hoping that Mildred and George wouldn't wonder what I was doing.

Taking a deep breath, I looked up and stood in front of the mirror. My tear-stained face looked foreign to me. I always used to stare at myself in the hopes that I would see my mother's reflection looking back at me. Now when I looked, all I saw was emptiness. My eyes were distant and cold. I could see the harsh realities of my circumstances consuming me. *What happened to the funny girl who loved to laugh? Why did it feel like I was always upset about something and that things were always going wrong?*

I could see the vein in my forehead pulsating. There was no goodness left in anything around me, let alone within me. Every time I got excited or I thought things were turning around, life ripped my heart out, bringing me to my knees.

Sliding the glass door on the vanity cabinet that was positioned just below the mirror, I stared inside. Though I didn't know what I was looking for, I knew when I found it: a small box of razor blades. I took it off the shelf, opening the box carefully, quietly grabbing one of George's razors. Returning the box, I turned off the faucet and looked deeply into the mirror once more before opening the door, and turning off the light.

My entire body was shrouded in numbness. I pushed my dresser up against my door and sat in front of it. I looked around the room. The afternoon sun

pushed through the white sheer curtains, illuminating my bedroom. My bed
was a pile of messy quilts and a knitted blanket that Mildred had made for
me last Christmas; several teddy bears lay around the perimeter of my bed,
Snowball and Freddy sat in front of my pillows as they had always been, for
as long as I could remember. I looked at Freddy's stained body, rusted brown
from my mother's seven-year-old blood. *How did I end up here, in this mess?*
My sobs had eased, but my rage hadn't. I lit a cigarette and stared at myself in
my full-length mirror. *Why did the world hate me so much? What made me so
horrible to have to suffer the fate of my very existence?* This couldn't be real. This
life couldn't be mine. I didn't belong here.

I turned on my alarm clock radio and stared at the tiny razor blade that sat
nestled in the palm of my hand. Picking it up between my thumb and index
finger, I gently raised it, inspecting the sharpened edge. The cold, thin blade
pressed against my wrist. I could feel the sharpened edge begin to cut through
the layers of my skin. I had to escape. I couldn't live here anymore. I pushed
it deeper into my flesh, blood pooling beside the thin blade. Relocating the
razor, I lifted it up and moved it to another spot. I lit another cigarette and
made cut after cut on my arms. As I looked down at the blood and cuts I had
made, I realized that it would draw too much attention. I took off my pants
and began to examine my scrawny pale legs. *My thighs would be a much better
spot to cut,* I thought to myself as I drew in another deep inhale of tobacco.
I hated everything about myself and my life but, somehow, with every slice of
my skin, I felt better—I felt alive. As I pressed the steel blade into my thigh,
a part of me wished for the blade to slip and cut too deep; I wished for the
courage to let every ounce of this life bleed out onto the floor. I couldn't break
into any more pieces. I had nothing left to give.

As the summer came to an end, the violation of my privacy and belongings
had still left me seething. I could not believe what I had returned home to.
What kind of life was this? I couldn't even leave my room without being
robbed by the very same people who were meant to look out for me and

protect me. These people, my so-called guardians, didn't care about me. To them, I was nothing more than a nuisance. Though I was still just a child, I knew that this world was cold, I was left to fend for myself, and no one would be there to watch out for me. I only had myself. My brothers loved me, no doubt, but at the end of the day, they too, were looking out for themselves. They had left. They had made the decision to take care of themselves, planning, ever since I was a small child, an escape from the same hellhole they had left me in. Now, all I had was Melanie, and even she was of the same mentality as my brothers: she looked out for herself first. She knew what she needed to do for her life and her happiness and that is what she focused on. To her, I was just someone that she loved and thought about when I was right in front of her face. We were sisters in this prison, sentenced to a life of uncertainty, poverty, and pain. And though I had tried to believe that my siblings would be there to support me, to aid me in this terrible life, I couldn't forget for one second that everyone around me was out for themselves and that I was very much alone in a cruel world where every day was a fight for survival.

This fight, this long, excruciating fight, was not just physical, but mental and emotional. I had been fighting for mental sanity, to conquer my Post-Traumatic Stress Disorder, to climb out of the hole of depression, loneliness and disparity that I had been tossed into. No one gave a damn about what I was going through, no one knew the horrible suffering that I endured inside my mind, or how desperately I wanted to escape. I would do anything to get away from this life sentence of misery. Why was it that I had to suffer when I didn't do anything wrong? Who did I kill? What did I do to deserve this life?

Holding on to the anger inside of me, I went through the motions as school began. Returning to junior high came as a relief. For seven hours a day, I could escape the confines of our decrepit apartment and pretend like my life wasn't what it was. Since Becky had defended me the year before, I no longer had any incidents or altercations with Julia. In fact, I had accumulated a decent number of friends, and one friend that was closer than the rest. Giselle, a fellow eighth grader, was absolutely gorgeous with jet-black long hair that hung almost to her waist. She was tall for her age and although she was only thirteen, she had the mature silhouette of an eighteen-year-old.

Freckles speckled the caramel complexion of her nose and cheeks; her laugh shook her whole body, and she was so alive when she spoke. It was no surprise to me that everyone loved Giselle. It was easy to see why: she was perfect and happy, and commanded the attention of every room she entered.

We met in the smoking alley across the street from the school, a sacred spot where a group of us would congregate every chance we could.

"Hey, how's it going?" Looking at me as though I was the only one on that street, Giselle had the most disarming charm about her. I smiled back at her words.

"Hey," I replied, offering her a lighter. "Pretty good. What's up?"

"I'm Giselle. I've seen you around. You're Becky's friend, right?" she asked in her bubbly voice.

"Yeah, that's right. I started here last year."

"You want to come to my place for lunch?" her head nodded toward the left, "I live just up the street. My mom will make us lunch."

I agreed in excitement. If it weren't for Giselle's offer, I would be left without a meal for the entire day. Quickly, a routine had formed. We would go to her house every day at lunch and her mom would make us tomato soup and grilled cheese sandwiches with Velveeta cheese that oozed between two slices of perfectly toasted bread. I finished every drop, despite my dislike for tomato soup, because I was too hungry to be picky.

Giselle didn't live too far from me. Her house, a simple two-storey, was only ten blocks from my apartment and in a much nicer neighbourhood. Her family was an average size of five: her mother, stepfather, two half-sisters, and herself. We would always enter the house through the back door which opened to the stair case landing where you could either go up to the main floor or down to the basement. The upstairs opened to a kitchen, formal living room, and three bedrooms where Giselle's parents and two sisters slept. The basement was where Giselle had her bedroom. There was another spare room, a bathroom, and a full living room where the family spent most of their time as well.

Giselle's stepdad was a Jehovah's Witness and so when her mother married him, she had converted and then had Giselle's two half-sisters with him. They all had to attend church and go door to door on the weekends spreading the word of God. Giselle, though she hated their religion, followed along out of obligation and duty to her mother. We made fun of their strange beliefs, sharing a mutual feeling of disdain toward following anyone over anything. We didn't want to be a part of anything except each other; we loved our friendship and our bond grew stronger day by day.

I went from spending lunch at Giselle's to also spending weekends there. I was so happy to have made a great friend in Giselle and to have a place to sleep on the weekends to escape the confines of the apartment I shared with Mildred and George. Giselle and I had common ground that I had shared with many friends I had in the past: we hated our family life and the circumstances that we felt powerless against. We didn't like the way our families tried to control us without really trying to understand who we were and what we wanted in our lives. Our parents didn't care about what we wanted, they only cared about their own agendas. Giselle's mom was just as blind to her new husband as Mildred was to George, and both women felt powerless without men, even if the men were losers.

The sounds of Melanie returning from work brought me to attention. Putting down the book I had been reading, I smiled at the thought of spending time with my sister. A muffled hello came from the living room as Mel greeted Mildred, and soon footsteps and the sound of a door closing followed. As soon as I heard music playing from her room, I rose from my bed and left my room, closing the door behind me. Though I knew privacy meant nothing in this house, closing the door at least created one barrier from Mildred and George. I paused, waiting to hear Steven, Melanie's boyfriend, come from her room. He had practically lived with us, and since Melanie would never be alone anymore, I was surprised to hear his absence. I knocked on her door.

"Come in!" Mel called above the music.

"Hey! How's it going, Smelly?" I asked, calling her the pet name I had given her since I was seven years old.

She was standing in front of her closet and there were clothes strewn all over her bed and on the floor. It took me a few minutes to notice that there were cardboard boxes stuffed with her things on the floor.

"What are those for?" I asked her completely confused and hoping we weren't moving again.

"I'm moving out with Steven!" She exclaimed, pulling shirts off their hangers with excitement.

"Wh-what!?" I couldn't believe what I had just heard. "You're moving out with him? You've hardly been dating. Why would you move away?" A knot began to form in my stomach.

"I'll just be downtown, it's not like I won't see you," as her eyes met mine, she paused. "I just can't stay here anymore, Iman. I mean, you know how it is…I just…I just can't stay here with Mum and George. I need to live on my own." She looked at me with sadness in her eyes and I could see her pleading with me to understand.

The knot had risen to my throat. I couldn't formulate a single coherent thought. "You can't leave me here, Mel!" My legs began to shake, as if my meagre weight was too much for them to support. "Please don't leave me here alone," my throat felt as though it was closing as I choked back tears.

"I promise I'll come visit you all of the time and you can come over whenever you want. You can come over every weekend, okay? I just really need to move out of here. I can't stay here."

I knew it was no use trying to convince her to stay. After all, I didn't blame her for wanting to go live in her own place. I dreamed of it for myself all the time. I couldn't wait to leave this shit-hole and I had no argument to make her stay. I couldn't sell something that I would never buy.

Resigned, I gave her a huge hug and stayed in her room while she packed her things, and silently watched a piece of my heart leave my body. What was I supposed to do without her here? Without Mel, I would truly have no one in this horrible place. And though I understood that she deserved to be free, I couldn't help but mourn my loss.

In the weeks after Mel moved out, a sadness took over me that I had never felt before—one riddled with loneliness and despair. She was the only person

I had left under the same roof and her leaving caused a chasm of betrayal in my heart that tore me open. *How could she just leave me like everyone else?* I asked myself. *Why was I always so easy to leave?* Over the years, I had grown very tired of goodbyes and all the new hellos that followed. Why couldn't everything just stay the way it was? This world, and how I fit into it, was a mystery that I could not solve.

When I was very little my mom used to talk to me about God and how he watched over me always. She reminded me of my name meaning faith in God, how I would always need to have faith and believe that there was something more: something worth believing in, even when I couldn't see it with my own eyes. She told me that I was never alone and that anytime I forgot that, I should pray and talk to God and that he would hear me. I wondered why God would let so many sad things happen to me. If he was always with me and I was never alone, then why did I feel so sad all the time? Why did everyone I love always leave me? Why was my existence so miserable? I was cursed. No prayers would save me from the darkness that consumed my heart. For the first time since my mom passed, I didn't believe in her stories of God. It was just like Shakespeare wrote: *Hell is empty and all the devils are here.*

The best I could do if I wasn't guarded by angels was to not be fooled by devils. I was done believing in anything that didn't believe in me.

Friday rolled around and the usual crowd of society's scum and misfits haunted our small apartment, indulging in a variety of alcohol and drugs of choice. It was odd. Though I had gotten used to the weekend routine of drunken stupor, as I grew older, I began to wonder what it was these fools were always celebrating. Their lives, like mine, were clouded in misery and poverty. A funeral would be more fitting.

As always, the best part of Mildred and George's parties, was the blessing of food. They would always buy chips, pizza, and late at night they would order Donairs. Grabbing a plate of pizza and chips and making my way toward my room, I pushed my dresser against my bedroom door and opened the closet. Within it was my secret hiding spot, where I would stash the stolen beer I had taken just moments before, eat my dinner, and watch my mother's small, black and white television.

After finishing my dinner, I went over to my window and hung my head out to have a cigarette. Hearing an odd noise in the dark night, I peered over to the rear parking lot. There was a man holding something in his hands but I couldn't make out what it was—a long stick or bar of some kind. I watched him shove the object into the crevice of car doors, forcing his way into car after car, rummaging through one before moving on to the next. Panic struck me when I realized what he was doing. I turned off my light for fear that he would see me watching him. My heart raced. I contemplated what to do as I watched him, taking pulls from my cigarette while ideas rolled through my head. Should I tell Mildred and George? Should I call out to him and frighten him? My mind stirred with thoughts of action, but as I contemplated what to do, in a blink of an eye, he was out of sight. Stunned, I lit another cigarette, thinking about what I should have done. I realized that the car thief's actions didn't differ much from what often happened in our house. Who was I to judge what level of wrongdoing anything was? Crawling back into my closet, I continued watching TV. I had enough things to worry about.

The party died down around 3:00 a.m. and I went out to the living room and kitchen to assess the damage. Surprisingly, Mildred had gone to bed and only George remained, passed out in the living room. The TV was on and I sat on the couch, watching whatever was playing as I nibbled on the chips that were conveniently placed in a bowl on the coffee table. It was hard to hear over his snoring and I was just about to get up and go to bed when he woke up. Barely able to hold his head up, he looked at me through half-opened eyes.

"What are you doing up?" His words were slurred, indicating just how incapacitated he was.

"I was just going to turn off the TV because you fell asleep," I mumbled as I began to stand up.

His large, calloused hands wrapped tightly around my left wrist as I tried to walk by. "No, leave it on," he pleaded. "Stay with me."

I pulled my hand away, and with my stomach turning and my entire body stiffening, I sat straight back down on the couch next to his armchair.

"I'm really tired, George." My voice shook. I could feel my fingernails digging into my palms before I realized my hands were clenched at my sides.

"I wanna talk to you," he slurred. "We never get time to talk anymore. Yer always off with yer friends," he paused. "Don't you miss me?" The last sentence seemed to make him laugh. His face contorted into a drunken smile that turned up the left corner of his lip.

Fumbling for his cigarettes, he dropped his lighter right next to my foot. He reached for the lighter while bracing himself with one hand on the coffee table, deliberately pinching my calf as he almost fell over to reach down to pick it up.

He fumbled through his cigarette pack, pulling out a slender white stick. After placing it between his lips, he offered me one. Hesitantly, I accepted his gift. It was a foreign offering—an act that he had never done before. As we sat in silence smoking our cigarettes, George's head bobbed back and forth as he tried with all his might to stay awake. I took long drags hoping that I could finish and go back to my room. I felt trapped in the living room and knew no good would come from conversing with George in his drunken, drugged state. His lack of coordination and balance, however, put me at ease.

"I have some really weird thoughts sometimes, y'know?" His head leaned against his right fist, unable to lift it high enough to look at me.

"Oh, yeah?" I had no idea how to respond to him; it was obvious I didn't want to entertain this conversation.

"You wanna know what I think about? I wanna tell you," he glanced at me as I took another pull of the cigarette in my hand. He seemed so vulnerable, I had never witnessed this side of him before. But, with every blink my eyes took, images of when he had confessed his love to Melanie so many years ago flashed before me.

I sat up in my chair, putting out my cigarette. "Not really, George. I'm going to bed," I replied without a shred of emotion in my voice.

As I rose from the couch, George began to cry, wiping his eyes in time with the sound of his own sniffling. I was the most uncomfortable I had ever been around him, but I did nothing to comfort him. I couldn't care any less that he was upset. I just wanted to disappear into my room. I wished I hadn't come out at all.

"Fine. I thought you were different but you aren't. You aren't special. You aren't anything to me." He wiped his eyes with his giant hands and looked toward the TV, "Now, go to bed!" he yelled.

I didn't need to be asked twice and gladly went to my room. *What a freak*, I silently said to myself. *I don't want to hear that idiot's thoughts.*

The next morning, I woke up and did my usual routine of listening to see if anyone was up and about. I did my best to avoid getting out of my room if anyone was in the kitchen.

Mildred wasn't home and George was passed out at the table snoring with one hand holding a beer can and the other holding up his head. By his position, it could be assumed that he had stayed up last night to cry some more after he had sent me to bed. I tiptoed into Mildred and George's room and quickly scanned it. The shades were closed and their bed was unmade. There were clothes strewn on the floor and a dresser by the door and another one against the wall closest to the door. I walked over to George's side of the bed and opened the box he kept on his nightstand. I knew this was where he kept his weed because he treasured it so much and I had seen him open it only to be surrounded in a cloud of smoke moments later. I grabbed enough to not be noticed, pulled a couple of rolling papers out of their blue package and headed outside.

I called Giselle from the payphone around the corner and told her to meet me at the park near her house. I walked down the alley behind my apartment building and headed toward Giselle's. I lit one of the cigarettes I had taken from George's pack while he was passed out cold in the kitchen and walked as quickly as I could to the park. Giselle was already at the park when I arrived. She pulled out two bottles: one filled with Coke and another bottle half-filled with vodka. We poured the Coke into the vodka and passed the bottle back and forth, adding more Coke when there was room.

We rolled up the weed into a joint and smoked it on the swings. We sat there for hours laughing and talking about our bullshit lives. Giselle was the only person on the planet that understood me. I would do anything for her and she was the only solace in my misfortune. When we were together it was as if we were the only people on earth. I felt so alive and like our friendship was my purpose. Somehow, Giselle and I could make the whole world disappear and suddenly nobody mattered. When we were together, I wasn't an orphan and Giselle wasn't stuck in her family. We were free and strong and powerful. The upside of hating your life is that you live each day as if it were your last; the only consequence being a chance to escape—whether it was an escape from home, life as we knew it, or earth entirely. We would welcome the opportunity with open arms.

As my mind filled with the fog of marijuana, my thoughts drifted off and I began to swing as high and as far as I could. I looked up at the sky and watched the clouds shift and dissolve. I loved how I felt when I smoked and drank. It was like taking a vacation from reality. A sweet escape where I could access any place on earth. If I couldn't join my mother or brothers and sister in a physical escape, I would have to escape the only other way I knew how. I wanted to bury myself so deep within my subconscious that my roots burst through to the other side of my heart and turned into wings. They could keep me in their foster care prison, starve me, beat me, and remind me of my worthlessness daily but they would never, ever break me. I would build walls far greater and stronger than anyone had ever seen and protect my inner freedom with my life. I didn't need any of them and one day I would leave and never ever look back.

When I went back home, Mildred and George were in their usual spots: Mildred was knitting in her chair and watching TV, a glass of rum and Coke by her side, George was sitting at the kitchen table, rolling cigarettes and drinking a beer while a cigarette hung from his mouth.

"Hello!" I called out as I kicked off my shoes. I didn't want to call attention to myself for having been out all day with Giselle. I was met with silence. They completely ignored me.

"Hello?" I said again this time only inches away from Mildred.

"Things are going to change around here," Mildred's voice was cold, and matter-of-fact. "We're not going to carry your weight and let you act like a kid anymore. You're thirteen years old and it is time you started taking care of yourself."

I paused in confusion. *What the hell was she going on about?*

"What are you talking about?" I could feel my defensiveness rushing through my words.

"Well, now that Mel is gone, we think you should have some more responsibilities," Mildred stated, putting a halt to her knitting as she spoke to me. "We can't keep carrying your weight around here when you don't even contribute to the household. From now on George and I need to be on our own. We aren't going to speak to you for a while so we can focus on ourselves. It's a lot harder than you think being a parent—*especially* to someone like you. I don't think you appreciate how much we do for you and maybe if you have to do it yourself, you will."

"I don't even know what you're saying…You're going to ignore me again? I live here!" In complete shock, I could feel the tears pressing against the back of my eyes.

"That's right, you *do* live here, and you should feel lucky that we don't kick you out on the street!" Mildred proudly barked from between her thin lips. "From now on, you'll clean the bathroom every day and the dishes will all be your responsibility. And we're not gonna cook for you anymore, which should make you happy since you've always been *too good* for our cooking anyways."

"Fine. I don't care!" Turning on my heel, I stormed to my room as my eyes began to cascade with tears. Though I didn't think it was possible, Mildred and George had managed to make me hate my life even more. *How could people ignore someone who lived with them? I was meant to be their child and they got money for looking after me. How could they just tell me I wasn't going to exist anymore?*

Grabbing my razor, I carved *FUCK YOU* into the flesh of my thigh. This was my way of expressing myself in a world that forced me to conform to its twisted ideals. I wasn't like them and though I didn't need a reminder, these types of situations made it so clear. I was tired of crying over these people, people who didn't even want me around! *Why wouldn't they let me go if they hated me so much?*

The next day when I woke up there was a list of chores scrawled on lined paper and shoved underneath my door. *Iman's Chores* was written on the top, followed by a list of my tasks for the day: dishes, clean bathroom, laundry, roll two packs of cigarettes.

The lump in my throat felt like it was going to burn through my neck. Mildred and George were nowhere to be found. They were probably out having breakfast somewhere laughing about how they were treating me. I couldn't help but wonder what George told Mildred about our late-night conversation. *Had I cursed myself by not listening to his creepy thoughts when he asked?*

I did my chores and made sure to roll myself a pack of cigarettes while I was making theirs. I ran down to the corner store with some of the pocket money that Ben had given me last time I had seen him. I bought some chips, licorice, crackers, cheese, and juice. I hid the supplies in my closet so I wouldn't have to come out of my room when Mildred and George returned. I couldn't believe my life. I was hoarding food and drinks in my room like a prisoner in my own home. I couldn't wait to be free. I would do almost anything for a chance to escape.

When Mildred and George came home Mildred came into my room. "Come here for a second." I followed her to the bathroom.

"You call this clean?" she asked while gesturing to the sink.

"I cleaned it today, I swear!" I looked around the bathroom and couldn't see anything that she could be referring to. I did all the laundry, the bathtub was spotless, there were no streaks on the mirror and the counter was bare.

"Open your fucking eyes, Iman. Look *here*, behind the sink," she barked. "You didn't even clean here." She looked at me exasperated, like I was missing the most obvious thing, but I was looking as closely as I could and I couldn't see anything.

She reached under the sink and grabbed an old toothbrush. "Here, take this and start again. I want you to clean the whole bathroom with this toothbrush and you better get it right this time or you won't be leaving the house next weekend at all."

She pushed passed me and shoved me as she pressed the toothbrush into my stomach and left the room. I stood there shaking wanting to scream but knowing full well that any defiance would have even worse consequences. I quietly closed and locked the door, turned on the water in the bathtub and fell to the floor crying as quietly as I could. I wouldn't let them know that they were getting to me. I cursed my tears as they fell and wished I didn't cry so easily. My second attempt at cleaning took over an hour and I inspected every inch of the bathroom before I told Mildred so she could come and inspect it. I didn't pass with flying colours, but it was enough for her to leave me alone for the rest of the day.

I couldn't wait for nightfall, all I wanted was to go to sleep and finally put this day behind me. Curled up beneath my blankets, as I drifted off to sleep, I thought about how my life would be after foster care: I would never let anyone tell me what to do again, I would be my own boss and I would control my own fate.

A few hours later I woke up feeling a strange sensation on my thigh. I couldn't quite make out what it was for several minutes. Suddenly, I registered what was going on: I could see George kneeling beside my bed, and it was his hand under my blankets, caressing my bare thigh. Panicked, I shot up in bed, pushing his body with all my might. He fell over and I hit him in the shoulder. He groaned and crawled out of my bedroom door. I jumped out of my bed and shut my door and pushed my dresser up against it.

I crawled back in bed and sat upright holding my knees against my chest. Adrenaline was running through my veins and I was shaking in a cold sweat. *What the fuck? Why was he in my room and why was he touching me? How long had he been there before I woke up?* My mind wandered. *It was happening—just like with Melanie.* I sat, remaining in the same position before I finally fell asleep again.

The next day the apartment was filled with a very strange low energy. Mildred sat in her chair watching television and chain-smoking; George hardly left his bedroom. No one spoke to me at all throughout the entire day and it was as though we were all in different world unaware of each other. Except, I was very aware of them. I knew exactly where they were at all times and, even though I barely came out of my room, I listened hard to see if I could hear what they were doing. I felt like I wasn't supposed to be there, like maybe I had broken in and didn't want them to know I was wrongfully in the apartment. I had never felt so out of place in all my life. I developed a sense of self-loathing so great that I continuously hoped I would die to escape my prison. Every day I would try to muster up the strength to push my razor too far into my flesh and cut too far so that I made one wrong move and I could leave everything behind. Each day I would awake to the same nightmare I had abandoned for sleep the night before.

I began to think about my life and how I wouldn't be suffering this way if it weren't for my father. *How could he do this to us?* Losing my mother was the most gut-wrenching, horrific experience of my life, and suffering with Mildred and George added insult to injury. *Why would he do this to me? How could he take away the most important being in my life? How could he destroy a family, destroy his children's futures, destroy my entire world?* My hatred for him was deep and furrowed within me, reaching into every part of my being. And while I, innocent by all means, was trapped here in a prison that he built, he still refused to confess to his crime. The only solace I had was knowing that he was still in Kingston Penitentiary and hoping that he was suffering the fate he deserved.

The last time I saw my father was years ago in the courthouse. I was an eyewitness to his crime, but since I was only six years old at the time, the courts had decided I was too young to testify, fearing that recounting the night's events would lead me to a deeper state of trauma. Sitting on a bench outside of the courtroom as Chokri and Adam testified behind the same closed doors that held the jury, judge, and my father, I patiently waited with Ben. Suddenly, I heard the muffled sounds of Chokri's voice shouting. An unseen chaos had erupted in the courtroom. Soon, the doors opened and my father, dressed in an orange jumpsuit, hands cuffed in front of him, was escorted out of the room. I let out a small gasp. I was in shock. The last time I had seen him, he was hovering over my mother's body.

"Princess! Princess!" his eyes had caught the sight of me, and he began to run in my direction, tears in his eyes.

"Daddy!" I squealed. I was unaware of what exactly he had done and how horrible it was, all I knew was that whatever he did that night, my mother would never return. In a mix of emotions, I was confused as to how it was possible to both love and hate someone simultaneously.

He had forgotten he was wearing handcuffs, and as he came toward me, extending his arms to give me a hug, the chain that connected his wrists wrapped around my neck. Immediately, I yelped. Winded and in pain, it felt as though my father was trying to choke me. Suddenly, a swarm of people rushed toward us, rushing to take him off me. Pulling him off, they escorted him away. I was confused. Rubbing my hand against my sore neck, I looked around. I knew that everyone had thought he was trying to strangle me, but in the seconds when everything had happened, I had known that wasn't the case. He was overwhelmed and, in the rush of it all, simply forgot to raise his hands above my head.

That was the last time I had seen my father and, unlike all those years ago, I now understood what he did. I understood that he murdered my mother, that he took her away from me and left me here to wither away and die.

I decided to write him a letter and tell him how much I hated him. In ten pages, I told him of all the suffering I had endured from the moment he stabbed my mother in front of me to the present moment. I took out school pictures of Adam, Chokri, and me and wrote on the backs letting him know how broken we were without our parents to take care of us. He had no idea what fate he left us to, nor did he give a shit about us at all. I spewed as much venom, anger, and hate as I could into that letter. *That bastard is going to know exactly how I feel about him,* I thought to myself, as I sealed the pages in an envelope with immense satisfaction.

I asked Mildred if I could spend the weekend at Giselle's house and after much deliberation, she decided that I could as long as I cleaned the walls of the apartment first. She told me I could use the toothbrush I had used for the bathroom. Luckily, I only had to wash the walls in the hallway, living room and kitchen and not the bedrooms. This cut down the chore in half. It took me all of Friday afternoon and night to finish but I felt extremely satisfied that I had fulfilled my end of the bargain. I packed my bag and ran out of the door toward Giselle's as fast as my tired feet would carry me. I just wanted to be free.

"You won't believe what I have!" Giselle squealed as she hopped down the street. Thrilled to see her, we met with shrieks and hugs.

"What?" I questioned excitedly. I was curious as to what she was talking about. "Tell me!"

"Well, I was over at Buddy's and got us a little something for the weekend," she smiled as she dug into her pocket. My eyes grew large with anticipation. Buddy was our drug dealer and by the look in Giselle's eyes, he had given her something special.

I watched Giselle open her palms and reveal a baggy with two little pieces of paper in them.

"ACID!" She held the baggy in front of my face with such pride.

"*Acid?*" I looked at her in disbelief. I had of course heard of acid, but I never thought about doing it before. We both had become obsessed with the movie *Dazed and Confused*, where everyone was doing drugs and partying on the last day of school. And though just a few weeks ago, we had discussed the seventies, how acid seemed to be a popular drug, and pondered what it would be like, I never actually thought of trying it. I looked at the baggy in her palm, both nervous and intrigued.

The bag had two simple squares of blue paper in it. We each took a square and placed it on our tongues as we walked back to Giselle's house. Giggling the whole way home, we were unsure of what to expect but looked forward to anything that came our way.

When we arrived at Giselle's we didn't feel anything quite yet, but just to be sure we didn't trip out in front of anyone, we went down to the basement to hangout in Giselle's room. After saying hello to her mother and two younger sisters, we vanished.

The effects of the drug started out slowly. And then I suddenly felt as though I had sunk deep into my body and was heavy and weightless at the same time. I was aware of every pore on my skin, I was made of light and could float through air. Giselle's bedroom suddenly looked completely new, like I had just discovered it for the first time. Everything around me was new and beautiful. My hands transformed into marvelous works of art that danced wildly with every colour of the rainbow following them as they moved through the air, and when I closed my eyes, I saw heaven: every shape and colour flashed behind my eyelids in the most miraculous patterns I had ever seen. Everything made sense. I was high above the clouds, but also grounded into a reality that I had crafted through thought. I was the freest I had ever been in my life. I felt as though I mattered, and the fact that I could hear my heartbeat pounding through my chest just confirmed how alive I truly was. Giselle and I giggled, as the colours that followed us as we moved, sparkled. We didn't need parents who only looked out for themselves. We could take care of ourselves because that was exactly what we had been forced to do for so long.

As we talked, our conversations seemed to have transcended, becoming more meaningful and profound. Confiding in each other with open hearts, Giselle told me how out of place she felt in her home and we imagined a world where we were happy every day: a place where we didn't worry about how to get food or if we were going to get beaten or molested. We made up our own fairy tale world, and in those moments on the edge of reality, everything seemed possible.

Everything was alive and every sense was magnified. There was nowhere else I would have rather been than in our escaped reality, discussing the problems of our worlds from the clouds that we sat upon. We had all the answers with no concern, no responsibility, and no fear. I felt transcendent, close to God and, most importantly, far away from the hell I woke up in only hours before. I wanted to stay like this forever, just Giselle and me living in this space between reality and desire. We had each other, and being lost in this glorious world together had made us feel more found than we had ever been before.

Chapter Fifteen

Age 14: Unholy Spirits

My fourteenth birthday loomed over me, and from behind my closed bedroom door, I could hear Mildred and George making plans for the annual family reunion at the hall they held it in every year. Once again, it felt as though my birthday warranted no real celebration. Ignoring my disappointment, I began to look forward to visiting the familiar rows of tombstones that studded my treasured cemetery. It would be nice to visit the friendships I had fostered with the stone sculptures and buried cadavers. In a childhood where changing houses, families, and schools was the norm, there was something oddly comforting about spending my birthday in the cemetery—like a homecoming. With such a tumultuous life, it's funny to think that the most absurd things can bring us peace. When my friends regaled tales of summer camp and vacations with their families, I would keep my secret birthday hideaway to myself. I had learned long ago that anything near to my heart must never be shared with anyone who might be able to destroy it.

I still felt like being with the dead meant I was that much closer to my mother. It made perfect sense in my mind that I had a better chance of reaching her through the dead as she was nowhere to be found among the living. Each birthday, I would walk up and down every row, paying tribute to each and every grave. I would read the stones, calculate the ages of the dead, and imagine what kind of person they might have been. Some I felt closer to than others, and I would stop and sit at their graves and tell them my woes. It was nice to be heard for once and be able to speak freely with the knowledge that I wouldn't be judged or yelled at. One sided conversations were something I had grown used to: from my farm animals to the small children I would babysit in the neighbourhood. In fact, it was just fine with me to have quiet friendships. The silence brought more peace than the shrill sound of Mildred's yells.

Grateful that the August night sky stayed light for so long, I rested in the grassy cemetery to look up at the stars and the moon. Imagining that there was a parallel world on the other side of the sky, my mind buzzed with the possibilities. I would be with my mother and brothers and we would always be laughing. We wouldn't have any idea what sadness was and I would only cry when I was bursting with love and happiness. I would be beautiful and all the boys would think so too. I wouldn't ever be mistaken for a boy with my perfect girlish figure, and my lioness's mane would be long and flowing. I would be rich and powerful, and no one would ever think of trying to hit me or hurt me. I would be successful and respected and never know the life of pain on the other side of the sky.

I loved these daydreams so much. I had come to think I was an expert at dreaming. The part I wasn't good at was real life.

The beginning of the new school year was only weeks away, and I was more than excited at the idea of returning to school. Aside from the ninth grade seeming like such an accomplishment, I loved having a reason to leave the house for the whole day. I missed my friends and looked forward to the freedom and independence to not have to hang around Mildred and George every day. Their decision to ignore me still stood and by then George had completely stopped going to work. Mildred and George's day-to-day activities consisted of moping around the apartment, smoking, drinking, and complaining incessantly about money. There was never enough of anything.

The cupboards were always bare and we had begun to rely more and more on the food bank for help.

Social Services had been called several times over the past few months. Social workers would come to the apartment or to my school and ask me all kinds of questions about living with Mildred and George. This process wasn't new to me and for as long as I could remember after my mom died, I had social workers visit my school to question me at least twice a year. I never trusted them or even got to know them, as it was always someone new who would come to my school, have my name announced on the intercom, forcing me to come up with some kind of lie to all of my friends as to why I was called to the principal's office. I would sit across from these strangers and wonder why they thought I would ever divulge anything to them, most especially my shameful life. The life I knew sounded far better than putting my future into the hands of a stranger who was just doing their job. They had no vested interest in me.

I thought if they came to our home they could see for themselves that we didn't have any food and perhaps notice the smell of weed and the endless empty bottles of booze in the storage closet. They would come into our home and ask me the same ridiculous questions about my well-being as they did at school. The only problem was that they asked me in front of them, as if I would say anything that would cause me any trouble once they had left. I could feel Mildred's eyes burn into the side of my head during these periods of questions. I was no fool and would never ever cause myself such harm by biting the hand that barely fed me, especially right in front of her.

By looking at my small, malnourished frame, it was obvious that my guardians hadn't been doing their duty to take care of me, but Mildred and George became so nervous about these surprise visits that they began keeping empty boxes of cereal, crackers, and cake mixes in the cupboards hoping to trick the social workers. When they looked in the empty fridge Mildred would giggle nervously and say how embarrassed she was and how she was just about to head to the grocery store right after this visit. Why didn't they find it odd that Mildred was always "just about to head to the store" whenever they visited?

Yeah, the liquor store, I laughed silently to myself. Conveniently, alcohol and cigarettes were the two things we never ran out of. If having no food in the cupboards was bad, having empty boxes of things I was never going to eat was even worse. The kitchen taunted me with all the possibility of food that it very rarely delivered. All the other girls in my class were blossoming into puberty and I did not look much different than I had in elementary school: I was underweight, my face was gaunt, my ribs were jutting out of my sides, and my hipbones could barely keep my pants up. Puberty for me was nowhere in sight.

Before the school year started I had noticed that my shoes had grown quite tight and there were holes forming in the soles. The black and white tennis shoes were a back-to-school gift from Ben and Elizabeth when they took me school shopping almost exactly a year ago. I loved them, and not just because they weren't hand-me-downs like most of my things, but because I got to pick them out myself. I was always so humbled and grateful that year after year, Ben and Elizabeth continued to care for me and my brothers. If it weren't for them, I would have gone without far more often than I already did. They bought my school supplies, my clothes, they gave me some pocket money now and again which I used to feed myself, but what was most impactful, was the time they spent with me throughout the years. Between the sleepovers, vacations, and summers in the country, I soaked up every minute of what they taught me. Often, I felt guilty because I knew I could never repay them. I felt bad that the family I lived with leaned on them so heavily, even though Mildred and George received income from the government to care for me.

Even after so many years, Mildred and George still resented Ben and Elizabeth. From her lowly position alongside the scum of the earth, Mildred constantly made fun of them. She would look down at them for what she felt was snobbery and "more money than brains." But I knew the truth. I knew that Mildred was deeply jealous of their success and embarrassed that she and George needed their help throughout the years. As before, her threats of making me live with them as punishment for acting up was more of a dream for me, and every time Mildred threatened to kick me out, my heart would skip a beat and I would fight with all my might not to let the smile forming on my lips show. My biggest dream was to finally live with them, but that would remain my little secret.

I walked into the kitchen where Mildred was standing at the counter making herself a coffee. "My shoes have holes in them," I paused for a reaction. "Do you think I can get some new ones for school? These won't hold the snow anymore."

I leaned against the fridge watching Mildred add her cream and sugar to the cup and stir.

"Well," she began. "That's too bad. We don't have any money to buy you new shoes." Her eyes remained on the cup.

"Don't you get money from the government for having me?" My face grew hot, the familiar lump in my throat forming, "Why can't you use that money to buy me new shoes?"

My curiosity was genuine. I had never asked, but it was about time I had an answer. I could see Mildred's blood surging through her body as my question hit a nerve. She slammed the spoon down on the counter and turned quickly to look at me.

"PARDON ME, YOU UNGRATEFUL LITTLE BITCH?" She spat the words as her lips pursed around her buckteeth.

My knees shook. Instantly, I regretted bringing it up.

"I-I just need new shoes, and these hurt my feet. You don't have to yell." I began to brace myself as any defiance in the past was always met with physical consequences.

"For your information, we *do* get money to take care of you. Who the fuck do you think pays the bills around here? Who buys the food and takes care of you, you ungrateful brat?" Mildred picked up her coffee and took a step toward me.

"In fact, we have been looking after you since your mom died, haven't we?" she sneered. "Nobody else cared enough about you to take you in did they? I didn't see Ben and Elizabeth going to court every week to fight for custody of you so that you could be with your brothers. Did they? DID THEY?" Her voice moved from tolerable to a shriek.

"No." I answered staring at the ground. I wished I hadn't said a word. Why did I think I could have a normal conversation with a drunk? My eyes began to well up and my body began to shake with anger and fear.

"You look just like your father. Did you know that, Iman?"

"No, I don't." I spat through gritted teeth, my eyes staring deep into hers, burning a hole into her head.

"Yeah, you do. You look just like him and you have a temper just like him, don't you? You'll probably end up in jail just like he is." The rigid creases of Mildred's face seemed to soften as she mocked me. I could almost see a smile on her face.

"No, I won't! I'm nothing like him!" I wasn't fighting the tears anymore and didn't care what I looked like.

"You're probably going to get so mad you'll kill someone, just like your father!" Mildred did nothing to hide the deep satisfaction her prediction seemed to bring her.

"FUCK YOU!" My anger burst through my veins as I screamed. "I FUCKING HATE YOU! I WISH YOU WERE DEAD, BUT I WOULD NEVER WASTE MY FUCKING TIME KILLING YOU!"

As I turned and began to run to my room, I felt something hard crack into my right shoulder blade. The scent of coffee was overwhelming, and the sensation of the hot liquid against my skin forced me to shriek. As her hand rose to strike me again with the mug of hot coffee, out of the corner of my eye, I saw the wall pattern with sprays of brown liquid and felt the remaining liquid sear my neck and back. The pain and surprise of the hot liquid scalding me brought a louder yelp from my throat. Running to my room, I slammed the door, bursting into tears. With only a moment passing, Mildred burst into my room, "DON'T SLAM THE FUCKING DOOR!"

My eyes quickly scanned my surroundings and, without thought or care, I instinctively reached for the half-empty glass of grape juice that sat beside my bed. Just as she began to close the door, with all my strength, I hurled the glass toward her head. Missing my target, the glass shattered against the door, and purple liquid burst all over my closet and bedroom door.

My whole head pulsed with anger. "DON'T FUCKING TOUCH ME OR I'LL…" my voice began in a strong yell, but quickly faltered as I stopped myself before I could finish what I so desperately wanted to scream. I was nothing like my father. Surely there were far worse fates than mine.

I collapsed onto my bed as my sobs took over my entire body. I cried for hours and it seemed the tears endlessly poured out of me. I cried for the horrible life I had to live, for the terrible injustice I was forced to live with every day, and for the way I let Mildred get the best of me. I cried for how much I missed my brothers, for my mother, and for the hatred that was inevitably burning its way through my heart. But, mostly, I cried because I was locked in a prison that didn't have keys, and it seemed the only escape was death. But I was too much of a coward even for that.

That week Mildred bought me new shoes. She didn't need to say anything but I could tell that she felt remorse for the fight we had a few days before. One morning she told me we were going to get a few things for school and we walked the ten blocks to the little mall in our neighbourhood and picked out some shoes. She even bought us lunch at a small diner and I ordered a big hamburger, fries, and gravy. Ben and Elizabeth, of course, took me for the rest of my school supplies and bought me lots of brand new clothes for my final year of junior high.

We stopped by the smoking alley before first class to catch up with our friends that we hadn't seen all summer. Giselle and I were so excited to start the ninth grade. We had talked about it all summer, anticipating the year to come, and how we felt so grown up almost being in high school. There was a new boy hanging out with the group of guys that was always there. His name was Karim and he was incredibly handsome. He was from Afghanistan and had olive skin and dark features. His love of sports was evident, by not only his need to talk about basketball, but by his athletic build. Unlike the rest of us, he didn't smoke but he hung out with some of the guys in our grade who did.

Quickly, we became acquainted. Immediately, I felt myself flush whenever he was around. He was funny, had a beautiful smile that lit up his eyes, and you could see that he was kind just by his face. I had gotten good at telling if someone was a good person or not just by how they looked at me; I had seen enough evil to trust my gut whenever someone looked me in the eyes, but Karim's eyes were pure and looked like beautiful pools of milk chocolate.

Luckily, Karim and I shared a lot of the same classes, allowing us the chance to sit next to each other and work on projects. It wasn't very long before I could see that Karim liked me too, and I felt like the luckiest girl in the world. I didn't get a lot of attention from boys at school and I certainly didn't know much about the opposite sex.

I thought back to when I met Noah in the seventh grade and how horribly that turned out. I didn't want to make that mistake again—although I knew that I was much smarter after that experience and that Karim was much sweeter than Noah could ever be.

Walking me to my locker after class one afternoon, Karim gave me a note to read at home. It was folded up into a perfect square and I could see parts of drawings that would be revealed once opened. Ecstatic, I put the note in my backpack, thanking him. He seemed extra shy and his face was flushed. I was blushing too but I wasn't sure how to react. I had never been given a note by a boy before and I was bursting at the seams to get home and read it.

I rushed home that day which was extremely out of the ordinary since I usually loitered after school and chatted with people until I absolutely had to go back to my prison. But I was so excited to read the note that I wanted nothing more than to beam myself into my bedroom and devour my message.

When I got home, I was practically skipping. I was so giddy that I could hardly contain my excitement. Mildred and George caught onto me right away. The interrogation began. Asking me thousands of questions about why I was so happy, I held strong, giving them absolutely nothing to go on. The last thing I wanted was for them to be able to take this away from me too. Making obligatory small talk, I quickly diverted questions about why I was so chipper and then made my way to my room. Closing my door, shedding my backpack, I rushed to sit on my bed, note in hand. Carefully unfolding the sheet of paper, I peeled back each corner of the delicately crafted square that Karim had so meticulously tucked each of the corners of the paper into. My eyes scanned the pages as they were filled with words but there were also so many wonderful drawings of butterflies and trees and birds and hearts. I giggled with delight at all the lovely craftsmanship that he put into this wonderful note. The note mostly talked about how we met and how much he liked being in the same classes together and seeing me every day. He wrote the sweetest words, calling me beautiful and sweet, and confessing that he thought about me all the time, especially when we weren't at school.

My heart raced as I read his words, processing what he was kind enough to share with me. I couldn't believe he felt the same way that I did! I was over the moon with joy with every word that I read. As I approached the end of the note, I glanced at the large cluster of hearts he had drawn. A thought bubble extended from the hearts: "Will you be my girlfriend?"

Stuffing my face into my pillow, I squealed at the top of my lungs in joy and excitement. Although I wanted to shout and scream as loud as I could, I didn't want to draw any attention to myself. *I can't believe that he wants me to be his girlfriend!* I thought. I was thrilled, nervous, and excited, but also kind of afraid. I suddenly realized I didn't really know how to be someone's girlfriend. I panicked as I thought back to Noah and how that hadn't worked out. Was that what it meant to be someone's girlfriend? *If that's true, then I wouldn't want to be anyone's girlfriend.* I didn't think Karim could ever hurt anyone and he already told me so many nice things in his letter. This was already a far more kind and thoughtful experience than I had in the two brief encounters I had with Noah.

I spent the rest of the night daydreaming of Karim and reading his letter repeatedly. I couldn't wait to see him the next day and tell him that I liked him too.

The next morning, I was more excited than usual to head out the door. Unable to sleep, I woke up earlier than usual. Mildred, when she came to wake me up as she always did every morning, was surprised to see me up. I was happier than I had been in a very long time and suddenly felt like I had a renewed look at life. I felt extremely special to know that someone thought I was beautiful and wanted me to be their girlfriend. It was like my life suddenly had purpose. No one ever told me that I was beautiful or pretty, most of the time I was mistaken for a little boy. I smiled to myself. *None of those things matter anymore,* I whispered to myself. *There's a very cute boy who thinks I'm beautiful.* I kept reading the letter over and over again on the bus, wearing out the creases in the paper as I repeatedly refolded and reopened the note.

My eyes lit up as I saw Karim at his locker. I felt a flush of red wash over me.

"Thank you for your letter. I really liked it," I smiled at him as I leaned against the locker beside his.

"Good morning!" A nervous smile crept upon his lips. "You did? Oh, good! I hoped you would like it." His face turned red, just as mine did.

"What did you think about the last part?" His eyes darted between my face and the floor and he nervously swayed back and forth, "About being my girlfriend?"

"I liked that part too," I felt sweaty and nervous. I had no idea what I was doing or how to talk to a boy.

"So, you'll be my girlfriend then?" As he asked me again, a flash of heat burned my cheeks. I still hadn't answered his question.

"Sorry! Y-yes, I'll be your girlfriend." Despite my attempts to seem composed, as I giggled and fidgeted with my books, it was evident that I was freaking out inside.

"Awesome!" he smiled. "That's great! Okay, we better get to class." He shut his locker and we walked to mine before heading to home room.

Although I was still beaming inside, I couldn't help but feel anxious. I had no idea what it meant to be a girlfriend, I didn't even really understand how to talk to a boy. We didn't hug or hold hands, and I wasn't sure how our relationship had changed from the day before. But, nevertheless, we were a couple now and I felt very happy about that. My world suddenly got less lonely.

In the evenings, I would go to a payphone and call Karim and we would chat for as long as we could before one of us had to go. I found out that he was the oldest child and had a younger brother. They lived with their mother who was a nurse and his father had passed away when they still lived in Afghanistan.

Over the next few weeks I understood more and more about Karim and I luckily had not shared too much about myself. I didn't want him to know about my life or what happened to my mom. My stories just made everyone sad, uncomfortable, or distant and I didn't want him to feel anything but adoration for me. My life felt purposeful and important.

We never hung out with one another outside of class although we did talk on the phone as often as possible. I could tell that Karim wanted to hold hands and touch more because when we were with our friends at lunch or before class he would put his arm around me or stand behind me and wrap his arms around my neck pulling me close. But, every time he touched me I froze. Instantly, my mind flashed images of Noah holding me down. I didn't like being touched, and I spent so much time avoiding George's nightly visits that I began to hate the idea of anyone touching me. Quickly, I began getting extremely anxious anytime I was about to see Karim. *What was wrong with me? Why couldn't I just be a normal fourteen-year-old girl who had a boyfriend that wanted to hold hands?* I was becoming more and more uncomfortable as time wore on because with each passing day I knew that he was going to eventually want to kiss me and I knew that I couldn't handle that. I didn't want to kiss anyone. I didn't want to hold hands. I didn't want to have anyone want to touch me. I hadn't realized it before having my new relationship but I didn't know how or feel comfortable being close to anyone.

I was fortunate to have received another one of Karim's amazing notes. It was colourful and I could see all the beautiful pictures he had drawn again. He was very talented and could draw anything. I had grown to love his letters and I cherished them deeply. To preserve them, I had even made a special box for them that I hid in one of my dresser drawers behind some old sweaters. When I got home that evening, I once again went to my bedroom and read the letter first quickly and then I went back and read it again, slowly taking in each word. I was immediately distracted when I got to the last page and saw that he had drawn a pair of lips and coloured them in red. Beside the drawing he wrote, "I think it's time we kissed." My whole body stiffened. My throat dried up. I thought I would be happy to kiss Karim when I had imagined it in the last few weeks since we become a couple, but I couldn't get past what happened the last time I kissed a boy, and how I thought it was just kissing, but quickly escalated into something so much worse than kissing.

As I read the letter over and over again, I realized that I must not like boys as much as I thought I had because I was almost sick to my stomach at the thought of having to kiss another one. I couldn't get the horrible night in Frances's basement out of my mind and how much shame and hate I had for myself afterward. My mind wandered to the handfuls of pills, the pool of vomit, and the immense shame I had felt. The last thing I wanted was to find out what would happen this time. I had to speak to Karim.

In a complete contrast to the morning after I had received his first note, I dreaded waking up and seeing him. I almost missed my bus because I was so slow leaving the house, as though I was preventing and sabotaging my encounter with him. I felt so nervous that I couldn't even feel the morning hunger pangs I had always felt when I awoke.

When I saw Karim in our usual spot in the hallway, I hung my head in shame. He looked so happy, smiling at me. I felt horrible that I couldn't feel the same way as him.

"Hey, beautiful!" He called out to me as he wrapped his arms around me. I froze and didn't reciprocate the hug.

"Hey," a giant lump formed in my throat.

"What's the matter?" It was obvious to see that I wasn't my cheery self. My whole demeanour had changed.

"I-I…j-just don't think we should be together." I couldn't even look him in the eye. "I can't kiss you, and I can't be your girlfriend. I'm sorry but I just can't." I thought I was going to burst into tears as I stood there saying words that weren't entirely true, but that I couldn't figure out how to say properly. I *did* want to kiss him, but I feared what that meant and what would happen to me if I did. I liked how much he liked me but I didn't know how to connect with him because I didn't do that. I didn't connect with anyone, besides Giselle of course, but she was my best friend and it wasn't this personal level that Karim—and boys in general—seemed to want to get to.

I watched his face contort with pain and sadness and then anger. He asked me why over and over again and when he realized that I really didn't have an answer he got frustrated and walked away.

I felt like the smallest person in the world breaking up with someone whom I cared for. It wasn't his fault that I didn't know how to connect with him, and it wasn't mine either. I thought of Noah. Who would have thought that his actions would have left such a stain on me? Or maybe it wasn't Noah—maybe it was me. I realized in that moment that the walls I had been building were real and they were high. I had done such a good job of withdrawing from my reality that I couldn't even let in the good stuff anymore. I choked back my tears as I watched him walk down the hall and I told myself it was for the best. *The good things in life and I didn't get along anyways*, I said to myself. *Girls like me don't have fairy-tale endings.* Girls like me only have chaos.

The weeks that followed my breakup with Karim were filled with a depression and sadness that I hadn't felt for what seemed like ages. His smile, his laugh, and the remarkably sweet letters he had written me weeks before swirled in my head. In the short time since I had told him that we could no longer be together, he had gone from being infatuated to refraining from making eye contact as we passed each other in the crowded halls of our school. Going through lengths to ensure that we were seated as far away from each other as possible, he wouldn't even acknowledge me when we were gathered among our group of friends. It was like I didn't exist. Just like when Mildred and George decided to ignore me for weeks at a time, the one person who treated me as though I mattered could no longer stand the sight of me.

I crumbled within. There was something about me that was easy to ignore. I was the girl you could forget. The one who was easy to not notice. Though I was aware that I had hurt him, and this was his way of processing the feelings of rejection, the cold side of Karim broke my heart. *Why did he have to try to erase me in the process? If only he knew how badly I wanted to erase myself,* I thought. He could never hate me more than I already hated everything about me.

A school-wide assembly had left the halls buzzing with students, marching like cattle toward the gymnasium. We often had speakers, awards, and announcements of sorts. As I walked in the crowd, the back of Karim's head was in front of me, just past a few other students. Though I lacked the courage, I desperately wanted to walk up to him, hold his hand, and make everything better again. But I couldn't. I hated myself for hurting him and I hated myself even more for being incapable of connecting with someone else. I had trained myself to close my heart at home, and now it was impossible to open the doors for anyone. Now, it would have to stay closed until I could move on into the world as an adult, away from Mildred and George, where I could make sense of myself again. With the walls, I had built so carefully, I had trapped myself, unable to talk to anyone about what I was going through. No one would be able to understand why I was so closed off, and I knew that. It was hard to see why it was necessary to protect myself if you weren't in my position, suffering every day in a household of neglect, abuse, and addiction. *I don't owe anyone an explanation,* I thought to myself, anger rising within me as I continued down the hallway. *I'm better off,* I concluded. *Men didn't have anything worth keeping anyways; at least not the ones I knew.*

The words of the Canadian national anthem rang throughout the gymnasium as the entire student body sang in unison. *Why would my parents move all to way to Edmonton from Tunisia, anyways?* I wondered as I stared at the red and white flag that hung against a white painted brick wall. *What would my life be if I lived with my mother's family?* I was given the opportunity, after all, but I had not taken it. *Would my life be as fucked up there as it is here?* There was no way to know. However, one thing was for sure, if I were in Tunisia, I would have food to eat every day. As I continued to daydream, spots began to sprout from the flag. I closed my eyes, reopening them to find that the spots had not only multiplied, but the room was on a tilt, rocking back and forth as if we were on a boat. A glaze came over me, I felt dizzy; it was as though my eyes were closed, but I was well aware that they were open. Finding my balance in the spinning room, I lost the little control I had left, and felt myself falling through the air.

I woke up to the fluorescent lights and sterile scent of the school infirmary.

"You fainted."

I looked over, seeing the school nurse by my side. My cheeks flushed with embarrassment. *Did I really faint in front of the entire school?* My heart imploded at the thought of Karim. *What did he think? Did he even care?* My thoughts were interrupted by the nurse. It was time to check me out, and as she did, she began to ask me a large list of questions.

"What have you eaten today, dear?" concern filled her eyes.

"Um…nothing yet." I couldn't meet her gaze. The last thing I needed was her prying into my malnourished life. I was ashamed of not having enough food.

"When was the last time you ate?" Her eyes searched my face for answers.

"Yesterday…sometime. I had lunch."

"How come you didn't have dinner, honey?" She had taken my hands into hers as she spoke to me.

"I dunno. We don't really have food." My body shook. With everything in me, I tried to hold back my tears, but my efforts were useless. I knew that this confession would get me into trouble, making my life much more miserable than it already was.

"Oh, dear," a crease formed across her face as she frowned. "Well, you wait right here and I'll go and get you something, okay?" A small nod was all I could give. Embarrassment had taken over me, and this entire situation was too much.

Returning with orange juice and a banana, I was instructed to devour them in front of her. As I chewed, she scribbled notes on her chart, and told me that I would need to go to the doctor for a full checkup.

"Umm," I began. "Can you please not tell anyone what I told you about not having food to eat?" She looked into my eyes, seeing my desperation.

"I promise," she said as she handed me the note that would excuse me from attending the rest of my classes.

Mildred seemed annoyed when she skimmed the note I had handed her. Grumbling, she said she would make an appointment for the next day. I walked away, toward my room. Living a mere block away from the clinic, I wasn't sure what the problem was. *It's not like she's missing a day of work to take me*, I silently mumbled as I closed my bedroom door.

I awoke early the next day and Mildred had booked the appointment. The doctor said I had extremely low blood pressure, and because of this, I needed more salt in my diet. "You're also twenty pounds underweight," he said, pointing at a chart on the wall that indicated what my body mass index should be for my height and age. I held my breath. Twenty pounds sounded like too much. I couldn't even imagine gaining that much, especially since it was a quarter of what I currently weighed.

"Take these so you don't keep fainting," he said as he handed me a pill bottle. "And don't stand for too long at one time." I couldn't help but be glad that I might finally get out of gym class.

I began to hate being at school since Karim provided a daily reminder that I wasn't as whole as I pretended to be when I walked out of the apartment every morning. His presence haunted me in each class that we shared, and just when I thought I felt as low as I could, our eyes would meet and I would wish I could just disappear and not have to face the discomfort that I now felt both at home and at school.

I began to head to class later and later until eventually Giselle and I decided to skip it all together. We would show up for our homeroom class and take attendance and then just walk right out of the school. We would spend our days roaming the neighbourhood, hanging out at our drug dealer Buddy's house, or just going to West Edmonton Mall and killing time.

The initial guilt I had felt about not attending classes eventually went away, and though I was still worried of the consequences of Mildred and George finding out I was skipping classes, for the first time I was glad we didn't have a phone and that the school couldn't possibly get a hold of them.

Life at home, however, continued to be unbearable. Mildred and George were proving to be more and more useless. They were fighting with each other more often and getting drunk earlier and earlier. Mildred spent as much time as possible at the bingo hall and George slept most of the time. They were the perfect example of everything I never wanted to be in life.

Giselle and I began hanging out with a girl in our school named Natalie— a very pretty, blonde-haired blue-eyed girl, who knew the same people we did. She was short, wore baggy clothes, and seemed as rebellious as we were. Though we would often see her in the smoking alley before school, we hadn't really said too much to her. It wasn't until we began to skip classes that we saw her more and got to know her.

One morning, we all decided that we should ditch class right after homeroom and Natalie said we could go to her place because her parents were out all day and her younger sister was at school.

We caught the bus and made our way to Natalie's place. We arrived at her townhouse and she showed us around. The house was nice and tidy, but clearly "lived in," as shown by the usual evidence of a family of four. There were some dishes in the sink, unopened mail littered the kitchen table, and laundry baskets filled with clothes sat on the living room floor. It was your typical household, and while they didn't look rich, they certainly didn't look like they were suffering. I couldn't help but notice the food in the fridge as Natalie opened it to look inside.

"Hey, you guys want some iced tea?" She asked with her head in the fridge.

Before we could answer she closed the fridge and went to the dining room and opened the hutch pulling out a bottle of Gibson's Finest Whiskey, "Or do you want a real drink?"

She held the bottle up at Giselle and me as we all looked at each other and burst out laughing.

"Hell yeah!" Giselle exclaimed.

"YES!" I was both surprised and excited for the way our morning of debauchery was unfolding. "That's a great idea!" I squealed.

The three of us sat around the wooden kitchen table and Natalie put a shot glass in front of each of us.

"I'll go first," she said as she filled the tiny glass up to the brim with whiskey.

She shot her head back and slammed the glass on the table while her twisted expression served as a prelude to what Giselle and I could expect.

"Your turn!" Natalie said. Wiping her mouth with the back of her hand, she passed the bottle to Giselle with the other.

Giselle giggled as she poured herself a shot and slammed it back with no complaint.

I was shocked at how easy she made it look and extremely nervous that I was next. I had some experience drinking, but never first thing in the morning and never as a shot. I had always mixed what little hard liquor Giselle and I had come by on our weekend sleepovers or hangouts in the park.

I took a deep breath as I poured myself a drink and realized that I didn't really have anything to lose. I didn't want to be at home and I didn't want to be at school, so sitting here drinking whiskey with my two best friends couldn't be so bad.

I closed my eyes and shot the liquid to the back of my throat. "*Aaaagh-hhh!!*" It began to burn instantly as it hit my mouth and slid down my throat into my stomach.

"That's fucking disgusting!" I squealed, jumping up from the table to help myself to the iced tea Natalie offered only moments ago. I had to get the awful taste of whiskey out of my mouth.

Giselle and Natalie burst out laughing at my reaction. I sat back down, with a glass of iced tea in hand.

Without a word, Natalie poured herself another shot and slammed it back before pushing the bottle to Giselle. Giselle poured her shot, drank it, and passed the bottle to me.

I looked at them both and back down to the bottle before filling up my glass and drinking it once again. Though it was just as horrible as the first time, I didn't make a fuss.

We passed the bottle around over and over again, each time counting out the number of shots we were on. Four, five, six, seven, eight, nine…we kept passing the bottle around and around and around.

"How many of these are we going to drink?" Giselle asked no one in particular.

"Let's have one for each year we have been on this shitty planet," I smiled as I looked at each of them.

Giselle lit a cigarette and laughed. Natalie smiled from ear to ear.

By the fourteenth shot, we were professionals. We had each created a system of pouring and drinking and mastered our unique techniques.

"We should get back to school." Giselle slurred, suddenly aware of the time.

Fuck. School. I hadn't even thought past hanging out at Natalie's house. It was 10:30 a.m. and we had wanted to get back by lunch.

"Yeah, okay. Let's head back." I slurred as I stood up for the first time since we began our little drinking game.

As soon as I stepped away from the table, I fell straight onto the kitchen floor face first.

"*Ouch!* Shit…I think I'm drunk guys." I couldn't seem to work my body and all my limbs stopped obeying me.

"*Oh fuck!*" Giselle roared with laughter as she tried to help me up.

With all my might, though I was trying to stand up, my legs and gravity both betrayed me.

"Stand up, Iman." Natalie came to the other side of me and helped Giselle support my body weight, "Are you okay?"

"I feel dizzy. I need to go lie down." I could barely keep my head up as the girls dragged me up the stairs toward the bedrooms. The entire house was spinning and I had never felt so dizzy in my entire life.

"You can come and sleep in my room for a bit until you feel better, okay?" Natalie and Giselle brought me up the stairs and down the hall to Natalie's bedroom and helped me up onto the bed that was right underneath a window. I collapsed into the big duvet momentarily before feeling sick to my stomach.

"I need to throw up! Open the window! Open the window!!" Though the words came out partially slurred, the urgency was crystal clear.

Natalie rushed to open the window as I sat up in the bed, hoping that closing my eyes would stop the room from spinning.

"Okay, it's open!" she said standing next to the bed.

In one fell swoop, I got up on my knees, turned to face the window and allowed the whiskey to eject itself from my stomach. My insides tensed up, contracting with a ferocity that I had never experienced before. To make matters worse, I hadn't eaten yet that day, and the pure whiskey, with nothing to cling to, forced itself out. When I felt my puke splash back onto my clothes and face, I was confused and I looked at the window only to realize that Natalie had opened the opposite side of the window and I had in fact just thrown up on the window glass, down the wall and onto the bed and myself.

"Oh shit, Natalie. You opened the other side! I–I'm so sorry…I just. I couldn't…" I didn't have the strength or sense to finish my thought and collapsed onto the bed, passing out to the sounds of Giselle and Natalie laughing from a million miles away.

Shortly after I blacked out I could hear Giselle's voice calling my name. She was lightly slapping my face while she said my name.

"Iman! Iman! Wake up! We need to go. You need to wake up now. Are you alright?" When my eyes opened, the room was still spinning and I had a hard time focusing on her face.

"We really need to get back to school. It's lunchtime, come on we gotta go! I'll drop you off at the infirmary okay?" She was trying to get me to stand up on my own and Natalie was desperately trying to wipe the vomit off my shirt with a towel.

"'Kay, let's get back to school. I'm coming." I had every intention of standing and walking but I still had not regained the use of my body. It was as though I was paralyzed and my brain was no longer connected to my body.

"I can't walk. I need to sleep." I longingly gazed at the bed, extremely resistant to the idea of leaving the very comfy, puke-covered haven I had made for myself, but Giselle and Natalie weren't having any of it. They each took one side of me and threw my arms around their shoulders as they carried and dragged me back outside.

Although we were all extremely drunk, I was the only one who had completely shut down because of it. It seemed that taking care of me had sobered the girls up a bit and they appeared to be in much better form than I was, even after having had the same amount to drink.

We made our way on a bus and sat at the very back. The motion of the bus made my stomach turn and once again I was hurling what was left in my stomach onto the floor between my legs.

The bus came to a quick halt as the bus driver slammed on the breaks and came yelling at us toward the back of the bus. She was not impressed with the mess she now had to clean up and kicked us off the bus eight blocks from school.

Giselle and Natalie apologized on my behalf and then had to half drag and half carry me to school.

As we arrived at the infirmary, the principal, Mr. Johnson, saw me and started asking a never-ending series of questions. What happened? Was I okay? What did I take? Giselle and Natalie told him they didn't know but that they found me like that and brought me in.

I was taken to the infirmary and the sweet nurse who had tended to me when I had fainted only weeks back, started to check my vitals.

"Well, what happened here, honey?" She looked over me with kind eyes and took my blood pressure.

"Looks like you have been drinking." I can only imagine what I smelled like and no doubt the puke on my shirt didn't do much to camouflage my morning adventures.

"Yeah, I don't feel so good. I just want to sleep." I could hardly keep my eyes open and as much as I would normally care that everyone was making such a fuss over my state, at that moment all I could think about was closing my eyes and having the room stop spinning.

"Alright, well you go to sleep then, and I'll speak with the principal." She turned off the light as she left and I faded quickly into sleep.

Once again, I opened my eyes to the bright florescent lights of the infirmary. This time, however, my social studies teacher, Ms. Wilson, was hovering over me. "Are you alright, Iman?" she asked. She was a beautiful, lively woman with gorgeous auburn hair and she always wore bright red nail polish and pretty dresses that hung tightly to every curve.

"Iman, what happened? Who did this to you? What have you done?" She looked frantic and I could hardly keep up with her questions.

"I did this to me," I opened one eye unsure if I was awake or dreaming.

"Why did you do this? We can't get a hold of your parents." She was getting more and more worked up as the questions poured from her lips.

I tried to sit up and the nurse came to help me. She also handed me some water and crackers. I slowly put a cracker in my mouth and drank some water. I looked up at the three people who were staring down at me with deep worry in their eyes: my principal, my teacher, and the school nurse. I recognized those looks and knew it was pity. I had seen them on the faces of everyone after my mom died.

I suddenly burst into tears. I don't know exactly why I was crying but it burst forth from my body like it needed to escape in the same way that I wished to escape my life. The tears drained from my head and I shook with sobs. My teacher came and sat next to me on the cot and pulled me close to her to comfort me.

"Please, don't tell my parents. Please, don't tell them. They'll hurt me! I can't go home if you tell them," I looked up at my principal with pleading eyes. I was begging him not to tell Mildred and George. I couldn't imagine what they would do to me if they found out I had skipped school to get drunk. They would never let me hang out with Giselle, they would ground me for the rest of the year, and my stomach turned at the thought of what physical consequences I would face. I wouldn't escape without some form of punishment, I knew that.

"Alright. I'll tell you what; I won't tell your parents you were drinking. But I need you to promise me you won't do this again, Iman. This could have turned out much worse than it did." The principal looked down on me with his kind eyes and I knew that this was as good as it was going to get for me.

"Okay. I promise, it won't happen again. Thank you, Mr. Johnson." My voice was barely above a whisper. My sobs subsided and I felt like I had gotten lucky this time.

I had gone from feeling extremely drunk to extremely hungover by the time I had to catch my bus home. My head was pounding and my body was aching. I felt weak and wanted nothing more than to go to bed, even though I had spent the better part of the day sleeping off the booze. I walked into the apartment and Mildred was in the living room knitting. I said hello and made my way directly to my bed. I collapsed on my blankets and stayed there for the rest of the night.

The next few days I channeled all my energy and focus toward my schoolwork and staying out of trouble. I ignored Karim and didn't want to skip school; I didn't want to call any attention to myself. I was humiliated when I had to go to social studies class and Ms. Wilson looked me right in the eyes as I sat in my desk. In that moment of eye contact, I tried to say a silent thank you, but for the remainder of the class my head was buried in my books. I couldn't believe that I had been so stupid as to try and drink my body weight in whiskey, thinking I would be fine. I really hadn't thought very far ahead on that one.

Chapter Sixteen

Age 14: Word of Mouth

I decided to call my sister on my way home from school, hoping that I could sleep at her apartment over the weekend. Since she had moved out with Steven, we had hardly spent any time together, and I missed her. I told her about George coming into my room sometimes and instantly, she was enraged. Apologizing for being out of touch, she said that she would try to have me over more often. Knowing that Mel almost always got what she wanted when she asked Mildred, I asked if she could ask her mother if I could spend the weekend.

Excitement took over me when Mildred told me that I could go to Mel's for the night. I packed my backpack and took the bus downtown, where Mel met me at the bus stop. I had never been so happy to see her. She and Steven lived in a big high-rise apartment building and they were up on the twentieth floor. Though the apartment was old, it was ten times better than the apartment I lived in with Mildred and George. The apartment was spacious, with two bedrooms, a bathroom on one end, and a galley kitchen with a little dining room on the other. A large living room sat on the other side of the kitchen wall. I was so blown away by how cool their apartment was and I hoped I could stay more and more often.

Mel showed me around the apartment and then let me get settled in. I could hear Steven come home and I came out of the bedroom to say hello. I had seen him many times over the year or so that he and Mel were dating, but I never really talked to him much. When Mel lived at the apartment they would be in her room the whole time, avoiding Mildred and George much like I did.

Steven had a handsome face with light brown hair and brown eyes. He was of medium height and build and had a friendly smile.

"Hey, kiddo! How are you? Welcome to our place!" His happiness at my arrival left me embarrassed.

"Oh, thanks. I'm glad I could finally come over." I felt shy around him.

Steven went to the fridge and grabbed a beer. "Hey, Iman, want a beer?" He held out the cold can and looked at me.

"Yes! Thank you!" I was so happy and I looked at Mel to see if she would protest my drinking. She grinned at me and gave me a very big sister glare to let me know not to get carried away.

We sat on the balcony with our beers and smoked and laughed. I looked over the edge and couldn't believe how high up we were. Everyone on the sidewalk looked so small and it was hard to imagine that there were so many different lives happening all around us.

We ordered pizza and watched movies and I was the happiest I had been in weeks. I loved my sister so much and I loved being able to hang out with her like old times. Steven didn't seem so bad either; he was so funny and nice to me. He treated me like I was just like them and not like some stupid teenager that didn't know anything.

It got late and Melanie went to bed. Steven said he was going to stay up a little longer and hang out with me. I had three beers throughout the whole evening and could feel a mild hint of intoxication sweep over me. I was still traumatized from my recent episode at Natalie's and was very aware of pacing myself. Also, Mel was watching me very closely and made sure she kept track of how many I had.

Steven, as he slurred his words and hysterically laughed at his own jokes, had quite a bit more than I did, and after Melanie had made her departure, he came to sit beside me on the couch. Paying no mind to his move, I found it understandable; the living room was large, and yelling from across the room at a late hour seemed pointless.

I was flattered by his obvious joy in spending time with me and including me in the conversation as it jumped from every topic his mind wandered to. Although I didn't really have a lot to say with my limited experience in the world, I was completely engrossed in everything he had to say. I thought he was so smart when he talked about travel and all the different countries in the world that he would like to travel to. He spoke about different cultures and the wild customs people had in Africa and Asia. He had strong opinions on politics and society, and though it was extremely hard to keep up with his drunken thoughts, I was having the time of my life. It was rare that an adult would spend so much time just talking and laughing with me about every topic under the sun.

An hour had passed before Mel reappeared in the living room, telling both Steven and me that we needed to go to bed. I had been getting tired for a while, but I was also having so much fun that I didn't want the evening to end. It was almost 3:00 a.m. and I couldn't believe how quickly the night flew by and how long Steven and I sat there talking.

I was extremely sad to have to go back the next day when Mel and Steven were driving me home. Mel promised that I could come back over soon and that the week would fly by.

When I got home, Mildred was sitting at the kitchen table. "Well, hello. How was Mel's place? Did you have fun?" She looked up from her crossword puzzle and peered over the rim of her glasses.

"Yeah, it was so much fun. We had pizza and watched movies." I stood behind the chair opposite Mildred at the table.

"That's nice. Well, I made some plans for you this evening. I got you a babysitting job in the building." She seemed to switch subjects quickly and I was surprised at what she had said.

"What? What do you mean? Whose baby?" I was completely annoyed at not having been consulted about my time and at how nonchalantly Mildred brought it up.

"Yeah, I told Tara down the hall that you would babysit for her. She just delivered her baby three weeks ago and she needs a night out. I thought it would be good for you." Mildred continued to fill in her crossword puzzle as I stared at her in confusion.

"Babysit a newborn?" I sputtered. "Isn't that a bit young for me to watch? I don't know how to watch a newborn."

"Oh, you'll be fine. It's a baby, they don't even do anything. Just pick her up when she cries, feed her, and change her diaper."

I could feel my body begin to stiffen and my face get hot. I hated that she would make plans for me without even asking me. How could I watch a newborn baby? Sure, I had taken care of the abandoned children left to their own devices when their parents came over, but I was just in the next room. *If Mildred liked babies so much why didn't she volunteer herself?* I asked to myself.

"Oh, for crying out loud! Stop pouting, would you? I told her you'd be over there in half an hour." She threw the paper down on the table and I turned and walked to my bedroom before she could get up and slap me.

Whatever, I thought as I filled my backpack with a book and my journal. Maybe I would make some extra money out of it.

Tara opened the door to her apartment and greeted me with a huge smile and hug. She was a big woman and almost the same body type as George. She was tall with long brown hair and a big smile. Tara was at our house often last year and less frequently the further along in her pregnancy she was. She was single and had become pregnant from a one-night stand she had—at least that is what I heard Mildred and George say one night.

"Iman! Thank you so much for coming to watch Alicia. I seriously need to go out and get drunk." She was all done up and I could smell her perfume instantly. Her eyes were covered in dark grey eye shadow and she was wearing a shiny black top and a pair of jeans. She led me through the small apartment to the living room. The apartment was much smaller than ours but had almost the same layout. It was dark, and although the furniture was mismatched and dated, the place was clean. There was a bathroom and the only bedroom right next to it. The kitchen and small dining room were exactly like ours. Even the living room looked like ours just in a different configuration.

"You can watch whatever you want and help yourself to anything in the kitchen, okay?" She opened a pack of cigarettes and threw two down on the coffee table next to the ashtray for me.

"Here, you can have these whenever and I can give you $20 for the night." She reached into her purse and handed me the crumpled bill. It felt good to already be up cigarettes and cash for the day.

"Let me show you the baby." She pointed toward the bedroom door. I followed her into the cramped bedroom. There was a queen-size mattress on a box spring, a dresser, and a crib between the two. The bed was covered in clothing that likely didn't make the cut for her evening out.

I walked up to the crib and looked down at the tiniest most beautiful little girl. She was wearing a yellow onesie and sleeping soundly. She looked so very peaceful.

"She will probably wake up in the next hour and you can just change her diaper and feed her. The bottles are in the fridge and you will need to heat them up. You know how to do that right?"

I looked up at Tara and shook my head no. My stomach was turning in knots at the very thought of doing something wrong and hurting the baby.

Gently grabbing my wrist, she walked me to the kitchen. There was a pot on the stove with water in it.

"Okay, you heat the water, put the bottle in, get the milk warm, and then take it out after a few minutes. Test it on your wrist like so to make sure it isn't too hot and burns the baby's mouth." She was spitting out instructions so fast and I was trying my hardest to remember every single word.

She demonstrated how to test the milk on my wrist and once again went over where the diapers were. I could see she was in a hurry to head out and nervous to leave her baby for the first time.

"You'll be fine. It will be great. If you need anything just go get Mildred, okay?" She looked down at me smiling with her hands on my shoulders.

I nodded in agreement. "Okay, I'll be fine. It'll be good. Have fun and I'll see you later."

I locked the door behind her and secured the chain on the door. I was excited, nervous, worried, and unsure, but I kept telling myself that I could do this and that it wasn't a big deal. Mildred was just down the hall if I needed her but I was going to do my very best to never need her. I could just see her smug face if I went there for help. She would never let me live down how I couldn't even take care of a baby.

I opened the balcony door and lit my cigarette, mindful to keep one ear listening for the baby. I was hyper alert and on the ready to do whatever it was that I would need to do to babysit this little girl.

I came inside and watched television for a little while before I could hear Alicia stirring in the next room. As I walked into the bedroom I realized that I had never met the baby and that she might be frightened having never seen my face before. I peered into the crib at her little body and her eyes met mine.

"Hello, little one. Are you hungry?" I reached in and scooped her up into my arms. I took her into the living room and changed her diaper. To my surprise, she just stared at me and didn't cry or fuss.

I placed her in a bassinet that was in the living room and went to heat up her bottle. I was feeling good and so far, the night was a success.

I tested the milk repeatedly as I had forgotten what Tara said it should feel like before giving it to the baby. I decided that too cold was better than too hot and sat down on the couch cradling my tiny companion. At first, she fussed and started to cry when I placed the bottle to her mouth, but within minutes she took the nipple of the bottle and sucked back the milk hungrily. I felt so happy looking at her little face and the fact that we got along so well made me proud.

"Well, look at us, Alicia. We're getting along just fine, aren't we?" I cooed to her as she ate, her little blue eyes staring up at me.

I thought of how my mom must have been when I was little. She had wanted a little girl so badly. I thought about how I would have curled up in her arms just like this and she would have looked down at me and smiled just as I was doing now. It brought me peace that I too was once loved as a little baby. Somebody chose to have me in their life and I wasn't just thrust into their existence like I was now. My mom wanted me and loved me and treated me the best out of everyone I had ever met.

I envied Alicia in those moments. She had a mother who loved her deeply and didn't have to live with strangers who treated her like a burden. I liked that I could enjoy this peace and quiet in my new job as babysitter.

I held her, burped her, and rocked her back to sleep and placed her back into her crib. She woke up again in two hours and we did our routine once more.

Tara came home just after 2:00 a.m. and I told her of our uneventful evening. She thanked me profusely and walked me to the door.

As I walked down the hall back to my apartment I couldn't help but feel sad to leave my new little friend behind. The evening had been filled with a sweetness and magic that you only get when you hang out with babies. It was like they brought a piece of another world along with them into this one.

I felt so proud that I had done everything right and that I didn't need to ask for help. *Maybe I had found a new way to make some money*, I thought.

I entered the dark apartment that I called home. The lights were off and everyone was sound asleep. Quietly shuffling in, trying earnestly to avoid waking Mildred or George, I walked into my room and crawled into bed. As I tucked myself under the sheets, the evening's events replayed in my mind as I drifted off to sleep.

Word of mouth had landed me a new venture. In the coming weeks, since my first babysitting job, news of my skills and service had made their way throughout the entire apartment building. Almost every weekend I was asked to watch a neighbour's child in exchange for a wrinkled twenty-dollar bill, and this little part-time job had become quite fruitful for me. I could make as much as forty dollars a weekend if I babysat two different times.

Directly below our three-bedroom apartment lived a family of five: a mother and father and their three young children. Provocatively dressed in short skirts and tank tops that left her midriff exposed, Candice, the mother, would stop by our place on the weekends for a drink and a joint with George before she left for work. She was petite and roughly around the same height as me at barely five feet tall. Her hair was short, blonde and wavy, and her face was sunken in, much like Mildred's, and her teeth were visibly rotting.

A chain-smoker with a very loud, cackling laugh, she was usually quite bubbly, but as I watched her from afar, I noticed she had a type of jitteriness to her—the kind that is common among those who were afflicted with drug addiction.

Her husband was a taller man with long brown hair that fell to his waist. Skinny and covered in tattoos, his face rarely expressed a smile and his eyes never met yours while he was talking. He made me uncomfortable, and though he had never done anything for me to feel this way, I would still stiffen in his presence.

Unlike her parents, Britney, their eight-year-old daughter, had long blonde hair and a beautiful smile. She was sweet tempered and always wanted to hang out and play dolls with me. The middle child, Alex, was four years old and looked much like his father, with dark eyes and hair and, like his father, his teeth were almost all rotten in his mouth: some of them were cracked and chipped, and several were severely decayed. Gabe, only eighteen months old, looked look like his mother and sister, with large blue eyes, wavy blonde hair, and a bright, happy attitude. His diaper was always in need of being changed when I saw him and it became a habit for me to change his diaper immediately when they came over. I could always smell the urine-soaked diaper before I even got close enough to pick him up.

One day after school Candice came over to our apartment and asked me if I could watch her kids for her that Friday night. Enthusiastically, I said yes. Besides the pocket money, I needed an escape from Mildred and George, and babysitting was the perfect way to get out of the apartment and be on my own. Since Giselle had found a new boyfriend, and she spent most of her weekends with him, I no longer had the luxury of regular weekend sleepovers at her house.

The muffled sounds of children screaming and crying got louder as I approached Candice's apartment door. My closed fist tapped lightly against the run-down door and was met with no indication that my arrival was heard. I knocked again, this time louder. Amid the loud yells of children, the sound of Candice screaming for me to come in broke through. When I opened the door, my eyes darted around from the floor to the kitchen to the walls to the living room. The layout was identical to our apartment, with the simple exception that it was an utter disaster. The floor was covered from wall to wall in clothes, pillows, and blankets; dirty diapers were piled in random spots throughout the apartment; and abandoned dishes with caked-on remnants of meals littered every surface. I peeked into the kitchen and it was the filthiest thing I had ever seen. Plates, bowls, and cutlery were everywhere; it was as though every single pot and plate had been used. Cups lined up next to the sink and the smell of garbage permeated the entire place.

I focused my attention back on the residents of the apartment, watching as Candice and her husband were frantically trying to get ready. It looked like the older boy, Alex, had just finished his bath as his hair was sopping wet and he had a towel wrapped around him. The little one, Gabe, was running around naked and had a wet red face as though he had just been crying. Britney was in her room playing and her mom called after her, letting her know that the babysitter had finally arrived. Stunned and overwhelmed, I stood there, not knowing what to do.

Candice was wearing a very short blue skirt that was so small I couldn't help but think it looked like she had picked it from her daughter's wardrobe. Her tiny breasts hung freely, moving slightly back and forth under her white halter top as she wildly sprayed herself with perfume. No surface was left untouched: she sprayed above her head, her neck once on each side and then stuck the bottle up her skirt and sprayed while laughing wildly and throwing her head back. "You just never know when that will come in handy!" she chuckled, walking back down the hall toward the bedroom. She returned quickly to the living room where I finally sat on the very edge of one couch, afraid to touch anything.

"Help yourself to anything you want. There are lots of movies and the kids can watch whatever they want. Put them to bed whenever you get sick of them, okay?"

I smiled and nodded

"Oh, and feel free to spank them if you need to," she added. "They can be shitheads sometimes."

Candice's husband came out of the bedroom and the smell of marijuana followed him. He didn't look at me, but mumbled something to Candice.

As she quickly repeated the instructions of watching whatever I want and helping myself to whatever I could find in the kitchen, Alex had seemed to finally have found some clothes and came out of his room, finding a place next to me on the couch.

"We shouldn't be too late, okay? Thanks for babysitting!" And with that, they rushed out the door, neither of them kissing their children goodbye or acknowledging them before they left for their evening out.

Letting out a small sigh, I went to pick up Gabe and put a diaper on him before he peed on the floor. Britney still hadn't come out of her room. I had been there for less than five minutes and I was already overwhelmed. *How am I supposed to manage the entire night ahead of me?* I wondered.

I decided to grab Gabe and Alex and go see Britney to make sure she was okay. I knocked on the door and then peered inside to find her playing with dolls on the floor of her very messy bedroom.

"Hey, are you okay in here?" She looked a little sad on the floor of her disastrous bedroom.

"Yeah, I'm okay. I was sad that my parents were leaving. Can we watch movies?" She looked a little less sad by the end of her request.

"Of course, we can! Come on, let's go and watch cartoons, okay?"

The four of us found our own comfy spots in the sea of blankets, clothes and couches that made up the living room and watched *The Little Mermaid*.

I got up to put Gabe to sleep in his crib as he had fallen asleep on the floor in front of the television. When I had finished changing his diaper and got him a final bottle and tucked him in his crib, I came out to let Alex and Britney know that their bedtime was soon approaching as well. They both began to protest and begged to watch one more movie. I told them we could wait for another half hour and made some popcorn.

True to my word, I announced bedtime had come and Britney got very upset. "I don't want to go to bed!!!" She screamed at me and crossed her arms across her chest in a huff.

I ignored her and looked down at Alex's face with his cheeky grin. "Come on, buddy, let's brush your teeth and get to bed." I saw him hesitate for a second and then comply and jump up and head to the bathroom to brush his teeth.

I cleared away the clothes and toys from Alex's bed and got him all tucked in before turning off the light and closing the door behind me. I made my way to Britney's room to get her bed cleaned off so that she could just get into it once she finished her tantrum.

I called after her from the bedroom and couldn't hear anything from the living room. I stood at the doorway and looked down the dark hallway that was only illuminated by the flickering television in the living room. "Britney? C'mon, that's enough. Time for bed." I listened and heard her shuffle at the end of the hall. I walked out of her room and turned on the hallway light and as soon as the light came on Britney began running toward me screaming.

"I DON'T WANT TO GO TO BED!"

With her two hands clutched above her head, I needed a second glance to see that she was holding a steak knife between them. My heart started beating faster. My hands start to sweat.

"Britney!" I yelped. "What are you doing?" To hide my fear, I didn't flinch, and, to my benefit, standing my ground stopped her in her tracks for a brief second before she began charging at me again, wildly waving the serrated knife between her small palms. I grabbed her wrist and twisted her arm behind her body until she squealed in pain.

"Ow!" she shrieked. "You're hurting me!" She seemed somehow surprised that I could overpower a child.

I grabbed her other hand and pulled the knife from her fingers. "Get to bed now," I grumbled through clenched teeth. I pushed her toward her bedroom, my voice a low growl.

Her head whipped back, her blonde locks flying behind her, as she turned to give me a look of hatred and disgust. The sound of her door slamming in rebellion echoed through the small three-bedroom apartment, and with that, I walked to the kitchen and began to search the drawers to find the knives. Gathering the small collection of sharp steel, I placed them on top of the refrigerator just in case she was brave enough to attempt to stab me again.

I made my way to the couch, chain-smoking while staring at the TV. The screen flickered with inaudible sound, allowing me to listen for any movement from down the hall where the children should be sleeping. Britney's ruthless stunt with the steak knife had triggered my PTSD, and with it in full effect, my awareness was in hyperdrive and my heart pounded violently in my chest. I still hadn't gotten used to knives since my mom's death. I could usually keep myself in check if I was expecting to be around them, but I was caught off guard being attacked by a child in a situation where I was meant to be in control. Closing my eyes and attempting to regain composure, I lit another cigarette as I sat in the dark living room, waiting for Candice to come back.

Loud stomps and the sound of the doorknob rattling quickly brought me to attention. Candice and her husband had returned. Though I thought I would be grateful to be relieved of my duties, the muffled yells that came from the hallway left a pit in my stomach. The door pushed open and their booming yells were matched by their drunken appearance.

"Whore!"

"Yeah?!" Candice sneered. "Well at least I'm working to provide for this *fucking family!*" Her retort left him fuming, and he stormed off to the bedroom, slamming the door. It seemed that slamming doors was a common occurrence in this household.

I was stunned and uncomfortable, unaware of what to do in a domestic altercation that I had no business being a part of. Slowly, I rose from my seat on the couch. They hadn't acknowledged my presence yet, and as I walked to the front door, I hoped Candice wouldn't notice. Unfortunately, she did. The sounds of my attempt to escape were heard and Candice, suddenly aware that her quarrel with her husband had an audience, looked at me as though she was surprised I was still there.

"Oh," a pitiful smile formed on her lips, "Hey, kiddo. Here's your money." She reached into her tiny purse, pulling out a crumpled twenty and pushed it into my palm. She murmured a quick goodnight and began to stumble toward the room her husband had entered moments before.

I made my way up to my apartment and was greeted by darkness and silence. Thankful that everyone was asleep, I locked myself in the bathroom and washed my face with scalding hot water before crawling into bed and falling into a deep sleep.

I was happy to spend the next weekend with Giselle. Although it meant I had to meet her boyfriend, Jorge, it was a sacrifice I was willing to make to spend time with my best friend. Although I had not met him, I already disliked him. He had taken up so much of her time lately, and hanging out in a group didn't compare to having the alone time I desperately needed with her. I also loathed the idea of playing third wheel. Giselle, however, had told me that Jorge had a friend named Lucas and that I might like him. My stomach churned. There was a worse fate than being the third wheel, and that was being forced to hang out with some strange boy while Giselle and Jorge moaned and grunted in the next room. I remembered exactly how that played out with Frances and I had zero interest in being trapped underneath another scummy boy.

Begrudgingly, I obliged. I was between a rock and a hard place: on one hand, I could swallow my pride and follow along with Giselle's plan, on the other hand, I could be stuck spending the whole weekend with Mildred and George. The former won. I made it very clear to Giselle that I was having nothing to do with this friend of her boyfriend. She laughed, "I promise you don't have to do anything with him, Iman. Relax!" I shrugged off her words. This time I wasn't going to be such a fool.

I met Giselle at the bus terminal and we rode the bus together to Jorge's house. I was surprised when I saw Jorge because he was nothing like I had imagined. He opened the door and greeted Giselle with a big kiss before shaking my hand and introducing himself. He was very charming and warm and I could see instantly why Giselle had fallen for him.

He looked like he spent a lot of time on his perfectly ironed appearance. He was eighteen, much older than I originally thought, wore baggy name-brand clothes, and had caramel skin that contrasted perfectly with his large, white smile. He was very short, had jet-black hair that was cut close to his head. As he welcomed us into the house, I could hear his mother and sister speaking Spanish in the next room, remembering that Giselle had told me that Jorge's parents had moved to Edmonton from Mexico when he was a little boy. We looked into the kitchen and waved, saying our hellos before heading down into the basement that Jorge had transformed into a small apartment of his own.

The overpowering scent of cologne hit me with such strength I felt as though I could taste it. Lucas sat on a couch that was against the far wall right below the only basement window. He stood up and came over to meet me. I couldn't help but stare in shock at how tall he was—I barely came up to his chest. He was slim and blonde, with very pale skin, blue eyes, and a pointy nose. Like Jorge, he was draped in oversize clothing: a crisp pair of baggy denim jeans and a designer shirt. He was also partly to blame for the smog of cologne that we waded through.

We spent the rest of the evening smoking weed and listening to the most incredible music. I learned that Jorge and Lucas spent most nights as DJs around the city. Sitting there in the basement with friends, music, and laughter was one of the best nights I had in a while. I guess it wasn't so bad to hang out with the guys if it meant that I had my best friend back.

The next day, Giselle's parents went out and Jorge and Lucas came over to Giselle's place. It was obvious that Giselle and Jorge wanted to be alone and they slipped into the basement after barely even thirty minutes of being in the house and pawing at each other desperately on the opposite couch from Lucas and me. I held my breath. This was all too familiar. I stole a quick glance at Lucas as we remained seated in the formal sitting room on the main level of the house. A sunny winter day, rays of light poured in through the open windows, illuminating the whole room. Silence cloaked the room. I stared straight ahead and could feel Lucas's eyes burning through the side of my head. He suddenly started to lie down and stretched his legs out onto my lap.

"We might as well make ourselves comfortable." He didn't seem to be phased at all by his decision to completely monopolize the couch and squish me with his giant legs. He was such a tall man and it was humorous to see him attempt comfort on this tiny couch while having to share it with me as well. I burst out laughing at the entire situation. Lucas soon followed suit and I watched his face turn red. We were both in a situation where we didn't know what to do.

"Comfortable?" I asked him while trying to wiggle into a comfortable position with his massive legs across my lap.

"Not really," he smirked at me sideways. "I have an idea. How about I lay here and close my eyes and you do whatever you want to me?" He proposed his strange idea with eyes already closed.

To say that I was uncomfortable was an understatement. Lucas's preposterous idea that somehow, I, the fourteen-year-old girl, should be in charge of an eighteen-year-old man-boy's body was one of the most ludicrous things I had ever heard. I said nothing and he seemed to take that as agreement to his ridiculously passive aggressive suggestion. We both just sat in silence for a few minutes until he realized that I was not moving and then he looked at me and lifted his torso off the couch.

"Hey, what's the matter? Why aren't you doing anything?"

"Umm, because I don't want to that's why," I began to push his legs off me so I could get up off the couch. "I don't want to do anything. I just wanted to come over to Giselle's house and hang out."

I was now standing up and making my way toward the kitchen for a drink of water.

"Oh, I just thought—well, I mean I like you and I thought, you know, you liked me too…" his words trailed off and I felt guilty for being so abrupt.

"I do like you. I just don't want whatever it is that you want to do right now." I knew I would probably get teased later by Giselle for being such a prude but I had no interest in being forced into a weird relationship just so Giselle and Jorge could run off and have sex.

I made my way to the basement and called Giselle's name. I heard scrambling coming from the bedroom and she called out to me to ask what I wanted.

"I'm going to take off. I gotta get back home!" I called down the hall.

I could hear Giselle and Jorge mumbling, trying to get organized fast enough to come out and catch me before I left.

"Iman? Where are you going? What's wrong?" Giselle came out into the living room in the basement where I was standing. Her hair was disheveled and she was pulling her shirt down and straightening up as she asked me questions.

"Nothing," I replied avoiding looking directly into Giselle's eyes as I spoke, fearful that I might burst into tears. "I just want to go home. I don't want to hang out with Lucas alone. I wanted to hang out with you. But it's all good, I'm going to get back home. I'll see you at school on Monday."

I wanted to tell her how uncomfortable I was being alone with him and how much I hated being put in a situation where it was just assumed that I would be someone's plaything while my friend got to go hang out with someone who she had gotten to choose. It was the same position that Frances pulled me into when she brought me to her mom's townhouse in Edmonton, just so she could have her boyfriend over and put me in danger. I was not interested in being someone's distraction or a way to pass time while their friends got laid.

"Are you sure? Just stay and hangout," she pleaded. I could see her eyes begging me to stay. "I know Lucas is a bit of a loser but he's Jorge's friend."

"I really just want to go home. Have fun and I will see you on Monday."

I made my way upstairs and Lucas was exactly where I left him on the sofa. He jumped up and came toward me when I stuck my head in to say goodbye.

"Where are you going? You're leaving already?" He looked nervous and embarrassed.

"Yeah, I gotta get home and finish some homework that's due on Monday."

I didn't care that that was probably the lamest most uncool thing to say to an eighteen-year-old guy that I was supposed to be impressing. I didn't give a shit about impressing anyone and I had grown tired of the situations I kept getting myself into that could result in danger and violence.

I walked home in the cold that afternoon and thought about all the things in my life that I wished were different. I knew I didn't want to go home to Mildred and George because I hated them and I hated living with them. I normally loved hanging out with Giselle and practically lived at her house,

I just didn't feel comfortable being dangled in front of Lucas, like I was supposed to entertain him while she spent time with her boyfriend. I knew I had my own hang-ups about men, and maybe I wasn't normal with how I felt, but for some reason I didn't care what I looked like, or if Giselle thought I was a prude virgin that had no idea how to act around boys. She had seen me freak out over Karim wanting to kiss and then breaking up with him and now she would see how when left alone with Lucas, I had no interest and decided to leave, even though I hated going home more than anything.

I wavered between caring what people would think about me and what Lucas would say happened, to complete and utter indifference to the whole situation. I danced between the two conflicting feelings as I trudged through the snow for the thirty-minute walk home.

I couldn't hear or see anyone when I entered our three-bedroom apartment and felt relief that Mildred and George had left for the day. With the weight of having to interact with my fair-weather guardians off my shoulders, I shed my winter jacket and scarf, letting the warmth of the apartment envelop me.

As I walked through the apartment, I stopped by the kitchen. It was funny to me how often I looked into the fridge, hoping that there would be morsels of food to greet me, and how often I was disappointed. Closing the refrigerator door, I went into the cupboard, retrieving a glass and filling it with tap water before I made my way toward my bedroom.

The door to Mildred and George's room was open. Absentmindedly, I glanced inside. Lying naked on the bed, with blankets barely covering the tops of his legs, George's eyes locked with mine. He continued to stroke himself as he looked at me, completely undisturbed that a child had caught him in such a grotesque act. I quickly diverted my eyes. I ran to my room, closing the door behind me. *What the fuck did I just see?* I shuddered in disgust and rage. *Why was he doing that to himself with the door wide open?* Surely, he had heard me come home and go into the kitchen to get my drink. *Where was Mildred?* I couldn't get the look on his face out of my head when we made eye contact for those brief but mortifying few seconds.

I need to get out of here, I panicked. My bag, still packed from when I had planned to sleep at Giselle's that night, sat slumped in the corner of my room where I left it after I had rushed in. I grabbed it and ran to the front entrance. The snow hardly had the time to melt off my winter jacket, some of it still sat on the front rug in clumps. Hurriedly, I slipped on the sopping wet outerwear and ran to the nearest payphone up the street.

Chapter Seventeen
Age 14: Idle Hands

Steven answered the phone and told me that Mel was at work.

"I really need to talk," I whimpered.

"You okay?"

"I just—I really don't want to stay home tonight. Can I come and sleep over at your place?"

He paused. "Yeah, I just need to ask Mel. Can you call me back in five minutes?"

I agreed, hoping that Mel would say yes, and hung up the phone. I walked over to the small plaza up the street so that I could wait inside and use the phones in there. My heart pounded in my chest as I waited for my five minutes to be up. When I called back Steven answered right away.

"Mel's working until nine o'clock tonight," he said through the receiver. "But I can come pick you up now and you can hang out at our place for the night."

A wave of relief hit me. I told him exactly where I was and eagerly waited for him to arrive.

I was so excited to see Steven's car pull up and quickly got inside. The heat was blaring. It felt nice to be in a warm, clean car. It was a sporty thing with an incredibly loud stereo and music was always blaring. Steven loved stereos he talked about them a lot and I remember how he set up all his equipment in my sister's old room when he used to stay over a lot of the time.

"Hey, kiddo!" he greeted me with a big smile and touseled my hair.

I laughed and felt instantly safe and my anxiety melted away. "Hey, Steve. Thanks so much for coming to pick me up," I looked at him with so much gratitude.

"Of course. No problem! Your sister told me to come get you and make sure you were safe at our place. I know it's no fun living with Mildred and George. You can stay with us anytime."

I had to look away so that I didn't burst into tears at everything that had happened that day. I just went from one horrible situation to the next. I would do anything to escape my life. I wanted so much to believe that it could get better and that I would wake up from the nightmare that was my reality. Deep inside of me, I knew that there was something far better than this waiting for me in life. I had faith that things would turn around and that I had paid my dues enough in this life that I could truly depend on happiness being just around the corner.

On the drive, Steven and I chatted about my schooling and random small talk until we got to their place, pulling into the underground parkade that sat below their apartment. I was so happy to have been able to leave the apartment so quickly and felt grateful for the fact that I had an escape plan from the day. I just wanted to hang out at my sister's place until she came home, where I wouldn't have to worry about going home until tomorrow. For now, it was Saturday night and I was truly free.

When we walked into the apartment I remember feeling a bit strange that my sister wasn't there to greet me. I had never been in her home without her and I felt her absence. Steven busily chatted away to me as he took off his coat and got organized in the apartment.

"Sorry for the mess. We were having a lazy morning today." He seemed nervous as he started folding blankets that were strewn on the floor in the living room.

Their place was always so spotless compared to the apartments that I was used to seeing. My favourite thing about my sister's house was that it felt so safe. I felt like it was one of the few places where I could just be myself and not worry about what to eat or what to say or that just being myself would get me into trouble. I was so happy that I had my sister and that I could count on her when I needed to.

"You want a beer?" Steven stood in the doorway between the kitchen and the living room holding out a can of beer toward me.

"Sure," I got up and met him halfway, accepting the cold can in his hand. "Thanks." He opened the fridge again and got one for himself, reaching out to clink our cans before we took our first sips. I made my way into the living room and sat on the couch. It struck me that I had never been alone with Steven before. Even when he sort of lived with us for a few months in the apartment, Mel had always been around. I tried not to get nervous and quiet as I didn't want to seem weird or uncomfortable. Steven was always so friendly and easy to talk to.

He made his way over to where I was sitting on the couch and sat next to me.

"So, what happened today?" Steven looked at me with deep concern. "Why did you feel like coming over tonight? You sounded upset on the phone." He leaned in and touched my leg when he asked me the questions.

Disarmed by his concern, I wanted to tell him everything but I was too ashamed of my life, embarrassed by Mildred and George, and the continuous humiliation that I felt being a part of their lives.

"I just hate living at the apartment." I looked away, swallowing a large mouthful of beer. "I don't like Mildred and George is weird. He gives me the creeps."

"Yeah, Mel's told me some stories about him. What a freak." Steven finished his beer and made his way to the fridge for another one and came back with one for me as well.

"Don't tell your sister okay?" he smiled. The sound of carbonation being released from the can broke the moment of silence as he placed the beer he brought me on the coffee table. "Drink up! You're behind." He pushed the bottom of my can as I held it to my mouth causing me to spill some beer on myself.

"Hey! Stop it!" I giggled, putting the can down and wiping my chin.

Steven stared at me for a minute and I could feel my face turning red the longer he didn't say anything.

"What?" I asked trying to break the discomfort I felt in the silence.

"You have really nice lips," he said, matter of fact. At a loss for how to respond, I stirred in the anxiety I felt from his words.

"Thanks." It was all I could say. I didn't like this kind of attention and didn't know what to say or do. *Is this just normal chatter?* I asked myself. I really had nothing to compare it to.

"I bet you are a good kisser," Steven's eyes were still focused on my lips and I could tell he wasn't changing the subject any time soon. I thought back to how only hours ago I was with Lucas who had similar thoughts. *Is this what every guy thought about?* Why couldn't I escape men today? What was so wrong with me that people had to think about sex when they were around me? I couldn't help but wonder what made every guy that I met think the same way. I felt even more like an alien for not sharing the same excitement for kissing and contact as the guys I had been around. There had to be something wrong with me, but I didn't quite know what it was.

"Tell you what. You let me kiss those beautiful lips and I won't tell anyone what we've talked about here. Your secrets will be safe with me, and George will never know what you told me. You can come and stay here whenever you want and I will come pick you up." He had moved closer to me on the couch. I sat there frozen.

Steven, seven years older than me, was twenty-one years old. At fourteen, I didn't really understand what he was saying to me, but I could tell that his ideas were more than just suggestions. He was blackmailing me, using my circumstances against me. I wished with all my heart that Melanie would come home any second. I just wanted my sister so badly.

"When is Mel coming home?" My voice was barely above a whisper.

Steven sat back and casually drank his beer. "Oh, she won't be home for another three hours."

My heart sank at the realization that I had to wait three hours for my sister. Three hours that I would spend here with Steven stuck in this apartment not knowing what would happen.

I sunk back into the cushions of the couch and slowly tried to move over to the end of the couch unnoticed. Of course, Steven was very busy noticing me and took my movement as an invitation to advance on me. He crawled up on the couch, pulling me under him. He forced his mouth onto mine, jamming his tongue between the lips he had admired seconds before. My entire being shut down. I felt my heart speed up and my limbs were paralyzed. My throat felt as if I had swallowed rocks and through my fear, I couldn't find a voice to scream out or to say stop. It was like I had lost the ownership of my body and now Steven controlled me like a puppet. I lay there frozen and terrified.

I could hardly breathe as Steven's mouth and tongue pressed against me. He was taking the oxygen right from my lungs. He stopped to look at my face and I can only imagine the expression of fear and terror that he saw.

The second of peace that came over me when he stopped soon disintegrated in a cloud of smoke all around me. He grabbed my legs and pulled me onto the floor, undoing my belt and with it, removing my pants and underwear. I froze, shaking with fear.

"W-what are you doing?" Barely above a whisper, these were the only words that escaped past the rocks that had nestled deep within my throat.

"You'll see," Steven looked down at me. "Don't worry, you're going to like it." He said the words as though we were talking about anything else other than him being on top of me, violating his girlfriend's younger sister.

Thoughts of panic and horror kept flashing through my mind in a terribly painful loop. *What is happening? How did this happen? What have I done? What's wrong with me? Does this happen to everyone?*

Steven was back on top of my half naked body. He had taken off his clothes too and continued to kiss me forcefully. Lifting my shirt, he began to kiss and bite at my breasts and stomach; licking and biting and grabbing at my skin as his hands made their way farther down my torso and between my legs. Tears streamed down the sides of my face and I shut my eyes so tightly, trying to transport myself to any other place than where I was. *What have I done to deserve this life? God, why do you hate me?*

Steven's puckered lips and wanton hands made their way to every part of me. My mind screamed out in violent terror as I lay there motionless, a prisoner of yet another man breaking into my body. I berated myself for not being able to move or speak. *Is this really what people do? Is this what it feels like to be with someone?*

My experiences with Noah, and now Steven, left me feeling even emptier than before I had met them. I was broken. Women were supposed to enjoy these experiences with men, but here I was: ashamed and splintered on the floor. I felt like dying. *What the fuck was wrong with me?* Didn't I want to be loved? Isn't that what I had always wanted? Did me not enjoying *this* mean I was gay?

In a blur between seconds and hours, he was done with what he had wanted to do. Removing his mouth from between my legs, he rose, picking up his clothes and dressing his naked body. "I've got to get ready to pick Mel up from work," he casually said as he made his way to the bathroom. It was as if this encounter was nothing out of the ordinary, and me lying motionless on the living room floor didn't faze him one bit.

I remained paralyzed. Closing my eyes, I imagined myself melting into the carpet below me—the same one that had left rugged burns and piercing scratches on my skin. *Just disappear*, I silently whispered to myself. Only death could leave me free. If I was dead, no man could ever want to know me, let alone touch me. I didn't even want to know me.

The bathroom door closed and the sound of the shower running soon followed.

Melanie returned home from work. As the invisible tears cascaded from my eyes, my body shriveled. I was unsure of what to say, or what to do. With Steven having told her how shook up I was when I called earlier that afternoon, my erratic state was blamed on George. My sister's imagination took over, leading her to the conclusion that it would be best if I spent weekends at her place whenever I could. She called Mildred that week and they both agreed that I should spend most of my weekends with Mel and Steven. I didn't know which devil was worse; I couldn't escape the darkness that followed me.

Instead, I would have to find a way to deal with my new problems. It seemed that no matter how hard I tried to stay on the right path, there were evils along the way that were far stronger than I could fight off.

A dizzying mess of anger, sadness, and the drudgery of my routine of home and school had blurred time. Although it was Steven who had proven himself to be a disgusting monster, it was I who was left with the torment of his transformation. I could feel the hate I had inside of me growing rapidly. I hated my life now more than ever and yearned for an escape. A heavy, poisonous ink stained every part of me. There were days that I wished I could just disappear and wake up in another life, one much different than the one forced upon me. There were days that I wished I wouldn't wake up at all. Perhaps I could disappear into the ether. Perhaps I could disintegrate into nothingness and reappear alongside my mother in an unknown world. What little care I had for my studies vanished—what little care I had for anything was gone. I didn't care if I was stuck at home, I just mostly laid in bed or hid in my closet anyways, and if I were at school, I skipped almost every class. I had as little regard for the world as it seemed to have for me.

My relationship with Mel had become strained in my heart. I couldn't bring myself to tell her what happened. Although I wanted nothing more than to tell her and be free of the burdens of this horrible secret, every time we spoke or spent time together, I was reminded that my truth would make her world a lie. I would rob her of her happy life with Steven, and maybe even make her hate me. It wasn't her fault that everything I touched turned to shit. I couldn't bear to bring her down with me, into a life of sorrow and despair. Melanie was one of the only beautiful things I had in this life, and as much as my heart begged me to confess, my voice betrayed me every time I tried. My big sister, my second mother, Melanie had spent most of her life dedicated to mine and I couldn't destroy the only good thing she had found in the world. Steven was her escape from George; and now, for better or worse, he had become mine too. I had decided to keep this horrible secret buried deep within my soul and under the cover of all the other shame that I carried. I would rather die than hurt my sister. My life was a mistake, a comedy of errors that seemed to get worse the older I got.

Chapter Eighteen
Age 14: Inside Job

Springtime came and ninth grade was almost over. School had gone from an escape to an annoyance to me. Giselle was hardly there and spent most of her time skipping class to hang out with her boyfriend. Most of the friends we had made together had either left, gone to juvenile hall, or had become drug dealers or prostitutes. My beloved ex-boyfriend, Karim, was now just a memory. It was as though we didn't know each other at all.

I wandered the halls from class to class with no direction or intentions. Occasionally an old friend would appear and we would ditch class, ending up wandering the city streets bored, or at someone's place smoking and drinking.

A classmate, Nina, came by the school to pick up some assignments that she needed to complete. She was drop-dead gorgeous, always dressed as though she had just stepped off the runway. Her creamy mocha skin and incredibly striking features complemented her petite physique and long dark hair. Underneath layers of eyeliner and mascara, her large, almond eyes shone. Her figure was years ahead of her and all the boys in school couldn't even pretend not to notice her; she paralyzed them with her sexual prowess and feminine energy.

"Hey, Iman!" She saw me walking down the hallway.

"Nina!" I ran up to her and gave her a big hug. "Oh my God, how are you? I haven't seen you in forever!" She was always so kind to me. I had missed seeing her for our lunch hour commiseration.

"I know," she smiled. "I've been working like crazy, and trying to finish school through correspondence." She pushed a loose lock of hair behind her ears. "I came to pick up some assignments. How are you? What's new?"

"Oh, you know, same shit," I laughed. "Just trying to finish school and get the fuck out of this shit-hole. I can't wait to be done with junior high. It's lame here now and Giselle and the old crew are hardly around anymore." When the words left my mouth, I realized how much I missed Giselle and feeling like I was part of something. Her friendship meant so much to me.

"Yeah, it's crazy how things have changed!" she smiled again. Nina had always been so kind; it felt nice to be in her warm presence again. "We should hang out. What are you doing right now? I have to head back to work but you should come by and keep me company."

"Yeah for sure. Let's get the fuck out of here." I needed zero excuses to leave that school.

Nina got what she needed from the office and we both walked out of the school, heading toward the bus stop. Our destination wasn't far from my house, which was nice—I wouldn't have far to go to make it home in time to make it look like I left school after the last bell.

We got off the bus and started walking up the familiar streets, toward Nina's workplace. My mind buzzed with curiosity. I still hadn't discovered what her job was. I asked some questions and she seemed to avoid answering me directly and just kept talking about how amazing it was and how much money she was making for hardly any work at all. My mind scanned my memory of the neighbourhood for a clue of what she might be doing.

We stopped in front of a house, only blocks away from my apartment. I was confused, I thought we were going to her work. It was an unimpressive old building that appeared to be two storeys; it's white paint was chipping, leaving brown scars beneath the peels. Nina let herself in like she had done it a million times before. She directed me inside, and I followed in after her.

We walked into the front entrance which had a small area filled with shoes. The kitchen was to the left and there was a living room to the right. I couldn't see anyone but I could hear music coming from downstairs.

"I'll be right back, okay? I gotta get ready for work. Just make yourself comfortable and give me like ten minutes."

She disappeared downstairs and I went and sat in the living room and lit a cigarette. The living room had a big window with a view of the city street, there was snow covering the grass on all the lawns. The inside of the living room looked comfortable enough; the couches looked only lightly worn but still comfortable and nicer than most of the houses I had been in. The décor was very bare and it didn't quite look like a home or a business. The ashtray on the coffee table was littered with different coloured cigarette butts, evidence that I wasn't the only stranger to pass through since the last time it had been emptied. I thought I heard sounds coming from downstairs and I was wracking my brain trying to understand what Nina could possibly be doing working here? What kind of home business was this?

Nina emerged from the basement moments later dressed in pink lingerie. My eyes bugged out of my head as I blinked at her trying to take it all in.

"Wh-what are you wearing?" I asked her, completely shocked and embarrassed at the same time.

"I gotta dress like this for work," she looked down at her pink-laced outfit.

"Are you a hooker?" The words left me before I could pull them back in. "Sorry, I mean…you know what I mean."

It was too late. I could feel her shame as my words slapped her across the face. She looked down and then almost as though she was convincing herself of her choices all over again, she looked me dead in the eyes.

"I know what it looks like, but it's really not that bad! I got, like, $40 for giving someone a blowjob." Her shame was quickly replaced with pride. I could see that she was genuinely impressed with how she was making money.

My stomach tightened. I couldn't wait to get out of that house. I didn't want to stick around for when the customers were expected to arrive. Why on earth would she bring me to this place? Did she really think that this was normal?

I picked up my backpack and stood up from my chair, "I am really happy for you, Nina. I gotta get going but I am so glad I got to see you. Let's hang out soon okay?"

"You're leaving already?" A quizzical look formed on her brow. "Just stay and hang out! I could get you a job if you want. It really isn't as bad as you think…after a few times you don't even think anything of it." She paused, waiting for a response. "I cried the first time," she continued, "But now I just act like it is any other job, you know?"

She looked at me, and for the first time that day I realized that I didn't know at all what she meant. My fourteen-year-old self couldn't pretend or play along with the reality or unreality that she was living. We were just teenagers, and I knew my life was messed up, but my entire body rejected her words and this house. I wanted to run far away from the entire experience.

I looked at her standing there in her lingerie, barely a teenager, entertaining grown men and my heart ached for her. I didn't know what Nina had been through in her life, but I could only imagine that she felt broken just like me. I wanted so much to take her with me and find a way for us to figure out this life together, but I knew that I couldn't save Nina. I was having a hard enough time just trying to save myself, and though I was certainly no expert at happiness or what I wanted in life, I knew very deeply that I didn't want to give blowjobs for a living.

She looked at me and nodded her head in resignation, "Alright, well, we should hang out soon. I get paid next week. Let's do something, okay?"

I smiled and agreed. It was a lie of course. I had no intention of ever seeing Nina again. It was bittersweet; never in my wildest dreams would I have guessed that Nina, the girl who sat next to me in class when we were bitchy thirteen-year-olds, was now holed up in a shitty house as a prostitute. I could never imagine doing that no matter how horrible my life was. I hated the few intimate experiences I had already had and couldn't even fathom doing it for a living.

As I ran home, I thanked God that my life hadn't taken the same turn that Nina's had. I struggled often with gratitude in my life because of how desolate it felt, but as I felt the cold air on my face and heard the snow crunch under my boots, I thanked my mom for always being by my side and guiding me. I knew she was never too far away and often felt her presence surrounding me, and this was one of those moments.

The next day I arrived at school and I could see Giselle across the street from the bus stop talking to some friends. My heart skipped a beat and I ran toward her squealing her name. She saw me and came running to greet me in a giant hug and shrieks of joy. I hadn't seen her very much the past few weeks and I missed her terribly.

"GISELLE!!" I yelped. "Where have you been? Oh my God, I am so happy to see you. Why did you leave me?" I asked and playfully punched her in the arm.

"OW!" She grabbed her arm, laughing as she gently yanked my ponytail.

I had missed my friend so much. I wished I could tell her everything that had happened to me lately. Flirting between happiness at her reappearance and anger at her absence, I knew that if she were with me none of the horrible things would have happened.

Her smile quickly vanished as she looked me directly into the eyes, "I need to talk to you." My heart skipped a beat. "Can you skip class?"

I skipped the day before, and to avoid getting in trouble, the least I could do was show up for attendance. I looked back at Giselle, my eyes scanning hers. I decided I could skip the first two classes of the day but I would head back before lunch and tell my teacher I was sick or something. I wanted to hang out with Giselle more than anything in the world.

Catching the next bus that came our way, we headed to West Edmonton Mall, a common backdrop for our weekends, where we would wander through the halls, passing time. It was perfect: there was so much to see and tons of places to sit and do nothing. We barely had any money, but when we did, we spent it on photo booth pictures and best friends forever necklaces. Lately, we had been sporting half of a yin and yang pendant that we had picked up last month.

We headed toward the back of the bus and sat next to each other in a two-person seat.

"I'm pregnant." Giselle stared straight ahead, focused on the invisible head in the seat in front of us.

"What?" I wasn't sure what I had heard, or if the words came from Giselle's mouth at all.

"I'm pregnant, Iman." She turned and looked at me, "I took, like, ten tests and I'm pregnant."

"Holy shit. Seriously? Wha…" My voice trailed off and I didn't know what to say.

"Yeah. Seriously. What the *fuck* am I supposed to do? I can't have a baby, Iman," she stammered. "I'm fourteen years old." Giselle's eyes were filled with concern. I realized that I had never seen her worry before, she was always the brave one.

"What are you going to do? Does Jorge know?" Too many questions bubbled up for me to be of any help. I paused, taking a minute to process what she was going through.

"Not yet. I don't know what to do. Maybe I can get rid of it or maybe it won't stick, you know?" She was looking at me for guidance, but I really didn't know.

We spent a couple of hours wandering the mall and talking about her options and what she could do. We didn't get any closer to answers by the end of our talk, but I knew Giselle felt better for having at least told me. Somehow, we each knew how to show up for each other even if we didn't have the slightest clue how to help. In our crazy worlds of constant chaos, it felt good to know that there was at least one person on the planet who had your back.

Giselle and I took the bus back to school and parted ways in the hallway heading to our different classes.

I waited until the bell rang and then entered my next class, slinking in a seat at the back corner of the room, I hoped no one would notice I had been missing all morning and the previous afternoon.

Chapter Nineteen

Age 14: Old Haunts

Unfortunately, as usual, luck was not on my side. As soon as the teacher walked into the classroom I was called to the front of the class and sent to the principal's office. My absence was very much noticed and, as punishment, I was suspended for the rest of the week. I wasn't exactly sure how my punishment for missing school was missing more school, but I felt my stomach turn at the thought of having to tell Mildred and George about my suspension.

I wished I could get Giselle out of her class to tell her what just happened. We should have skipped the entire day and hung out if I was just going to get sent home and miss my assignments anyways. I left, wandering the city and taking the bus to different terminals with no idea what I was doing. There was one thing I was sure of, of course: I didn't want to go home. I knew that what waited for me there would not feel as free as roaming aimlessly throughout the city.

My heart felt heavy as I walked up to the apartment. I knew that I would for sure get grounded for getting suspended and wouldn't be allowed out for a long time. I walked through the door and Mildred was sitting in her chair smoking and watching one of the few channels we got on the television. She looked over at me through a cloud of smoke, "How was your day?"

"I got suspended." I walked over to her and handed her the paper that the school gave me explaining my punishment.

"What in the hell did you do now?" Mildred snatched the paper out of my hands and scanned it quickly.

"You little shit," her wiry voice pierced the air. "Get your ass to your room until George comes home and we figure out what to do with you." She slammed the paper down on the small table beside the chair and forcefully extinguished her cigarette.

I rolled my eyes and made my way to my bedroom. I had become all but immune to how she spoke to me, expecting nothing less than drama and anger when telling her anything. She never asked me why I did anything. She only highlighted the worst parts of me.

I sat in my room until I was summoned to the living room to receive my punishment.

George was sitting on the couch and didn't even look up at me as I entered the room. "Sit down," his voice boomed in its usual growl.

"I don't even need to tell you that skipping school is wrong. You are grounded for a month. No TV, no phone, no friends over, no going to your friends. You're not to leave this house unless you're at school. You understand?" He looked up at me with his bloodshot eyes.

"Yeah," I stared back at him in disgust. How dare he try to show *me* some sort of moral fibre. His very presence disgusted me.

Never one not to share her two cents, Mildred piped in, "Starting Monday I am going to call the school every day to make sure you are there, you understand? You better get your ass to every fucking class or you'll be dead fucking meat."

I knew she was lying, since she didn't have the discipline to get a job or pay the phone bill, never mind make a call every day to check on me.

I lowered my eyes to my lap, seething in anger. I loathed them so much and could not understand how such morons could oversee anything, let alone my fate.

The next few days of being a prisoner in my own home was devastating. As much as I skipped class, I needed the escape from this apartment—from these people. I spent almost every moment in my room, writing, reading, or hanging my head out the window smoking. I still had my mother's small television in my closet that no one knew was there, and I would wait until Mildred and George were sleeping to watch it. I would set my alarm for the middle of the night and sneak into the kitchen to grab whatever food and drink I could to keep in my room, avoiding having to leave my sanctuary unless absolutely necessary. I did everything I could to avoid being reminded that I lived with such idiots. Finally, Monday rolled around and my suspension was lifted. I had never been so excited to go to class. I could hardly sleep the night before and left the apartment as soon as I could.

The next couple of months I did my best to go to class on time and get my homework done. I finished the rest of my punishment with as little resistance as possible and I longed for summer time which was just weeks away. Although there would be no school, the weather would be beautiful and I could spend all day out of the house, away from Mildred and George. My relationship with them was nonexistent, which was better than the alternative. To them, I didn't exist—unless they were drunk, of course. But I had learned to manage them, and now that I wasn't grounded anymore, my sister had fought to have me spend weekends at her house again. I still couldn't bring myself to tell her what Steven did and although I didn't want to ever see him again, I didn't want to stay at the apartment either. The next time I saw him I was extremely guarded and shot daggers at him when he looked at me. I could see his regret written all over his face and at the way he feigned a smile and looked at me with concern. I didn't care if he was sorry. I had more than earned my freedom to be in their apartment and I had nothing left that he could take from me anyways. Luckily, Steven didn't try anything else with me and I made sure that I was never alone with him.

Disguised in baggy clothes, Giselle's pregnancy had advanced and she was growing bigger by the day. She still hadn't told her parents and they thought that she was just gaining weight. By now, Jorge knew, but he and Giselle still hadn't come up with a plan to tell their families. I worried for her, and I could tell that this was all too much for her to handle. We did our best to act as though it wasn't happening, hardly mentioning all the changes that she was going through. Like so many things in our lives, it seemed easier for us to process things if we just acted like they weren't happening.

When June rolled around, we had created a list of summer plans and dreams. Giselle and I would finally be finished with junior high for good and entering high school in the fall. I would be turning fifteen soon, and that meant that I only had to wait one more year until I could legally move out of Mildred and George's guardianship. That was my biggest dream. I would do anything to be free of people who didn't care about me; people who didn't care if I ate or had new shoes; people who only cared about the cheque that they received from the government. They didn't care about my health; they didn't care that I was too young to watch a crowd of belligerent drunks doing drugs and collapsing on the floor. No one was there to protect me from George's visits in the middle of the night, or Mildred's temper that regularly resulted in me being hit to the floor, bruised inside and out.

There was so much to look forward to once I broke free from the hell I had inherited from my father's choices. I couldn't wait to see what waited for me. Often, I would pray to God and tell Him that I knew that this horrible childhood must mean that there was an incredibly beautiful adulthood waiting for me. I rested my faith in the fact that I had suffered enough for this lifetime and whatever was beyond this hell had to be paradise.

As ninth-grade graduation approached, my classmates buzzed with excitement about what they would wear and their summer plans. I couldn't help but hope and pray that Mildred and George remained oblivious that there was an event to celebrate our junior high graduation. The only thing worse than being with them in private was being with them in public. I was so glad that we didn't have regular phone service at the apartment, and that Mildred and George had zero involvement in my education. Life, as overwhelmingly miserable as it was, was looking up.

I made my way toward the smoker's bathroom. As I sat in my stall dragging on my cigarette, I heard someone come in. I paused. Usually, this was a secluded area of the school—no one came here. My heart pounded in my chest as I quickly flushed my smoke down the toilet, leaving the washroom in a hurried blaze, brushing past a girl I didn't recognize. I hid around the corner and waited until she came out of the bathroom. I watched her walk directly toward the principal's office and hoped she would keep walking past it. I followed her anxiously willing her with my eyes to change direction.

Within minutes the principal came out of the office and saw me standing there.

"Iman, were you just smoking in the girl's room?"

"No!" I yelped. "She's lying, I wasn't even in there." I was a terrible liar.

Mr. Johnson went down the hall himself and poked his head into the girl's washroom and quickly turned back and started walking toward me.

"It smells like smoke in there, Iman. Come to my office." He was seething and could hardly look at me.

He was normally one of the kindest men ever and had been very lenient to me over the years. He had always turned a blind eye with much of my skipping until he had no choice to suspend me months ago, and hadn't even gotten me in trouble when I had come to school drunk. But, this time I could tell that he had had enough.

"Listen, I'm sorry. I don't know why I did that. I…" I started rambling an apology but Mr. Johnson cut me off before I could finish.

"I don't want to hear it, Iman!" His voice was cold and distant, dripping with anger. "I am *done* covering for you. I have gone out of my way protecting you, and turning a blind eye ever since you came to this school in the seventh grade, and this is how you repay me?" He paused, letting the silence fill the room, suffocating me. "You smoke in the bathroom? Why couldn't you just go outside?" I was familiar with the exasperated look on his face. It seemed I had a knack for bringing people to their breaking point.

"I don't know. I wasn't really thinking I just did it." I was consumed with shame for turning one of the few people on my side against me.

"I am sorry to do this, Iman." He let out a sigh, "but I think it's best if you leave and don't come back for the rest of the year."

I felt as though I had been slapped in the face.

"WHAT?" I was in disbelief. "You're expelling me? Seriously? F-for smoking…that is ridiculous." I felt my face get hot and my shame was replaced with outrage.

"I'm sorry, but you leave me no choice. I can't very well let you do whatever you want. You obviously don't want to be here and you are disrupting the other students."

We sat in silence for a few moments and I could feel the tears welling up in my eyes. I didn't say another word. I got up and stormed out of the office and lit a cigarette as I walked toward the front doors.

Fuck this place. Fuck him and fuck everyone. I never needed anyone and I wasn't going to start now.

Once again, I was grounded. Only this time, much worse: they had taken away my sanctuary. Mildred and George had filled my days with tasks that forced me to leave my room. Keeping me busy with dishes and rolling cigarettes, sending me to the store to buy what little groceries we could afford, it was torturous to be stuck with them and not have privacy. Although I loved being outside, when I returned, I would be forced to sit across the table from the disgusting pedophile George. I just wanted to be alone in my room writing or reading…or even just sleeping. I had tried to sleep as much as possible to pass the time.

Summer had started and I was still serving my time in hell. With the warm weather, perfect for doing what they do best, Mildred and George began to party harder which, in turn, resulted in them being more lenient with me. New drunken and strung-out faces filled our apartment as summer kicked into full gear, and as much as I hated being surrounded by drunks and drug addicts, it took the attention from me a little bit, which I liked.

As soon as I was no longer grounded, I made plans to stay at Giselle's for the weekend. I couldn't believe my eyes when I saw her and how big her belly had gotten. She had finally had to tell her parents and Jorge told his as well.

Their families had come to some agreement that Giselle would keep the baby and they would all work together to raise it.

Giselle said that her family took the news surprisingly well and began treating her better because of it. She was no longer subject to her stepdad's beatings since she was pregnant, so life got a little more bearable for her. She completed the school year and would go to tenth grade until she delivered the baby. Then she would finish high school through correspondence.

I was happy that she had found some peace and had her family's support, although it still didn't really register that she was having a baby or what that would mean exactly. What I did know is that I would be sad not being in the same school as my best friend.

Ever since we had known each other, whenever we would hang out, we would meet each other halfway between our two homes and then we would always walk the other home at the end of our weekends. Falling in line with our ritual, Giselle and I headed toward my apartment when the weekend had come to an end. A few blocks into our journey, the summer sun blaring, I turned to Giselle as she slowed down. Her face was flushed, her breathing heavy.

"I need to sit down for a minute," she apologized.

"Are you okay?" I had never seen her so physically exhausted before.

"Yeah, I just need a minute." She was holding her bulging stomach and trying to control her breathing.

After a few minutes, we kept walking, but had hardly made it to the end of the block when Giselle cried out, "I can't do this, I need to go home."

I had never seen Giselle in such pain. "Are you okay?" I panicked, staring at her belly. "Do you want me to walk you back?"

"No, it's okay, I just can't walk you home. I'm sorry. I need to go home." She looked so uncomfortable. I hated that I couldn't ease her burden.

"It's okay. Just go home and I'll call you later, okay?" I gave her a big hug and watched her walk slowly back toward her house.

It felt so foreign to watch Giselle in such pain, to see her swelling belly get bigger every time we saw each other. She was changing, her body was changing, and our friendship would have to change right along with it.

I thought about my sweet friend all the way home and hoped that she was okay and that whatever our futures held, that we would find a way through them together.

Preparing for grade ten ignited a flame fueled by excitement and anxiety. Growing comfortable in the last three years in one school, I began to panic at the thought of once again being labelled as the new girl. Not only that, I was finally entering high school—a world of new beginnings—and I would be starting from the bottom. Since not everyone from my grade nine class would be attending Glacier Springs High School, I would know even fewer people.

My one saving grace was that Giselle would be with me until she gave birth. Although I didn't know if we would be lucky enough to be in the same classes, it would be comforting to have her there—even if it was just until November.

Ben and Elizabeth took me shopping for new clothes, instilling me with a huge sense of relief and joy. I wanted nothing more than to fit in seamlessly at school and not receive any unwanted attention. It had always felt as though I stuck out no matter where I went. I couldn't even blend in at home. And tenth grade could make or break me since school was my now only escape since Giselle had found out she was pregnant. I barely even had my best friend anymore. Soon she would have a baby to worry about, and the preparation and reality of her looming motherhood had already taken up all her free time.

Making new friends was my only option if I wanted to fit in at Glacier Springs and get through the tenth grade. My only hope was that playing the new kid would be easier there than it had been in the past.

Mildred stood in the kitchen in her pale pink robe as she made her coffee. She was up earlier than usual.

"Morning!" Mildred's voice was unusually chipper and her hair was a mess.

"Morning!" I replied, my tone a blend of excitement and nervousness. Dressed in a pair of brand new jeans and a long-sleeved black shirt I had bought with Ben and Elizabeth, I felt unstoppable.

"You wanna coffee?" she looked up from the sugar bowl briefly to look at me.

I paused. Mildred had never allowed me to drink coffee before, let alone offered it to me. It was as though we both felt a little different that morning, as though I had grown up overnight. I accepted her kind gesture and we sat at the table together and made small talk and drank our coffee. In those moments, it was hard to remember the usual animosity we had for each other.

Mildred gave me a big hug and told me to have a great day. I felt so special and like we had passed a barrier that was between us only the night before. Her vulnerability and kindness were so rare that I briefly wondered if something was wrong before I grabbed my coat and backpack. Ignoring the fleeting thought, I ran to the same bus stop I had gone to since we moved into the apartment almost three years ago. I smirked at myself, *I was fifteen and ready to conquer high school.*

As I boarded the bus, my stomach twisted into intricate knots. I took a deep breath, saying a silent prayer to see at least a few familiar faces at school. When the bus pulled up to the building it struck me how Glacier Springs High School was so much bigger than my old school. Although it was only two storeys of brick and glass, it spread out far across the property and had to have been at least double the size of my old school.

With nothing to lose, I walked into the building and made my way to the office to find out where I would be going for my classes. I was quickly assigned a locker and given my schedule for the semester, and began to wander the hallways in search of my locker. As I made my way through the crowded halls, it was like I was a needle in a haystack. I was shocked at how many people there were in the hallway, how much older they all looked, and the array of cultures within my view. Up until junior high, I was always the odd one out—the only non-Caucasian person in any of my classes. But, as I looked around, I saw every skin tone and hair type; people wearing hijabs and Arabic being spoken as a group of gorgeous girls giggled and chatted on their way to class. There was a breathtakingly handsome group of boys with the most beautiful dark skin, dressed in crisp new clothes and the whitest sneakers. As they passed me I couldn't help but stare. I had never seen so many hot guys in one place and my teenage heart was beating out of my chest as my eyes followed their every step.

"Hey, Sticks!" One of the boys called out to me before he and his group of friends burst out laughing.

"Oh shit, did you see how skinny that girl was? She looks like she has twigs for legs." A volcano of hysteria erupted as each boy turned to look at me and confirm just how skinny I was.

Walking just steps behind them, three beautiful, voluptuous blonde girls each turned to look me up and down and smirk before tossing their hair, snickering to each other as they kept walking past me. My heart sinking with each step I took, the all too familiar feeling of my own alien hideousness presented itself. I suddenly felt naked in my new outfit. What was I thinking, wearing fitted clothes on my malnourished frame? In that moment, I wished I could disappear off the face of the earth. I would never be glamorous, or perfect, or a woman; I was destined to stick out with my untamed afro hair and my hip bones that burst through my skin.

Finally, I arrived at my locker and found my way to each class. When lunch approached, I wandered out to the courtyard for a cigarette and saw Giselle talking to a group of people. I ran up to her and tugged at her ponytail. She turned around and gave me the biggest hug in the world. We squealed and gossiped about our classes and the people we had met. Regardless of her efforts, her large belly showed beneath her baggy clothing. She only had two months left before she would deliver the baby. Our fifteen-year-old selves could not fully comprehend the magnitude of what it meant to be a mother and to have a child. But that same ignorance, paired with resilience, was what had gotten us this far in life. We didn't always understand the situations that were forced upon us, but we always conquered them. Our fiery spirits knew that whatever the world had in store for us, we would overcome it. We might suffer, we might struggle, but we would eventually come out of whatever hell we endured. It was this tenacity that made me love Giselle so much because without ever speaking the words, we each knew that we would fight with our lives for the other.

The first few weeks of high school were awkward and filled with insecurity. Not being in any of Giselle's classes had brought the familiar feelings of isolation to the surface. I felt so far away from her. From time to time I would see familiar faces, but never a face of someone I had been close to. Lunch hour had become my most feared time of the day. I was starving— which apparently was very physically evident. Luckily, the cafeteria was stocked with hot food, which caused huge excitement and change from my diet of bread, crackers, and peanut butter. The moment I stepped into the cafeteria, the succulent scent of deep-fried food hit my nostrils, causing my stomach to gurgle with anticipation. I looked around as the entire school made their way to either line up for food or meet up with friends at a table. I was almost paralyzed with fear as I scanned the room wondering what to do next and where I should sit.

With an order of French fries and gravy on my tray, I walked toward the endless sea of tables, scanning furiously trying to find somewhere to sit. Suddenly, I heard my name, "Hey, Iman!"

I turned my head and looked behind me to find an all too familiar face looking at me.

"H-hey, Julia." I was both surprised and somewhat relieved to see Julia standing there. She and I hadn't really gotten off on the right foot since she screamed at me on my first day of seventh grade after she thought I was staring at her boyfriend. Luckily, she was nothing but kind to me after Becky stood up for me the next day. We hadn't really crossed paths since that incident as she kept a fair distance and I didn't go out of my way to be her friend either. However, seeing her standing in a room filled with strangers made me feel so happy to know at least one person and not feel completely out of place.

We smiled at each other and I knew that whatever awkwardness was between us vanished and was replaced with pure comfort in not being alone.

"Do you want to eat lunch together?" she asked nervously.

"Yeah, for sure." I was equally as uncomfortable in my own skin.

We brought our trays to a table and began talking about how different school was and the new classes we were in. We reminisced about our wild junior high days and the antics we got up to back when we were "kids" a few months before.

Julia still dressed provocatively and was wearing a very small black shirt that exposed her midriff paired with skin-tight black leggings. On her feet she wore black, chunky-heeled ankle boots. She somehow made it work with her curvy figure, and I admired the courage she had to dress that way. I was dying of discomfort wearing full sleeves and jeans. Of course, I didn't have curves. I was all bone and no meat, not to mention the fact that I hadn't developed breasts yet.

As Julia and I laughed and chatted the lunch hour away, we instantly forgot that any quarrel had occurred between us. She even brought it up again shyly, apologizing, and I brushed it off with instant forgiveness. I had never been so glad to have a friend to navigate the unchartered territory of high school with.

We quickly became inseparable, meeting before school, at all our breaks and spare classes, and even started to hang out after school. Giselle was at school less and less and I was deeply grateful to have a friend who made my days much more fun.

As time wore on, I succumbed to the ebb and flow of my new school. As I began to make new friends, I noticed that the kids in high school hung out mostly in groups based on their heritage. I would see groups of Asians, Latinos, Afro-Canadians, Caucasians, and Arabs. Although it was uncommon to see the groups mixing, every now and again you would see the odd one or two people in a group where they were a visible minority. I wondered which grouping I would fit into. Though I was Arab, I never really fit in anywhere—I had mostly been raised by white people. My family was African, and although I took after my mother's light skin, my brothers had beautiful chocolate colouring. I had never been to a school that housed so much ethnic diversity, and although I was very excited to no longer stick out like a sore thumb, I also realized how even more confused I was when faced with so many options. Where did I fit in?

I knew how important it was to belong, and with intense desire, I wanted to be with people that accepted me and had things in common with me. But since I felt more like I was from another planet anyways, I decided that I would try to make friends with as many people as I could.

Eventually, the Lebanese girls in my cooking class and I became friends and I loved hearing them speak Arabic. They didn't understand how my parents could be from Tunisia and I couldn't speak the language, but I didn't bother explaining all the wild and heartbreaking events that had robbed me of my family, my heritage, and my language. I didn't want anyone to know of the horrible things that I had lived through, so I just never talked about my family or went into any details about my mom. People assumed I lived with my parents and I didn't correct them. It was somehow easier to just stay quiet and not call any more attention to myself.

I loved having a group of girlfriends who reminded me of my own family from so long ago. They made me feel a sense of belonging I hadn't found before and I loved their friendship. Even though I knew I didn't fully belong, when I was with them in the hallway between classes where we laughed about boys or parents, I could forget that the life we had in common had slipped away from me long before high school.

As I walked to class I heard a familiar voice just behind me. I turned to look and I saw Karim just steps away from me with a couple of his friends. He had grown in the last few years. He looked so different, yet still as handsome as he had always been. His face was covered with specks of facial hair and he had grown taller. Perhaps the most surprising thing of all was how he was dressed. Seeing him in jeans and a T-shirt was odd since he always, *always*, wore track pants and a white shirt. We used to joke that he loved basketball so much that he was always dressed for it.

My heart pounded faster in my chest and I looked at him hoping he would see me. So much had changed in the past years, and yet looking at him felt like coming home to an old friend. I wanted to tell him how much I'd missed him and how sorry I was for breaking his heart. I wondered if maybe now that we were both in high school and more mature that we could be friends again and laugh as we used to.

As though feeling the heat of my eyes burning into his face, he looked up from his conversation and saw me. I smiled and his face lit up. I could see he was surprised and slightly caught off guard but he was still polite and didn't look away this time as he had so many before. We walked toward each other and awkwardly said hello.

"How are you?" I beamed at him with the biggest smile on my face.

"I'm great," his face still turned red when he spoke to me, and his eyes darted from mine to the floor. "Just getting used to the new school and my teachers, y'know?"

"I almost didn't recognize you! I mean, you look so different. I've never seen you in jeans…Are you still playing basketball?" I was instantly embarrassed at the string of thoughts that poured out of my mouth without me first checking them. I was so nervous.

"Oh yeah, that was a long time ago. I used to be such a dork." He laughed and I could see his face and body language change and grow less friendly. "I needed to grow up and not dress like such a dweeb."

"You weren't a dweeb," my thoughts trailed off and I could feel the sadness of our breakup flooding back into my memory. How I wished I could just say all the things that I wanted to and let Karim know just how much he meant to me and had always meant to me—that he hadn't done anything wrong and it was just me and the giant fucking brick wall that I had built around me so no one could hurt me because everyone always hurt me.

Before I could say anything else, a beautiful, petite, dark-haired girl with big brown eyes appeared from behind Karim and threw her arms around him. He looked down at her and his whole face lit up and he pulled her under his arm and kissed her passionately on the forehead.

He quickly forgot about me standing there and as they walked away he called back, "I'll catch you later!"

I turned and walked away as fast as I could, running into the washroom and locking myself in a stall to silently sob. I felt so stupid. *I'll never think about him again,* I vowed to myself, trying to cheer myself up by remembering that I was the one who hurt him first. My efforts backfired, somehow making me feel worse. I wished so much that there was someone who would love me so hard and never ever want to let me go. I prayed that a beautiful man would come and save me from the horrible life I was destined to be a part of and whisk me away to my own Happily Ever After.

Days had passed since my encounter with Karim and I had finally regained my composure. As I headed to my locker, Amina, one of my new friends, stopped me.

"Hey, Iman," she said. I looked up at her and smiled. She quickly looked down before raising her eyes to meet mine once again.

"Um, are you the same Iman whose father killed her mother years ago?" she looked at me with shame in her face at asking the question, but as though she wasn't asking to embarrass me.

"Wh-who told you that?" I stammered. Her question had taken me aback. I had tried to keep the horrors of my past cloaked in secrecy, but regardless of my efforts, the truth had outrun me.

"Well…I'm sorry to pry," she began. "It's just I was telling my mom about school and I said that you were one of my friends. She asked about you and said that some friends of our family once looked after a little girl for a while after a tragedy happened and she and her brothers were orphaned. So, um… is that you?"

The lump in my throat had almost choked me. With my mouth paralyzed, all I could do was nod. Everything she said brought a flood of memories and it was taking all my strength to hold my tears back. I remembered having to live with the people she spoke of and the humiliation of sleeping on the floor and how they treated me like a dog came rushing back into my brain. They took my things, my pictures of my mom, and what little money I had. I stood frozen in front of Amina as she searched my face for a reaction.

"Look, I'm so sorry to bring this up. I promise I won't tell anyone. I just wanted to give you this phone number. They want you to call them." She shoved a crumpled piece of loose-leaf paper into my hand and gave me a hug before she walked off.

I shoved the paper deep into my pocket and made my way to my next class.

When I got back home I went to my room and dug out the crumpled piece of paper and unfolded it and smoothed it out against my thigh with my hands. I stared at the number for a long time wondering what they wanted. Why hadn't they thought of me before now? If they cared so much why didn't they keep in touch for the past eight years?

I walked out of my bedroom and into the kitchen where George was reading and Mildred was in the living room watching TV.

"What are you looking at?" She seemed annoyed by my presence instantly.

"Do you remember the family that I stayed with after my mom died? Well, one of my friends at school said they were looking for me and gave me this." I handed her the piece of paper.

She snatched it out of my hand and inspected it very closely before looking up at me, "Who gave this to you?"

"Just some girl that is in my class. I guess she was telling her parents about school and mentioned me and they asked if it was the same Iman." I suddenly regretted telling her.

She looked at me and then at the paper. "You are not *ever* going to contact these people. Do you understand?" She tore the paper into shreds as she looked me in the eye. "I got you. *I* fought for you, and they don't get to fucking contact you!"

Tiny pieces of paper fluttered around as Mildred's face grew red. I looked to the ground as she continued to shred the sheet of loose leaf long after the number was unsalvageable.

"What's your problem?" I snarled. I didn't see why she got to choose who I contacted or not or why she was freaking out so much.

"You're my fucking problem!" she barked. "You have no idea what I did to get you, and I will *not* let these people just come in and act like nothing happened. Nobody wanted you. I helped you when *no one even wanted you.* You're so fucking ungrateful, Iman!"

Surprised by her own words and her lost temper, Mildred picked up the tiny remnants of the phone number and threw them in the kitchen garbage.

When she came back to the living room she calmly sat down, lit a cigarette and picked up her yarn and knitting needles.

"Iman, never talk to that girl at school again. She's bad news and those people don't give a shit about you." She didn't look up at me when she spoke and just continued knitting until I got up from the couch and made my way back to my room.

What a mistake it was to tell Mildred anything. Her emotions were an unpredictable rollercoaster that could go unhinged at any moment. I couldn't understand her anger. Contacting the family that had taken me in all those years ago and treated me like nothing more than an animal was never my agenda, but I wanted to make that decision on my own. It was as though what I wanted never mattered.

By the time October rolled around, I felt like I knew my way around school. Getting lost on my way to class was a rarity, I had friends to eat lunch with and even did my homework and got good grades. I had finally settled into life as a high-schooler. But with that newfound comfort came new challenges: I had developed my first high school crush.

Eric was a year older than me and in the eleventh grade. We had met in the hallway at lunch while our groups of friends were chatting together. He was tall, dark, and very handsome with a smile that lit up his entire face. I loved the way he looked at me and how I felt like nothing else existed when we talked. He was so funny, smart, and very sweet. He also was very well spoken and polite, with impeccable manners. I began to look forward to seeing him every day, praying that I would bump into him between classes or at lunch hour. When he walked passed me on the way to his next class, he would always smile or nudge me playfully while asking me how I was, or say my name like he was an announcer—"*IIIIIImmmmaaaaaan Boussssaaaaaada*"— and I would laugh shamelessly at everything he said.

With my science textbook in my arms, Julia and I made our way to our lockers after class. A smile spanned across my face as I saw Eric walking by with one of his friends.

"Iman!" he chimed. His eyes lit up when he saw me and it made my legs feel weak, "How are you?"

"Hey, Eric," I smiled. "I'm great. How are you?" As usual, I melted into butter when he spoke to me. I couldn't imagine a more beautiful boy than him.

"Do you think we could talk on the phone sometime?" he asked shyly while pulling gently at my arm.

My heart pounded. *A boy likes me,* I excitedly thought to myself. It was a dream come true.

"Yeah," I muttered, fearful that my excitement would show. "I'd like that. What's your number?"

Pulling out a pen, he reached toward me, grabbing my textbook to scrawl his number onto the inside cover.

"Thanks," I smirked. "I'll talk to you later."

Julia and I casually walked away, waiting until we were out of earshot before rejoicing in celebratory squeals and jumps. I felt like I could run laps around the moon, like I had just won at life. A boy liked me, and that meant I was special and that I existed—that maybe someone cared about me.

That night I asked George if I could use his cell phone, knowing that we hadn't had a phone line for months. Unless I wanted to go use a payphone, I would have no choice. Under his instruction to make the call quickly, I took his large phone to my room and practiced what I would say in the mirror a couple of times before I called Eric.

"Hello," his voice came through the receiver. I almost choked on my words but quickly regained my composure. Just as he was in the hallways at school, he was sweet and friendly. Our topics of conversation knew no bounds. He talked about his family and friends, and we discussed Michael Jackson—his favourite musician—comparing our favourite songs and music videos. Basking in his kindness, I was overjoyed. He was kind, sweet, and funny. Although he was oblivious to this, he was the best part of my day, and it wasn't because I was infatuated with him, but because no one in my life ever bothered to ask me what I thought, what I liked, or made the effort to make me laugh. He was very kind and I liked how fun he was and how nice he was to me. For the first time in a long time, I felt special—and that was a feeling that I wished I could bottle and take with me wherever I went.

Fearful that George would barge into my room and embarrass me, I cut my conversation with Eric short and told him I had to go.

"Can I have your number?" he asked. My stomach churned. Desperate to avoid the embarrassment of telling him our phone was disconnected, I quickly recited George's number over the phone. Hopefully if he called I would be around to answer.

It wasn't long before talking to Eric every night was part of my routine. I did my best to call him first since I didn't want to see what would happen if my drunk guardians answered the phone. I would always make sure that Eric and I had discussed and planned when we would talk so I could be ready and not leave it to chance. The last thing I wanted was to taint our budding romance with the truth of my home life. I just wanted to be a regular fifteen-year-old girl, who liked a boy, who liked her back and did and said the right things. I didn't want to be overshadowed by my past and the mayhem that followed me around, and although deep down in my heart I knew the chaos always caught up with me and eventually would ruin this too. For now, I was just a girl who laughed every day because someone had finally paid attention to her. It was both magical and terrifying.

I began to measure my days by when I would get to talk to Eric. During the day, I looked for him in the halls, and at lunch we would occasionally sit together in the cafeteria or outside if the weather allowed. Due to his part-time job at the mall, before the end of each day we would discuss our evening phone call schedule, just in case he would be working late and wouldn't be able to call.

I waited patiently for the sound of George's phone to ring. It was Eric's turn to call. With my radio turned on low, my ears blurred out the sound of music, eager to dash to the phone. Looking at the clock, I went to the kitchen twenty minutes after Eric had promised to call.

"Did the phone ring?" I looked at George, trying to hide my eagerness. He shook his head. Sauntering back to my room, I sat next to my door, listening in case Eric was simply running late. Time passed and a lump began to form in my throat. I knew he wouldn't try calling. Resigned, I retreated to my bed. As I nestled under the covers, I wondered why he hadn't called and hoped he was okay.

The next day at school I didn't see him all day. I walked the same halls, at the same times I normally did and I looked for him on the way to each of my classes, but I didn't see him. I asked Julia if she had seen him and she hadn't. It felt so odd that he didn't call and that he wasn't at school and I wondered if he would call that night.

I paced my room for hours replaying our last conversation and wondering if I said or did something wrong to make him change his mind on me. I couldn't think of anything. I went back to ask if anyone called for me. Again, George said no.

"Who are you waiting on, Iman? Why do you keep asking if someone called?" Mildred looked like she had had a few drinks already.

"No one," I muttered. "Just a guy from school. He was supposed to call me."

"Well maybe he doesn't like you!" she laughed. "What kind of boy says he is going to call and then doesn't? He sounds like a loser." She went to the kitchen and poured herself another drink.

"He's not a loser. He said he would call. He probably had to work or something." I snapped back.

"Or maybe he just doesn't like you. Did you ever think of that? Not everyone is going to like you. You really can't be so full of yourself, you know." I wanted to strangle her and her smug little face.

I stormed to the bathroom and drew a hot bath and cried in the tub. I was such a loser to think that he was a nice guy. Mildred was right. He probably found out about me and my family or, worse yet, he probably met some other girl and forgot about me. I felt so stupid for thinking that such a gorgeous and popular boy like Eric could ever fall for an orphan who lived with drunks. Who was I kidding anyway? It's not like it would have lasted.

Chapter Twenty

Age 15: Enamoured

I spent the weekend at Mel and Steven's place, happy for the distraction and change of scenery. Luckily, they had plans to go out to the bar, which meant I could just stay at their place by myself and watch movies and listen to music. I loved having the place to myself and knowing that I didn't have to hang out with Mildred and George and listen to their weekend drunkenness.

The phone rang and I answered it in case it was my sister checking in on me as she sometimes did. A man's voice I didn't recognize was on the other side of the phone.

"Hey, Mel, it's John. I'm at the door."

I quickly changed the channel on the TV to show the camera downstairs in the main lobby. There was a man with blonde hair, blue jeans and a black jacket standing in between the main doors.

"Umm, this is Iman, Melanie's little sister. My sister isn't home right now." I wasn't sure what to do.

"Oh, hey! I'm Steven's cousin. Can I come up quick? I need to use the bathroom." He laughed as he said it.

I held down the number 9 and could hear the door release in the lobby through the TV and watched as John walked toward the elevator.

I felt instantly nervous. I didn't know this person and in any moment, he would be knocking on the door.

As I heard his knuckles rap against the wooden door, I went and opened it and said hello properly. He was way cuter than he looked on the camera. He had piercing blue eyes and huge dimples that exploded on his cheeks as he smiled. Although his teeth were crooked, his face more than made up for it. I could smell his cologne and feel the cold air from outside by looking at his rosy cheeks and the way he rubbed his hands together.

"Thanks for letting me up. It's getting cold out there." He took off his coat and after he used the restroom, we made our way to the living room. I sat down on one end of one couch and he sat adjacent to me on the other leaving the round coffee table between us.

"You're Mel's little sister, eh? I've heard about you, but it's great to put a face to the name."

I blushed and laughed realizing I had no idea what to talk about with my new houseguest.

I lit a cigarette to ease my nerves and John followed right after. He was very friendly and made conversation quite easy. We started talking about everything from music to my school to how much I hated living at home. He was so full of life and wanted to ask me about everything: my favourite colour, what I liked to do for fun, my dreams for after high school, and even asked me if I had a boyfriend and what kind of boys I liked. I told him I didn't have one and that the boys at my school were immature and stupid.

John was a 21-year-old man and worked in construction. As he puffed his cigarette, he went into detail about his life, telling me that he didn't really love his job but it paid the bills for now. Enraptured by the conversation, I barely noticed the time. Two hours passed and Mel and Steven were still not home, which made sense, since it wasn't even 11:00 p.m.

"Well, I gotta get going." John rose from the couch, putting his half-empty cigarette pack into his pocket. "Let Mel and Steven know I stopped by, okay?"

I smiled and nodded. "It was great talking to you," he added. "We should hang out next week sometime if you're free."

He wrote his number on a piece of paper and handed it to me. Looking at the seven digits scrawled on the piece of paper in my hand, I promised to call him on Sunday to set something up for the week.

I closed the door behind him and my face grew hot. The last two hours of conversation were just what I needed—I had almost completely forgotten how heartbroken I was over Eric. John's attention gave me a refreshing distraction, and left me feeling special. Finally, someone had treated me like an adult and not some stupid fifteen-year-old girl. It didn't matter that he was six years older than me and that I wasn't *technically* an adult, I felt like one on the inside, and life sure as hell treated me like one too. *Besides that, I don't really have that much in common with kids my age anyways*, I thought to myself. Other than Giselle, not many people my age understood me or what I had been through.

I walked back to the couch, lighting up another cigarette. Quickly, I turned the television to the security camera feed so I could watch him leave. My heart raced at the excitement of what just happened. I was smitten, lost in a trance of heartbeats and daydreams so encompassing that I had hardly noticed when Melanie and Steven returned. As John requested, I told them that he had stopped by and excluded the more treasured details, trying my hardest not to smile. Finally, when they retreated to their room, I closed my eyes to fall asleep, eager for Sunday to arrive.

Seconds felt like hours as I counted down the minutes until Sunday. My excitement to call John and make plans for our next encounter was all-consuming. The prospect of seeing him gave my life a new sense of purpose; my spirits were soaring and the realities of my life were suddenly more tolerable. Common sense told me not to disclose my plans to Mel. As my older sister, and a friend of John's, I knew she would disapprove—she would treat me like a child and tell me I was far too young for him, even though I didn't see myself as the child she thought I was. And my perception of myself wasn't unfounded either—John had even brought it up when we were talking. He said that, like me, no one really understood him either, and that Mel and Steven would probably try to stop us from being friends if they knew that we were going to hang out again. Enamoured by his truth, I told him that I wouldn't tell anyone and he promised that he wouldn't either because he didn't want to get me in trouble. His consideration for me was flattering, especially since we had only known each other for a short time. I had known people for years who didn't seem to care about me at all, let alone think ahead as to how a situation would affect me. John understood me on a deeper level than anyone else. I couldn't wait to see him again and bask in the glow of his gaze.

After dinner on Sunday I offered to go to the store for Mildred. Eagerly putting on my shoes, I scrambled out the door, heading to the pay phone to make plans with John. My heart fluttered as he picked up the phone on the second ring.

"Hello?" His voice sounded slightly different but I recognized it right way.

"Hey, John? It's Iman. How are you?" I prayed for my voice not to give away how nervous I was.

"Hi!" I could see his smile in my mind. "I'm so glad you called. I was beginning to wonder if you would," he let out a nervous chuckle.

"Of course, I called. I just had to get away from my apartment and use a pay phone. I can't talk long but I wanted to make sure I called you." I knew I had to hurry or I would be interrogated for my absence when I got home.

"I am so glad you did. Listen, do you want to hang out with me tomorrow? I have some time around lunch if you're free. I could come by your school and at least see you for a bit."

My stomach flipped with excitement at the thought of seeing him again so soon.

"Yeah," I coolly said. "That would be great. I can meet you outside of the main doors at around noon…if you're good with that." I tried to be calm and conceal the squeal that was brewing inside my throat.

"Perfect. I'll see you then. Have sweet dreams, beautiful…and I will see you tomorrow."

"Goodbye!" I hung up the receiver.

Beautiful? Oh my God—he thinks I am beautiful. Without a moment to waste, I ran as fast as I could to the store to get Mildred the pop and chocolate bar she requested before I headed back to the apartment.

Our conversation was on a loop in my head. It was short, but perfect, and I wanted to memorize every word. The more I thought about how he called me beautiful, the more beautiful I started to feel. I wondered if this was what love felt like and how someone could give so much meaning to my existence after only one meeting. I thought about how true that was for Romeo and Juliet, and hoped that I had finally gotten my fairy tale ending.

The next morning, I took extra care in getting ready, knowing that I would be seeing John. In a storm of wardrobe changes, I had finally found an outfit that I deemed acceptable, put on some makeup and headed for the door. My mind was fixated on the clock throughout my morning classes and as noon drew nearer, my stomach filled with butterflies. With the ring of a bell, I headed toward the front doors and sat outside on a bench to look out for John, nervously looking down at my light sweater and favourite jeans that had made me feel so confident only hours before.

He arrived after a few minutes and our faces were covered in giant smiles as we saw each other. I walked toward him and he opened his arms and gave me the biggest hug and I melted into him and wished that hug would last forever. I could smell his cologne and leather as his cold jacket pressed against my cheek.

"It's so good to see you again." He whispered in my ear like an old friend who had just returned from a long absence.

"Yeah, thanks for coming to see me. What should we do?" I looked up at him with curiosity and the realization of our limited options.

"Let's go explore," he smiled. Grabbing my hand, he led me toward the bus stop. We got on the next bus, sitting at the very back. Wedged between the window and John, I beamed as he continued to hold my hand. We rode the bus all the way to the mall, went to the food court and dined on Chinese food. Between bites, he told me more about himself, and we laughed and talked the hours away. Before I knew it, the school day was nearing an end, and I would need to head back home.

I had never felt so special in all my life. It was like this unexplainable connection like no one else existed in the whole world—just the two of us and our laughter. I could have spent days just sitting across from him, plastic plates of westernized Asian cuisine between us. *Is this what true love feels like?* I wondered. *Does it feel like someone thinks you're the most important person on earth, and cares about you?* I didn't know what I was feeling, but I knew it was new, and I never wanted it to end.

John rode the bus with me all the way back to the stop near my apartment. He said he wanted to see where I lived in relation to him. We walked around to the side of the building so no one would see us and he held me close. "I have a day off on Wednesday," he smiled. "Promise me you'll see me again?"

Returning his smile, I agreed and we decided to meet at the same place outside of my school first thing in the morning. He said that we could go to his place if I wanted and we could hang out there. I nodded excitedly. Taking my face into his hands, he titled my chin upwards, toward his and kissed me sweetly on the lips. I swooned; my legs felt weak and I could barely stand as I looked up at his piercing blue eyes.

"Remember, we have to keep this as a secret for now. Nobody will understand us and they'll try to come between us." He kissed the top of my head and held me close against his body.

"I won't tell anyone. Nobody understands me anyways and I can't wait to move out of this shit-hole."

We hugged, kissing again quickly before I ran around the corner toward the front door of my apartment. Leaping up the stairs to the second floor, I stopped to look out the window to catch one last look at John to see him sitting at the bus stop. My heart pattered quickly. I felt like I had just won the lottery and finally found someone just for me. When I finally reached our apartment, I took a deep breath before opening the door.

I had to protect this happiness with everything I had. Nobody could ruin this for me, which would happen if anyone ever found out that I was dating a 21-year-old man. Everything I had ever loved was taken away from me, and with all my heart I knew that I had to keep this to myself.

With the intent to keep my love affair a secret, I kept to myself as much as I could so that time would pass and I would once again get to see John. I replayed every second of our day together a million times over, and wrote about him endlessly in my journal. Knowing that my diary wasn't as sacred as I would have hoped, I didn't put his name or age and just referred to him as "my man" for fear that someone might find my journal and ruin everything.

Chapter Twenty-One

Age 15: Winged Cupid

As I rode the bus to school on Wednesday to meet John my heart was beating so fast. There were drawbacks to our budding relationship, of course: he was much older than I was, and I couldn't tell Melanie about us. Keeping a secret from her was killing me, but I knew she wouldn't understand. I was always misunderstood and I didn't want to keep fighting for everything I wanted. I just wanted to be happy. I would do anything to be happy and no one would ever take that away from me. I had finally found something that was just for me. It wasn't perfect but it was mine and I couldn't remember feeling so cared about.

We made our way to John's apartment across the city and on the way, he told me that he lived with two other guys. He had recently moved there and didn't have a lot of stuff but was planning on getting things set up soon. After getting off the bus, we walked about a block before stopping at a store to buy some Cokes and cigarettes. Within a few minutes, we arrived at a standard four-storey walk-up much like the one I lived in. I wasn't familiar with the neighbourhood—I hadn't ever ventured off this far from my part of the city. We walked up the stairs and before we opened the door John stopped and looked at me.

"If anyone asks, you're eighteen okay?" His eyes were serious. "We could get into big trouble for this, and I don't want to do that, okay?"

I nodded in agreement. *What kind of trouble was he talking about? Would I get kicked out of my place?* I mean, that wouldn't be the worst thing that happened to me—people would judge me based on my age, even though I wasn't living the life of an average fifteen-year-old.

The apartment was very bare; you couldn't really tell how many people lived there because it hardly looked like anyone lived there. The balcony looked out over the busy city streets and the kitchen didn't even have a table. I walked through the entrance that opened to a long hallway with three bedrooms and a bathroom before opening to a living room and kitchen. There were two mismatched sofas in the living room, a coffee table, and a TV.

We spent the day together laughing, talking, smoking, and making out— never once seeing either of his roommates. As the hands of the clock neared closer to three, my heart grew heavy. I didn't want to leave such bliss only to go home to people who didn't even see me. I was invisible at home; Mildred and George didn't acknowledge me or encourage me, or notice anything about me. *I could be dead,* I thought, *and they would be relieved.* I ached for freedom.

John walked me to the bus, accompanying me to the terminal where I transferred to my next bus home. As we made plans for our next encounter, our goodbye was cloaked with sadness. "Could you just tell Mildred you're staying at a friend's this weekend?" he asked. I quivered—I was a terrible liar but I agreed, spending the rest of the night practicing my story and covering my tracks. I asked if I could spend the weekend with Giselle and made sure I told Giselle my plan in case someone tried to get a hold of me.

The next few nights went by excruciatingly slow and I counted down the seconds until I could escape back to my secret paradise. With permission to spend the weekend at Giselle's, I began to gather my belongings, but as I was packing, it suddenly dawned on me that I would be spending the night with John. I had never spent that much time with a boy and certainly had never slept over before. I panicked at how that would be and hoped we wouldn't get sick of each other. Knots twisted the insides of my stomach as I thought about the very likely event that John would want to have sex. I had hated that thought as long as I could remember. I wished it didn't come up so often in my short life. Taking a deep breath, I calmed myself down. I would do whatever it took to escape the hellhole that I lived in and that this was my way out.

John and I would fall in love and run away, and I would never have to see Mildred and George again. It really was just like Romeo and Juliet—only I hoped that neither of us died at the end. I just wanted to escape. Either way, it probably would be completely different to be with John because of how we felt for each other. It had been less than a week, but I could tell that this was real love. Why else would it feel so perfect?

I brought my packed overnight bag with me to school and John came and met me just after the last bell. I couldn't think of anything else all day; I just wanted to be with him and I was both excited and terrified that we would have the entire weekend together. I had played it over and over in my mind all day as I watched the clock, waiting for my Prince Charming to come and pick me up. I prayed that we didn't get caught and that Mildred and George forgot about me just like they always had.

I could tell John was just as nervous as I was. He looked shy and I could see his face turn red whenever I brought up the fact that we were spending the weekend together. We made our way to his place and I recognized the buildings that we had passed just days before. John held me tightly on the bus and kissed the top of my head several times. I could feel his excitement and, once again, it made me feel like the most important girl in the world.

When we arrived at the apartment, John reminded me that when I saw his roommates to tell them I was eighteen. Making a mental note not to talk about school, I wondered if I needed to make up a job—I didn't have the slightest idea of what I would say if someone asked. I normally wasn't a very good liar, although lately I had become an expert.

My nerves quickly dissipated as we curled up on the couch. We talked about everything—that's what I liked about being with him, he really listened to me. I didn't have many people like that in my life, and most days I spent in my own company trying to avoid upsetting anyone.

Later in the evening John's roommates, Matt and Kyle, quickly made an appearance. Matt was around the same medium build as John and didn't really say much more than hello before disappearing into his room and then leaving. Kyle was much warmer and had a big smile on his face. His six-foot-two frame loomed over me as he came to shake my hand and introduce himself. He had brown hair, dark eyes, and looked like a very nice man. He seemed to be around John's age and sat with us in the living room for a few minutes before heading back out to meet with friends.

John and I ordered a pizza and drank beer while sharing stories of our childhood. It was mostly I who shared—John seemed to get very serious and sad whenever I asked questions and I decided to change the subject to more cheerful topics. We talked about my sister and Steven a bit and suddenly a feeling of dread washed over me as I realized that John knew nothing of what had happened between Steven and me. I wondered if I was meant to tell him since we were dating and Steven was his cousin. I decided to say nothing, hoping that both my guilt and my memories would leave me.

As the night grew late, John suggested that we go to the bedroom and get some sleep. My heart beat feverishly at his words and my stomach turned into knots. I wasn't sure what to expect, although I had an idea. I took my bag to the washroom, washing my face and brushing my teeth. I looked at myself in the mirror and took a few deep breaths followed by a prayer to God and my mother to keep me safe.

The room was very empty and I was surprised to see that there wasn't any furniture in it. There was a makeshift bed on the floor made up of just some blankets and a couple of pillows. There was a pile of clothes in the corner and my small bag leaned against the wall. No dresser, no nightstand, no sign of home.

"I need to go and get some furniture still. Sorry, it isn't much to look at." I had forgotten that John was watching me and I must have looked as surprised as I felt.

"Did you just move in?" I completely knew what it was like to have to move. *Perhaps John hadn't had a chance to go get his things yet,* I thought.

"Yeah, kind of. I had to get rid of my stuff and so I don't have much… but I will soon." He looked slightly embarrassed and I sensed he didn't really want to get into it.

John turned off the lights and I felt less shy in the dark. I kept my T-shirt on and took off my pajama pants and crawled under the covers on the floor.

"Are you doing okay?" As our eyes adjusted to the darkness I could see him looking at me.

"Yeah, I'm fine." I giggled nervously as I lay on the hard floor.

"We aren't going to do anything, okay? I just want to be next to you." He reached over and placed his hand on my face and I breathed a giant sigh of relief.

Oh, thank God, I thought to myself. My relief quickly transformed into flattery. I was amazed that John didn't try anything with me, even though he had me alone and in his bed. I don't think I could have cared for him more than I did in that moment. The men in my life had often disgraced me and paid no mind to what I had wanted or even thought of my feelings at all. John was so different from anyone I had ever known. I was consumed with gratitude that I didn't have to experience something I had grown to hate so much but that men wanted so badly. I thought about how much he must really love me as I fell asleep in his arms.

The next morning, I woke up to John watching me sleep. I felt instantly embarrassed and wondered what I looked like and if he had been awake long.

"Good morning, beautiful." He leaned over and kissed my forehead.

"Good morning," I curled up into the nook of his arm and closed my eyes. For the first time in a long time, I woke up happy and excited for the day ahead.

We got up and John made coffee and then gave me some towels to take a shower while he made breakfast. I was in heaven and all I could think of in the shower was how truly happy I was. I was so elated to be able to spend the entire day and another night in our little paradise so far removed from the whole world. I felt so grown up and so deeply loved. After all, look how wonderfully he treated me—and he didn't want anything in return besides my company!

We spent the day doing some shopping at a nearby mall and getting some groceries and beer for a planned night in. We laughed so much all day and once again did not run out of conversation. I felt like I could tell John anything.

We started drinking and smoking weed late in the afternoon, entertaining ourselves with each other's company. I felt so free and so far away from the world I had grown to hate so much.

I had grown increasingly nervous about not having told John about Steven and I couldn't hold it in anymore. As we sat on the couch together I grabbed his hands and looked him in the eyes and said, "John, I have to tell you something about Steven." I scanned his face for a reaction and saw concern in his eyes.

"What about Steven? Did he touch you?" His face grew serious and I suddenly felt scared for what might happen if I told the truth.

"He kissed me." I thought I would test the waters and gage his reaction.

"*What?*" His body stiffened. "*When?* At his and Mel's apartment?"

I nodded yes. He seemed to get angrier as he talked, but then tried to compose himself.

"What a fucking pig he is. I should go kick the shit out of him." John's face turned red and he spit the words out of his mouth with a hatred I had never seen from him. I was frightened at the reaction I had provoked.

I panicked at the thought that my secret would be out and begged John not to say anything. I told him how much I would hate for my sister to find out and how mad she would be at me. I would ruin everything she loved and she might have to move back with Mildred and George, and I would feel so horrible. I burst into tears at the thought of it.

John wiped my tears away with one hand while pulling me closer with the other and promising not to say anything. I decided not to mention anything to do with Steven ever again. I regretted bringing it up at all and did my best to compose myself and change the subject.

I spent the rest of the weekend trying hard to make John forget what I had said and thankfully it wasn't brought up again.

I dreaded heading back home to Mildred and George all Sunday, and when the time came for John to take the bus with me, we were both upset that our weekend was coming to an end.

"Don't worry, sweetheart. One day it will be just you and me and you won't have to leave me." He tipped my chin up toward his face and kissed me on the nose.

My whole heart swelled at this idea. *Was he serious? Could he save me from Mildred and George?*

I had so many questions and very few answers. All I knew was that I was completely infatuated with John and nothing else existed when I was with him.

Chapter Twenty-Two

Age 15: Between Two Worlds

When I got home the apartment smelled like food, which was very rare. George was in the kitchen making roast beef, potatoes, and cream of corn. It smelled incredible.

"Hey, stranger! You're back!" He looked at me and smiled.

I couldn't help but laugh and wonder what had gotten into George. He was almost never in a good mood these days, and to see him cooking so happy, seemed completely unusual for him.

It seemed his good mood was contagious as Mildred was also in good spirits. I couldn't help but wonder how drunk they were. They were usually only happy when they were drunk or high, and I could never predict what mood they would be in as it didn't have anything to do with circumstance, day of the week, or time of day. It was a wild combination of the dozens of pill bottles on top of the fridge, booze, weed and hash that I could never calculate or understand. I was at the mercy of their inconsistency and I would take the good whenever I could.

We ate as a family that evening which was rare but nice. I was grateful to eat such a wonderful meal and ate until I could hardly move. After dinner I washed the dishes, pots and pans, while daydreaming about my magical weekend with John. I missed him terribly already and it had only been hours since I saw him last.

The next week John had to work more and I needed to attend my classes for fear of being caught. We spoke on the phone but didn't see each other until the following Friday when he came to spend the afternoon with me. We talked about when we could spend another weekend together and planned for two weeks later, when he didn't have to work and I could get permission to be at Giselle's again.

Giselle hadn't been to school in a couple of weeks and one afternoon she called me to tell me that she had given birth to a sweet little boy name Isaiah. I couldn't believe it—we had talked about it for so many months and now he was here! I was so excited for her and I couldn't wait to meet him.

The next week Giselle's mom dropped her off at my place with Isaiah so we could meet. She lugged him up three flights of stairs to our apartment in his car seat. He was all snuggled up and covered in blankets to ward off the November chill and keep warm. I peered inside beneath the layers of blankets at his darling little brown face. He was absolutely perfect, with chocolate-coloured eyes and smooth mocha skin. I couldn't get over how this tiny little human came out of my best friend.

Giselle looked healthy and happy, beaming with pride at her little son. Mildred was all over Isaiah and couldn't put him down—she had always loved little babies but didn't know what to do when they grew old enough to talk back.

I sat thinking about Giselle and Isaiah long after they had gone. My friend was a mom now. I couldn't fully wrap my mind around it, but I knew I loved that little boy as much as I loved his momma.

The next weeks passed quickly as Giselle got used to motherhood, and I dug deep into my imagination to get to John's house whenever I could. I wanted to spend every moment with him and had soon realized that I was infatuated with him. I fantasized about running away with him and getting our own place together. I wanted to live with him and get as far away as possible from where I was.

That weekend I wasn't allowed to go out because Mildred told me that Giselle would be too busy with Isaiah to have a friend over and that I should give them space. I knew she was right, but I just wanted to go to

John's place. I didn't have an alibi to use if I couldn't get permission to go to Giselle's.

In preparation for the weekend at home, I took my usual precautions and loaded up my closet with whatever food and beverages I could find so that I could hide in my room as much as possible over the weekend. Since one of my jobs was to roll Mildred and George a pack of cigarettes a day, I would roll myself a pack as well and stash them in the back of my sock drawer.

As usual, strangers piled into our apartment as early as 5:00 p.m. and our apartment filled with people as quickly as it filled with smoke. With music blaring and people competing to be heard, I made my way to my bedroom and put my headphones on and daydreamed as the Wu-Tang Clan drowned out the chaos of my living nightmare.

As the evening wore on, I missed John terribly and hoped that I could at least sneak George's cell phone into my room after they had passed out and call him. I only left my room to use the washroom and I tried to open my door as quietly as possible so as not to even cross Mildred and George's mind.

Throughout the evening, as George grew more intoxicated, he would bang on my door for kicks and then run into the bathroom as though it wasn't him. After the third time, I stopped getting up to look at the door and see who was there. *Such a loser*, I rolled my eyes. I hated getting any attention from him.

Not long after the last time he knocked, I heard anther bang on the door only this time it was followed by a loud buzzing noise that didn't go away. I ripped off my headphones in utter annoyance at yet another disturbance and pulled open the door and looked at the floor and instantly my body filled with disgust. The buzzing was coming from a white, plastic vibrator that was on full blast and vibrating against my door.

I was mortified. I didn't want to touch it, but didn't want it next to my door either. After kicking it into Mildred and George's room in a fit of rage, I ran into the kitchen right up to George and yelled, "What the fuck is wrong with you?"

His eyes bloodshot and glassy, he looked up from his beer with a ridiculous smirk on his face, "What's your problem?"

Laughter surrounded him as his drinking buddies heard his response.

"George, what have you done now?" Mildred chimed in.

"He thought it would be funny to leave a vibrator at my bedroom door!" My blood was boiling and I wanted to reach over, grab him by the hair and repeatedly smash his face against the table.

"*George!* Smarten up!" Extremely intoxicated, Mildred's words slurred over her buckteeth. He could never do anything wrong.

"Oh c'mon, Iman. You are so uptight. I just thought you could use a little loosening up. I put fresh batteries in there for you!" He could hardly contain his laughter as he took a swig of his beer. The room erupted in laughter.

"Get a fucking life, you disgusting pervert! And leave me the fuck alone or I'll call the cops." I stormed to my room, slammed the door and pushed my dresser up against the door and collapsed on the other side of it crying into the carpet. I couldn't hate living there any more than I did in that moment. I felt like a trapped rat in a cage with no escape.

Shortly after, Mildred tried to come into my room. Not answering her calls, I glared at the door, relieved that I placed the dresser against it. She tried to console me at first and quickly got annoyed. Soon, she angrily yelled at me to stop being such a baby. She was never on my side. She never stuck up for me and was never ready to protect me when it came to George.

I grabbed one of the straight razors I had hidden in my room that I used to carve into my legs, sticking one end of it into the eraser of my pencil. I taped it in place as tight as I could and I put it under my pillow, promising myself that if that piece of shit pedophile tried to come into my room one more night I would slit his throat and kill him. I didn't care if I went to jail. I would be better off anywhere but where I was. I felt like I was losing my mind. I wasn't safe. I wanted to die. I just wanted it all to stop.

The next day was the usual hangover and silence after the chaotic drunken storm. Mildred and George stayed in bed most of the day and I read in my room.

By mid-afternoon I could smell weed and heard Mildred and George discuss going to the liquor store. I knew they were going to just repeat their drunken escapades, so they didn't have to face reality. I could hardly blame them sometimes—I didn't want my reality either and it was far better than theirs.

George and I ignored each other for the entire day and evening, which was more than fine by me. I didn't like him any more in the daylight.

The apartment wasn't as packed as the night before, and things were a little quieter. I kept to myself and watched Mad TV from the small black and white TV that was still stained with my mother's blood. It had given me a sense of comfort, as though part of her were still with me. I felt the same way about my teddy bear Freddy and how every night I held his blood-soaked body tight next to me as though I were squeezing my mother once more.

I had crawled into bed early with a book and had fallen asleep with the lights on. I shot up in bed when Mildred's shrill voice called out to me louder and louder until she was hovering over me.

"*Iman!* Get up! Why are you sleeping? Wake up!"

I looked at her confused as my eyes adjusted to the light.

"What? What's wrong?" My heart was beating fast inside my chest—I had still not grown comfortable with being awoken abruptly.

"Why are you in bed? Come read us poetry. I was just telling everyone how beautiful your poems are." She could hardly keep her eyes open when she spoke, her body swayed from left to right as she tried to keep her balance in such an inebriated state.

"I don't want to," I glared at her. "Please, just let me sleep." I couldn't believe what I was hearing. The last thing I wanted to do was read poems to a bunch of alcoholics and drug addicts in the middle of the night.

Mildred's face changed from playful to furious at my denial of her request and she clumsily grabbed a corner of my blanket and ripped it off my body.

"GET UP AND READ US POEMS! You're always writing in your fucking book, and now you can share it with us. Unless you think you are too good for us?"

I knew better than to argue with her in this state.

"I never said I was better than you," I quickly scanned my memory and wondered what poem I would read.

"Good," her demeanour changed instantly. "Then come and read one to us. I told everyone how proud I was of you." She smiled at me as her eyes struggled to stay focused. With a grimace, she mumbled to herself as she made her way back to the kitchen.

When had she ever bragged about me? I wondered. She was always teasing me about my writing.

I glanced at the clock next to my bed. It was 1:28 a.m. Things must be getting lame out there if they needed a fifteen-year-old for entertainment. I grabbed my poetry book and opened it to the last poem I had written. A knot formed in my throat at the thought of sharing my very private poems with fools.

There were only four people sitting around the kitchen table: Mildred, George, George's cousin Jimmy, and a woman who I assumed came with Jimmy.

"Well, what are you waiting for? Read your poem!" Mildred hissed impatiently.

I stood at the end of the table, partially in the living room and opened my book as my knees shook and my palms grew sweaty:

> *I am like a bird locked in my cage.*
> *My chapter of imprisonment is over, as I am about to turn the page.*
> *I have earned my wings. Now I must fly free.*
> *I was born to soar high,*
> *No one can capture me.*
> *In the air is where I belong.*
> *I am going to fly far 'cause my wings are strong.*
> *How I have waited for this day.*
> *When I could go far, far away*
> *My wings are spread, I spread them wide.*
> *I close my eyes and let the wind be my guide.*
> *When I am up here, I clear my mind.*
> *No worries, no cares, peace is what I find.*
> *I need not boundaries to feel safe and loved.*
> *All I need are my wings and to soar up above.*

I closed my book when I finished reading and nervously looked at my intoxicated audience.

"Whoa! That was really good, Iman!" Jimmy's eye lit up and he clapped his hands together in applause.

"Thank you," I was blushing at my one rave review.

"Alright, well that was a bit of a weird one. You can go back to bed now." Mildred didn't even look at me as she stood up and went to the kitchen to pour herself another drink.

I quietly made my way to my bedroom and went to bed. I felt secretly proud that I had read my escape poem to my hideous captors.

The next weeks went by so quickly as I did everything in my power to spend time with John. I missed almost every class I could and took the bus to his apartment at every chance. Being with him gave me such happiness inside. It pained me deeply to have to leave him at the end of every day—I wanted nothing more than the perfect existence we created when we were alone. It was like my very own secret paradise; my perfect escape from the horrible hand I had been dealt. Well, it wasn't *always* perfect but it was awfully close.

From the first time John and I had sex I could tell something was different about him. He would get very angry and shy and demand that I not look at him. I was so startled the first time he acted so strangely that I didn't know where to look or what to say. I decided it was best not to say anything at all and just closed my eyes. He would turn off the lights and then undress in the far corner of the room while yelling out for me to not look at him. Sometimes I would lie and pretend I wasn't looking while I squinted through the darkness to see if he was a deformed monster and what he could possibly be hiding. I could never find anything and when I touched his body in the dark he felt perfectly normal.

It wasn't until several visits later that John was drunk enough to share his past. He had had a lot to drink and was in a state I hadn't seen him in before. He seemed tormented by the fact that he never told me about anything and loved me for not pressuring him to tell me. He confessed that before living in this apartment he had been in jail and that is why he didn't have many belongings. He didn't say for how long but he said it felt like forever and that horrible things happened to him in there.

My heart broke listening to his stories of prison and some of the degrading things that they did to him and forced him to do. He had been terribly abused in every way and I could see now where his crippling insecurities had come from.

As bothered as I was by what John had to go through, I found myself secretly wishing that my father had found an even more painful fate in prison. I imagined John's crimes were not even slightly comparable to my father. Surely, the other criminals didn't take lightly to a murderer.

"Why did you go to jail?" I couldn't help the words as they flew out of my mouth.

John looked at me for a long time in silence, trying to read my face and pre-judge my reaction.

"I hurt someone pretty badly." He lit a cigarette and looked away from me.

"How badly? Who did you hurt?" I felt a chill move up my spine as I suddenly realized I was alone in an apartment with a man I thought I knew but knew nothing about.

"I smashed someone in the face with a beer bottle and fucked them up pretty badly."

I brought both of my hands to cover my mouth in shock, "Oh my God! Why?"

I wasn't sure I wanted the answer but I was dying of curiosity and hanging on the edge of my seat.

"I got in a fight with my ex-girlfriend. It was horrible. I shouldn't have done it, I know. I just got so mad at her and she was trying to break up with me." Shame covered his face and he got up and walked over to the window and stared outside.

I suddenly felt nauseous and terrified. *He hit a girl? His girl?* My sweet and gentle John? I didn't want to believe it but he was confessing and I could see through his shame that he wished what he said weren't true.

"It wasn't supposed to happen. I fucked up, you know? I didn't mean to hurt her." He anxiously ran his fingers through his hair and paced the room.

"You believe me, right? You know I would never hurt you, right?" Suddenly he was kneeling in front of me, grabbing both of my shoulders tightly while gently shaking me. He began to cry and collapsed into my lap and sobbed.

"Of course, I know that. I know you would never hurt me." I spoke the only response I knew to be correct in that moment. The truth was that I was afraid for my safety. I thought of my mom and how she would be so disappointed that I was with John. I knew I had to get myself out of this.

I instantly regretted that I had arranged to spend the night with John and what became even more worrisome was that no one knew where I was. Although Giselle knew who I was with, she didn't know where he lived.

I was alone with a violent criminal and once again found myself feeling trapped.

I did my best to not let on to John that his words had shaken me. I maintained my previous behaviour, smiling and chattering the evening away, and when I felt it unsuspicious, I feigned exhaustion and excused myself to sleep. Though it didn't happen often, as I closed my eyes I couldn't wait to get home.

Christmas was approaching and with it came the usual mix of cheer and discomfort. In the weeks that had passed since he had told me what he had done, I had begun to distance myself from John. Although I knew he could feel me slipping away, both he and I refused to even bring it up. A fear had grown within me. I'd grown afraid that I would say or do the wrong thing and be positioned on the other side of John's rage, and I swore to myself that

I would not follow my mother's fate—extinguishing my soul at the hand of a man with no control of his temper.

I had deliberately not brought my report card home over Christmas break, and with an entire winter break trapped with Mildred and George, I had prayed that it would go unnoticed. I hadn't really thought ahead to the repercussions of my report card when I skipped classes to hang out with John, but the last thing I needed was to be yelled at for my terrible grades and the overwhelming amount of absences that had outweighed the number of classes I had attended.

As my terrible luck had never failed me, it wasn't until school resumed when Mildred asked me where my report card was. After telling her I didn't get one, her eyes narrowed as she walked toward the phone and called the school. I stood silent as I heard her request for one to be mailed to the apartment, aware that when it would finally come, there would be hell for me to pay.

Sure enough, when the mail arrived and Mildred had looked over my grades and attendance, I had to endure another horrible lecture, filled with yells and screams—she slammed doors only to open them immediately after, coming into my room after sending me in only to berate me.

Finally, as the evening drew on, I thought I was safe to enter the kitchen and stealthily retrieve a glass of water.

"You're a real piece of work, Iman!"

I froze. I turned to meet Mildred's gaze.

"Where have you been going every day, huh? What do you have to do that is so fucking important that you only attended *twenty-three days in four months?*"

I assumed her questions were rhetorical since she went from one to the next without stopping.

"Answer me!" She shrieked as she lunged at me.

In a blur of instinct and fear, as I watched Mildred raise her hand to hit me, I grabbed both of her wrists, finding the strength to slam her against the kitchen wall. Shock filled her eyes, and I froze as I realized what I had done. I had discovered a strength I didn't know I even had.

"Let go of me!" Mildred tried to wiggle free but I overpowered her without much effort and pinned her against the wall.

"Don't hit me," I hissed. "Never hit me again. Do you understand?"

It was as though someone had taken over my body—everything I did and said surprised me.

In the last nine years, I had lived with Mildred and George, I had never stood up for myself. I never hit back. Never defended myself. For the last nine years, I simply took all the beatings and kept all my pain buried deep inside, but that day something cracked inside of me. I felt different and I could no longer tolerate one more second of abuse.

"Let me go!" Mildred was helplessly looking at me.

"Don't hit me." I repeated my words with as much authority as I could muster.

"Okay—just let me go." A defeated look was on her face

As I let go of her wrists, I could see she was shaking in fear. She grabbed her purse and jacket and ran out the front door.

George sat merely feet away in the living room as though nothing had happened. He didn't even flinch at what just occurred. I smiled to myself, happy that Mildred could see what a coward she had married.

Mildred and I never spoke of our confrontation, but I could feel a shift in how she treated me the next few weeks. She and George kept to themselves, ignoring me for the most part. I didn't mind. Deep down I knew that she would never lay another hand on me again. I could tell that the power had shifted and that *she* was afraid of *me*. It felt good to see her scared. Now she could have a taste of her own medicine.

That weekend, Giselle came over to our apartment for a sleepover. In preparation, I had been stealing weed and rum from Mildred and George all month. As soon as she arrived, Giselle and I went to the park up the street and got drunk and high. As I told Giselle about my amazing confrontation with Mildred, we laughed endlessly. Giselle talked about how good it felt to leave Isaiah at home with her mom and for it to be like old times again—just the two of us without a care in the world. I loved her so much. When we were together, it was as though nothing else existed.

We made our way back to the apartment and tried to act sober enough to get back to my bedroom. Luckily, Mildred didn't ask Giselle too many questions on our way back in. I wondered if our perfume and bubble gum was enough to mask the smell of booze and cigarettes.

Having spent the past couple of months completely sober and breastfeeding, our escapade had a much more potent effect on Giselle. She was delirious and a complete mess and we did our best to not draw too much attention to ourselves in my bedroom. Retiring to bed early, when I came back from brushing my teeth, Giselle was out cold on my bed. Letting a small smile creep upon my lips, I turned off the lights and crawled in next to her and fell asleep.

I woke up to the light being turned on and a sharp pain in my ribs as I felt someone hit me while shouting for me to get up. I opened my eyes and recognized my sister's voice right away.

"Mel? What are you doing?" I tried to shield my eyes from the blaring light.

"You fucking bitch. Get up! How could you?" The smell of alcohol violently hit my nose. Mel was frantic. Beside her stood Erin, her friend, who also happened to be John's sister.

"What are you doing? What's wrong?" I was trying to understand what was happening and kicking Giselle to wake her up to help me.

"What are you doing here?" My groggy brain couldn't make sense of everything happening.

"We climbed up the balcony and broke in to come and talk to you." She was out of breath and completely enraged.

"I know what you did, you fucking slut! You kissed my boyfriend?" She was shaking with rage, "How could you?"

I had never ever seen my sister look so upset.

"How could you do that to me? Why would you kiss my boyfriend? John told Erin everything. You're such a fucking bitch. I HATE YOU, Iman. I hate you. I can't believe you did this to me. After everything I have ever done for you. I'm your sister—no, you're *not* my sister. I wish I never met you. I fucking hate you. You are NOT my sister and I never want to see you again."

My heart sank and I couldn't form any sentences. I was enraged that John had broken his vow to keep what I told him a secret and hurt at the hate that Mel spewed at me. In a panic, I kicked Giselle again, hoping this time she would finally wake.

I looked at my sister standing there, her anger radiating off her like the smell of booze, blaming me for everything. How could she blame me for what he did to me? Why was everything always my fault?

"You *are not* my sister, Iman. Do you hear me? I never want to see you again. You are nothing to me. *Nothing.*"

I felt my heart harden at every venomous word. *Fuck you,* I silently barked at her. I didn't need any of these idiots.

"That's fine, Mel. How about you get the fuck out of my room and go back to your perfect boyfriend." I pulled the covers over my head and rolled over hoping they would just leave.

She stormed out and slammed the door and all I could wonder was why no one woke up. No one came to see what was happening. Stunned in silence, I buried myself beneath the covers. With Giselle still dead to the world, all I could do was hide beneath the blankets as I silently sobbed.

In the morning, I explained everything to Giselle and she couldn't believe what I was telling her. She showered me with apologies, remorseful that she hadn't woken up. We were both thankful that Mel and Erin hadn't tried to hurt me.

Nevertheless, I couldn't shake Mel's words and how angry she was. We had our fair share of fights over the years but she had never ever told me she hated me and that I wasn't her sister. The thought of living in a world without my sister was devastating. All I could do was sit in bed and sob. I wanted to die more than anything and wished there was some way I could just disappear.

Mildred and George were ignoring me and now my sister disowned me—one of the only people who always had my back. I felt so ashamed at what had happened between Steven and me, but it wasn't even my fault. All I wanted was to take it all back and tell her how much I wish that hadn't happened. *Everything I touched always turned to shit,* I sobbed to myself. *My curse hurts everyone that ever encountered me.*

That week Mildred and George acted as though I were invisible and I wished I was. I wished I could disappear.

As I stirred awake one Saturday morning, I woke up to an empty apartment. It was strange. I went from room to room, searching for some evidence of life. From the corner of my eye, I saw a sheet of paper on the table.

It was a note, addressed to me.

Iman,

You have three days to leave our apartment. We don't want you anymore and you obviously don't want to be here.

If you are not gone by Wednesday, we will change the locks and throw your belongings in the street.

Mildred and George

My whole body started shaking and I wavered between extreme joy and fear. I had wished for this day almost all my life, but now that it was here, what would I do?

I couldn't help but wonder what Mel had told them. I knew it was no coincidence that her giving up on me was the straw that broke the camel's back.

How could John betray me and tell my secret?

Now where would I go? Would I have to live with him?

I was rich with questions, but lacked money and answers. I was finally free—and honestly, I didn't care where I went, so long as it was far away from this hellhole.

I sat on my bed for hours, contemplating my next move.

Thoughts of Ben and Elizabeth came to mind. Suddenly I was filled with shame. What would they think of all of this? Would they be disappointed that I had messed up and had no place to go?

My body was surging with adrenaline yet the apartment was so quiet. The stillness reminded me of the way it felt moments after my mom was killed.

There was the same heaviness in the air and I was filled with the same mix of grief, anticipation, and curiosity. In those strangely quiet moments, it feels as though both nothing and everything is possible at once. A crossroads of sorts, that requires immediate action but I lacked the time or the ability to properly process it all.

Eventually I lit a cigarette, called John and left him a message, and started packing my suitcase.

Mildred and George didn't want me anymore? Fine by me.

I had been counting down the days for years until I was sixteen and no longer under their guardianship.

An hour later, the buzzer rang and I ran down the hall to answer it. I thought that maybe John had gotten my message and decided to come over and get me.

"Hello?" I answered anxiously.

"Hey, Memo. It's Adam. Let me in."

ADAM! I was so surprised but happy to hear my brother's voice on the intercom. I had just spoken to him over Christmas but it felt like a lifetime ago.

I opened the apartment door and waited for my big brother with excitement. I ran down the hall and jumped into his arms as soon as I saw him come up the stairs.

"How are you, Memo? What happened?" He looked at me with so much concern in his big brown eyes.

"I don't know. They left me a note and told me to get out. Did they call you?" We sat in the living room and I curled up in my brother's lap. Having him there made me feel safe and optimistic about what the future held for me. Oh, how I had missed him.

"Yeah, Mildred called. She said that she couldn't handle you anymore and that it would be better if you moved out." He sounded so worried about me.

"Well, I agree with the witch for once. I don't want to be here and I will be better off anywhere else. Can I live with you?" I looked up at my brother, hopeful.

"Maybe. Let's see. First, we need to call Ben and Elizabeth—they want to talk to you."

Adam dialed the phone and passed it to me. As I held it up to my ear the shame I was filled with earlier began to creep back in. Would they be disappointed in me? Would they finally realize that I was no good and didn't deserve them? Surely, they would wonder what was wrong with me if Mildred and George no longer wanted me.

I held my breath as the phone rang.

"Iman?" Elizabeth's voice came through loud and clear. "I hear you are moving." She always said things in such a matter of fact way.

"Yeah, I guess I am." My voice dropped slightly as I imagined all that was to come. The knot in my throat began to throb and I could feel the sweat on my palm as I held the phone.

"Well, here's the deal. We are coming to pick you up and you are going to come and live with us. I don't want to hear any arguing. Do you understand? I will be there in a few hours so pack your stuff and be ready."

I finally let go of my breath in a giant burst of happiness and relief. I had dreamed of living with Ben and Elizabeth for nine years. Just like that, my prayers were answered. A flood of emotions filled me: gratitude, hope, excitement. I knew only good things were waiting for me outside of this dingy, dark apartment.

I hung up the phone and did a little dance around the living room making Adam laugh.

Adam stayed for another hour and then left me at my insistence that I would be okay. I had not heard from Mildred and George. Adam said that they would not be back until I left.

Once I had a plan, I kicked it into high gear. Elizabeth would be bringing her car so I knew I could only bring my suitcases and my backpack. I grew very sad when I realized I couldn't bring everything. I just didn't trust Mildred and George enough to schedule a time to come back with a truck. Plus, Ben and Elizabeth lived five hours away.

Once I walked out of that apartment, I had no intention of ever returning.

I looked at my mom's television and realized that I would have to say goodbye.

I knew I couldn't bring my past with me if I wanted to start fresh.

With just over an hour before Elizabeth would be arriving, I sat on my bed, feeling overwhelmed with sadness and fear. I let the magnitude of what was happening wash over me. I was free! I was finally free after nine long and grueling years and what felt like several lifetimes of heartache. I tried to imagine what it would be like to live with Ben and Elizabeth. I had imagined it so many times and now that it was coming true, I felt nervous and unsure of what to expect. I prayed that I would be good enough for them and that the dark curse of my life wouldn't follow me into their home. I just wanted everything to work out for once.

With my freedom on the horizon, I knew I had to change my frame of mind and think only about the good that was to come. I was ready and eager to leave everything else behind.

I pulled out my book of poems and began writing:

> *Look ahead, don't look behind*
> *Open your eyes and you will find*
> *That my love for you is growing strong*
> *We have had some troubles and I know I was wrong.*
> *I am not too stubborn to admit or too proud*
> *To confess but through all of the pain, I hope you don't love me less.*
> *Tears streak my face as we say our goodbyes*
> *Try to remember our happiness and see beyond the lies.*
> *Look at the good times and forget about the bad*
> *And think about the love and trust that we once had.*

I didn't know if I was writing it to myself or to Melanie or to Mildred and George but I copied my poem onto a sheet of paper and left it on my bed.

I didn't want to bring any of the resentment and anger that I had nurtured all of these years with me. I wanted to start anew and move into the next phase of my life. I wasn't going to ever be this sad or poor or hurt again. I hoped I would never see Mildred and George again. I knew I wouldn't keep in touch with John, even though I told him I would. I wanted nothing to do with anyone or anything that reminded me of my horrible past.

This was my one shot at becoming all of the wonderful things I had been reciting into my mirror for most of my life. A time to not only remember who I was in my mother's eyes, but to bring that girl to life. I had always known something better was waiting for me. My prayers had been answered. I was finally free.

I gathered my bags and took one more look around the apartment. I left my keys on the table, and walked out the front door where Elizabeth was waiting for me.

Epilogue

As I sit here writing this, it has been over twenty years since I left the "home" I shared with Mildred and George.

I wish I could tell you that I left my guardians that day and walked into the most perfect life.

But life did get so much better. Ben and Elizabeth were, by far, the best guardians I had ever had—besides my own mother. I lived with them for three years. They spoiled me, showed me so much care, and loved me dearly. They taught me life skills like how to cook; helped me get a part time job; showed me the meaning of hard work; and comforted me through many nights of tears and sadness as my trauma reared its ugly head. They invested in tutors so that I could catch up on my studies and they took me traveling which sparked my passion for seeing the world.

Six months after I moved out of Mildred's apartment she wrote me a letter. It was the first time I had heard from her after she kicked me out. She wrote that had she regretted kicking me out and that it was the biggest mistake of her life. She also shared that she had contracted HIV. She wasn't exactly sure how but thought that it might have been either from a blood transfusion she'd received in the '80s or from the tattoo she had gotten in her friend's basement months before.

While I was still in high school my brother Adam got married in Las Vegas. Ron, Chokri, Mel, and I ventured to Nevada to attend, along with

Ben and Elizabeth. It was the first time I had seen my sister since the night she broke into my bedroom and disowned me. I was so nervous to see her but once we laid eyes on each other everything that had come between us melted away. Melanie ran toward me and gave me the biggest hug in the world. I had never been so excited to see her in my life. I had missed her desperately and enjoyed every second of our reunion. We didn't bring up what happened with Steven but I was glad to hear that they were no longer together—Mel had eventually come to her senses and broke up with him. We would speak about it deeply in the coming years and cry and laugh and forgive each other for everything. We have never been closer and see each other often. I know we will never let anything or anyone come between us again.

With the help and support of Ben and Elizabeth, I graduated high school and moved to the west coast of Canada to attend college to become a travel agent. I spent the next few years travelling as much as I could to get as far away as I could from my past. Something about travelling made me feel found—as though I belonged in all of the faraway places where no one knew who I was. I used to pretend that the reason I lost everything I had loved was because I was a child of the Universe. In my heart of hearts, I knew that I was meant to roam free and be raised by everything that I encountered.

Whenever I stood still long enough to make a home, I invested in various therapies and counselling to begin to understand and heal all of the pain and anguish I felt in my heart. I was diagnosed with Post-Traumatic Stress Disorder and began to finally make sense of everything I had experienced throughout my childhood. I lived in various cities throughout Canada, trying to find a place to unpack and build a new life, but I could never quite feel settled enough before my heart would yearn for the next adventure. I even tried to live in Toronto to get to know my aunts and cousins—in an effort to reconnect with the culture that was taken from me. I didn't last very long there and realized that as much as I longed for the parts of my mother that made me feel connected to her family, I didn't belong there. They had left my brothers and me so many years ago. That separation was wedged between us in a way that made it hard to find my way back to them.

After a year in Toronto, I moved to Scotland where I lived for two years. Scotland provided some of the best times of my life and so much of me healed there. My spirit needed to be away from everything that haunted me, and Scotland welcomed me when I needed a home the most. So much of me was mended there and it gave me the strength and reprieve I desperately needed to get back to Canada and face my demons.

When I returned from Scotland I was hit with unexpected, yet welcome news. I finally found out what happened to my high school crush, Eric—the guy who never called me back! I found an ad looking for actresses to shoot a music video. I was in love with all things performing at the time and reached out to audition. In a hilarious turn of events, the artist turned out to be Eric. We laughed at how young we were and I told him how hurt I was that he never called me back. He shared that he had in fact called me and that George had answered the phone and told him I wasn't interested. George had threatened to harm him if he so much as looked at me. So, Eric avoided me at all costs. I was blown away at learning this information and so grateful to reconnect after all those years.

As with most wounds, when you are finally ready to clean them, you are faced with the task of moving through some pain to actually administer the salve that heals them. When I returned from Scotland, I moved in with my brother Adam in Edmonton. It was the first time in my adult life that all of my siblings and I would be in the same city at the same time.

At this point, I was 24 years old.

Adam had divorced his first wife and remarried; Chokri found love and got married; Melanie had met the most incredible man and married him while I was in Scotland; and Ron was set to marry the love of his life. It brought me so much peace and happiness that my siblings and I had managed to defeat so many of the odds that were stacked against us our whole lives. We had made it through to the other side of our shattered childhoods and remained as close as ever to one another.

I discovered that Mildred and George had split up and that George had moved to the east coast of Canada to live with his parents. Although I was shocked to hear the news and still repulsed at the thought of him, I couldn't help but wonder how many demons he was living with. I hoped that he could finally be free to live a life that felt authentic to him and that he never ever tried to harm another child.

Mildred on the other hand, wasn't so free after their separation. Her health had deteriorated considerably because of the HIV, as she didn't make the necessary changes to her lifestyle to compensate for her illness. A tumor the size of an orange grew in her brain and she was hospitalized. When I heard the news from my sister, I knew that I had to go and see Mildred. I was torn between the resentment I had held for her for so many years and the humanity I felt for her illness. I do not want to deceive you into thinking that some holy love draped over me and suddenly forgiveness washed through my soul—I had too much bitterness in my heart for her at the time to come to that place. I grew angry thinking of her being released from a lifetime of guilt, suffering, and poverty. As much as I felt justified for how I felt toward her, part of me knew that if I didn't make my peace before she died, I would never forgive myself. I had been working so hard for so many years on releasing all of the pain of my past and I sure as hell wasn't going to let her sting me one last time by dying on me while the pain of our life together festered in my soul.

I forced myself to visit her. I swore that I would not be her victim ever again and winning that battle meant swallowing what I wanted, to come to what I needed the most: to be released of this pain I felt for her. I sat by her bedside many days and nights keeping her company and working with the doctors to ensure she received all the help that she could. She mostly slept or stared into space. I sat and cried and prayed that somehow, I could ease the pain I felt that had become inseparable from the memories I had of her. She was nothing like I remembered. She was frail and sad-looking and at the mercy of everyone around her. My heart felt pity for her for the first time since I could remember. She was weak and delirious. The tumor was growing so quickly that the pressure to her brain caused most of her memory to fail.

But she recognized me immediately and her eyes lit up when I walked in the room. She told me she loved and missed me. Whenever the doctor would come around and do his tests, he would always ask her the date and where she was. Sometimes she couldn't remember the simplest of facts but one question she consistently answered was, "How many children do you have?" She always responded with, "Five."

It astounded me that after all of this time and everything we had all been through, she considered all of us her children. I could feel the pride with which she answered radiate through my whole body. I could suddenly see how hard she battled to have us all under one roof. How much she fought for three orphans even though she didn't have the emotional, mental, or financial capacity to care for us. Her intentions were noble but it was her execution that I judged her on. I suddenly saw her as a child and realized that the same way she held me to a standard that felt impossible to fulfill, I, too, held my expectations over her all the while, dooming her to fail.

In those final weeks, I decided to just show up and be still. To surrender to what was. I didn't ask her for anything, I simply sat supporting her in the small way that I could. One day, I knew it would be my last visit. I got up after a few hours and stood at the foot of her bed with my hand on her leg. "I have to go now, okay? I love you, Mildred." She had been staring at the wall for some time and when I spoke she looked me straight in the eye and a small smile crossed her lips as she whispered, "I love you, too."

She passed away days later in early June, in the middle of the night, mere weeks from the anniversary of my own mother's death. My heart broke for Mel and Ron. I knew all too well the unrelenting pain from losing their mother that would tear at their hearts for the rest of their lives. My siblings and I were not new to adversity and much like the rest of our lives, this tragedy only brought us closer together.

The five of us were all we had left.

Grieving for Mildred was so much more painful than I had imagined. I used to think that I couldn't wait until she died so that I could be at peace in my heart but it wasn't how I imagined it at all. I spent weeks screaming and crying in my apartment. One night I missed her so much that I searched everywhere for the letter that she had sent me after I had moved in with Ben and Elizabeth—the letter she sent me saying she regretted kicking me out, and telling me she had HIV. I couldn't find it anywhere. I sobbed until my eyes nearly swelled shut. I found a new depth to my trauma that I didn't know was there. I hated that I had hated her at all.

Through my grief, the torment that I carried inside of me had surfaced tenfold and I found a new level of self-loathing that was harrowing. I knew that I still had one more dragon to slay if I ever hoped to find myself again. I didn't know if I had it in me, but I knew that if I didn't face him, there would be no life left in me to live.

I looked up and saw a very short, bald, fat man with a long beard walking toward me. He was wearing a dark blue shirt and pants. I stared at his face while he walked toward me and I tried to find something that I recognized. I stood up beside the table until he was just a couple of feet in front of me.

We looked at each other for a few seconds until he spoke first, "Are you with the press?"

I was confused. Didn't he recognize me? No words came to my throat.

Then I saw a spark of recognition light up his eyes. "Princess, is that you?" He finally saw me. I still couldn't speak but I nodded. He took a few steps toward me. "Can I hug you?" I just looked at him and nodded.

I melted into his arms and we hugged tightly and cried on each other's shoulder. Something inside of my soul snapped and let go. A ferocious sob escaped and my whole body shook and collapsed into my father's arms. The six-year-old girl inside of me cried for her father and cried for her mother. I cried for the life that I had lost—been robbed of—and I completely surrendered to the situation I found myself in twenty years after that horrible night.

I sat down across from this familiar stranger who had haunted my life for as long as I could remember. I had given him so much of my strength and power over the years. He had ruled every single moment of my being since the day I was born from hero to villain. I looked at his small frame and wondered how the years had treated him.

I yelled at him and told him of all the injustice that I had been dealt. "How could you do that to us? Why did you kill her?"

I could hardly speak as my throat was coarse and my soul was weary from the journey.

"Princess, what do you mean? I am so sorry that your mother is gone, I can't believe someone took her from us. I dream of her every night."

My body stiffened at his words. "What do you mean, someone? It was you. You took her!" I snapped at him with every ounce of venom I could muster.

He shook his head. "No, no, no, I would never do that. I love her. She was my wife and I loved her. I didn't take her, princess, they didn't find who did it and I have been here for so long, waiting for them to find who is responsible." He was looking me straight in the eyes and I couldn't believe what I was hearing. I stared at him waiting for him to tell me that he had misheard me, that he didn't know what I was saying, and that he, of course, killed my mother.

I knew then that an apology was never coming. I felt stupid for thinking that this man was going to be able to redeem himself or heal the pain that his actions had put me through. Suddenly, when I looked at him, I saw a broken shell of a man who was very sick.

I suddenly realized that he didn't have what I was looking for.

He didn't have my peace.

He didn't have my apology.

And what would that apology even do? She was gone.

Even though I could see that he didn't have what I was after, I didn't want to go home empty-handed. I needed whatever pieces of my mother he had left and so I decided to shift my approach. I decided to take what little he did have to offer and I asked him to tell me about her. What was she like? What made her laugh? Why did she marry him?

When I asked him about her, his eyes lit up—he came to life. He told me stories about her. It was as though we brought her to life and she was sitting at that table with us. I laughed at how funny she was, and I cried at how much I missed her. He told me that I looked exactly like her and I never felt so close to her. I loved her so much in those moments and as much as I wanted to, I couldn't summon the hate that I had harboured my entire life for this cruel monster of a man. He had somehow become more human and so had I. The more he shared, the more I loved her, and the more I could see all of the pieces of my chaotic life come together. I could feel how much I carried her around with me—inside of me and how she had never fully left me. She had led me here to be healed.

We sat there for nearly seven hours. I could hardly keep my head up. I was starving. I had never felt so empty and full at the same time. I told him I had to get going. When he asked me to stay in touch, I smiled.

We hugged for a long time and I knew that I did the right thing. I brought her back to me and that was all I ever wanted. I found the key to the prison I had been living in all of my life.

I felt the air hit my face as I stepped outside and I knew that it was a luxury that not everyone got to experience. My whole body filled with gratitude at everything I had ever lived and even more for the fates I had avoided. I made it. I did it all for her. I did it for us.

As I walked down the street toward the bus stop, I noticed that something was missing. I felt lighter, like I had truly freed myself of the chains I had carried for so long. For the first time in forever, I wanted to live more than anything in the entire world. I felt myself come alive and I promised that as often as possible, I was going to bring myself to life for the rest of my days. It was the first day of my forever and I wasn't going to waste another second of my future looking over my shoulder for my demons to catch me. I was willing to let it all go for a chance to change the course of my future. The one that I was creating anew.

I would go back and visit my father several times after that. Each time, I would get more and more memories of my beloved mother and take them with me. There came a day when I knew it would be my last visit in that prison courtyard. Just the same way I knew leaving Mildred that day would be my final goodbye. I felt as though I heard all that I needed to and that he had given me everything I needed to move forward in my life—that was all I really ever wanted. To move forward. To heal. To awaken the dormant dreams that had been crowded out by old traumas. The day of that final visit I felt something inside of me shift back into place. I knew I would never allow anyone else to hold the key to my happiness again. From then on, I would remain in charge of my life.

In the years following that last visit, I continued to do the work in order to work through the lifetime of trauma. I threw myself into therapy, meditation, and exercise. I read everything I could about how to heal from the inside out. I was determined to not waste another second of the life I had so often taken for granted.

My relationship with Ben and Elizabeth remained strong until they announced their divorce. It came as a complete shock as I had no idea that they were struggling so much. They had forever been my example of perfect love, and hearing of their split tore through my insides. It wasn't amicable and because it was Ben who initiated the divorce, Elizabeth spiraled into a deep and dark depression. One day she emailed me and told me never to contact her again. She said that she couldn't bear to be in contact with me or my brothers knowing that we still spoke with and loved Ben so much. She said she didn't want us to be stuck in the middle of their breakup and that instead of asking us to choose sides, she would simply remove herself from our lives. I couldn't believe what I was reading. I begged her to change her mind. She was the closest thing to a mother I had ever had—save for my own—and I loved her with all of my being. Adam tried to see her in person and reason with her as well, but she had made up her mind. And just like that, she closed her door and her heart to us and never made contact with us again.

The pain of her absence was excruciating. Ben was heartbroken for us and couldn't fathom how she could just stop being our family. For me, her self-imposed exile was the cruelest thing she could ever do to me. She knew all of my history, all of my suffering and pain, everything that I had had to deal with in my life. In fact, she had soothed so many of my wounds over the years and I had confided everything to her. She called me her daughter and I had joyfully claimed her as my mother. For twenty years, she helped nurse me and remedy the distrust I had from my foster homes and the ways in which I was mistreated by the women who claimed to care for me over the years. Her sudden choice to remove herself from my life crippled me.

Today my family means more to me than I could have ever imagined. Ben and I remain close. He has been my champion of love since I was six years old and he assured me that he would never leave or abandon me. My siblings and I also remain close. It has been incredible watching my brothers and sister start their own families—making me an auntie seven times over!

As with most losses in life, they allow you to see all that remains. We made ourselves into a family and those bonds were forged with blood, tears, trauma, and time. Kindred souls who had been on the battlefields of life together and who knew deep in our souls that nothing would ever tear us apart.

I have started a family of my own.

Last summer Ben walked me down the aisle to give me away to my husband. I will cherish that walk for the rest of my life because there is no other person on this planet who is more of a dad to me than he is. I know it has a lot to do with my beloved Ben, that I was able to meet the love of my life: my incredible, selfless husband Jeff. His love is beyond anything I could have imagined for myself. Every day I am so grateful to wake up to him and share this life together. We are expecting a daughter early next year. I can't help but think of my mother and how desperately she wanted a girl. I know that I am being given a chance to raise my daughter with the same love and conviction that was given by my own mother. The serendipity is not lost on me and I know in my heart of hearts that my own sweet child will always know how deeply loved and cherished she is.

So here I am now, 36 years strong.

As I look back at my story I am humbled, happy, proud, and relieved.

The further I moved through my own healing, the more I was called to help others heal as well. In discovering my own path, I knew becoming a coach, author, and speaker was what I was born to do. My childhood spent speaking into those mirrors and repeating my mother's words was preparing me for this divine purpose!

My willingness to heal, and to do the work (so much work!) that was required to be able to be a happy, successful, and purposeful adult has been the best decision of my life. I am so grateful that I took the long and painful road back to who I truly am.

I have been given so many incredible gifts in this life. And as wildly outrageous as it may sound, I wouldn't trade a second of my life for a different one. I have suffered deeply at the hands of others and also by my own doing. I have made bad choices and brought more pain into my heart than I care to admit. I have fallen countless times and stayed down far too long. But something I always, always know to be true in my life is that no matter how many times I have fallen, I will always, always get back up. In fact, I don't even worry about getting knocked down anymore because that is simply one of life's conditions: we will fail, we will hurt, we will be pressured so much that we crack and feel as though our souls cannot bear another second.

Throughout all of the hardships and pain and heartbreak, I have also been shown so much love and compassion and beauty and forgiveness. I have forgiven others for their wrongdoings and I have forgiven myself for the parts I had to play. One thing I know for sure is that the beauty in my life far outweighs the pain I have endured.

No matter how it felt during my darkest times when I thought my soul would perish, I was being filled with more light. If I had to do it all again, I would, because I now know where I was being led: back to myself. And that is a prize worth fighting for. There were many times I thought I was broken beyond repair and couldn't bear another second of this life, but I can see now that I have never been broken. I was simply being cracked open to let more love in so that I could find my way back home.

Mommy and me, Summer of 1987

My Dad, Ron (aka Ben) and me at my wedding, August 26, 2016

Acknowledgments

To my incredible husband, Jeff: I love you so much. You make everything worthwhile and I am so grateful for you. Thank you for your endless support, encouragement, and love. You have truly shown me the depth of my heart and how sacred true love can be.

To my daughter, before you are even born, you have already filled me with a love I didn't know was possible. I cannot wait to experience miracles with you.

To my sweet and loyal dog Charlie, you truly are a best friend. You have licked so many tears, kept all of my secrets, and ever so faithfully, loved me back to existence time and time again. You graciously sat with me through every word of this book. Thank you for your endless devotion, my sweet prince.

To my amazing siblings: Adam, Ron, Chokri, and Mel—I couldn't have been given a better team to conquer this life with. You have held me up and guided me more than you could ever know. I love that we have created a family on our own terms and that we have a bond that is far beyond this lifetime. I am so proud to be your little sister and thank each of you for the love, devotion, laughter, protection, and safety you have provided me throughout this crazy life. I owe so much of my heart to each of you and I love you with all of my being.

To my dad Ron, it will take me more than one lifetime to show you my gratitude. You are every daughter's dream. Thank you for never giving up on me and for showing me so much magic in this beautiful world.

To Sonia, Ken and Tanya, I am so grateful for you.

To my Campbell Clan, thank you all for the many ways in which you have helped to raise me and give me a feeling of belonging.

To my incredible in-laws: Patti, Vince, Eleesha, and Grandma Helen— thank you for raising the man who would become my everything, for bringing me into your home and hearts, and for continuously supporting my dreams and doing whatever you can to help make them come true.

To my first coach and dear friend, Heidi, I will forever be grateful for you! Thank you for all of your guidance and constant encouragement as I was writing this book. You came into my life and truly heard and saw me, for what in many ways, felt like the first time. You have always believed in me and never let me forget about this dream. Your friendship means so much to me.

To my sweet soul sister, Jill, the ways in which you bless my life are endless! I adore you and our sisterhood. You helped me so much with this book and did everything you could to make it come to life. Thank you for coming into my world and making a home of our friendship—in this life and the next, I will always love you.

To my incredible friend and love warrior, Mel H., I am so grateful for you! Thank you for always bringing so much love to the table and for your infinite example of courage and faith. I adore you!

To Ruby, thank you for showing me new ways to rise up and for always believing in me.

To Kerissa, you have always been an incredible example of perseverance and strength. I admire you in a million ways and I love how you shine, sister!

To Andrea, it is no coincidence that we met and that at just the right time, you knew to guide me to my publishing team.

To Gabrielle Bernstein, my mentor, teacher, sister, and friend, thank you so much for cracking me open to the miracles of this path. I am eternally grateful for you.

To all of the amazing women of LIT, I am ever better for knowing each and every one of you. Thank you for your grace.

To my Spirit Junkie Family and the sisterhood of Kate Courageous and my Courageous Living warriors, you have given me so much belonging and love. I can't imagine this path without you.

To the many Earth angels that have worked tirelessly to help create this book:

Rose and Con Boland: Thank you for the most incredible photos I could ever imagine for my book cover. You are both so wildly talented and I cherish our friendship dearly. My darling Con, we have always had a special friendship and I have loved you deeply all of these years. Neither of us could have known that you would depart this earth weeks after taking my photo and that my cover photo would be the last photo you ever took. I will hold this gift dear for the rest of my life. May your soul rest in peace knowing that all of the beauty and passion you have created here on earth will never be forgotten.

To my phenomenal team at Purpose Driven Publishing: Jenn, Heather, and Niki—thank you for treating my book with such love, seeing my vision, and working so hard to bring it to life just as I dreamed. I am honoured to have the privilege to birth this book with you.

To my first editor, Jennifer Sintime, thank you so much for helping me get my book in order and for spending countless hours editing and working on this project. You helped guide me when I needed it the most.

To my first readers and extra eyes, Emily, Suzanne, Heidi, Dana, Rachael, Mel and Kate—I am so grateful to you for reading my book baby with such care and for all of your support and guidance. Each of you inspires me so much. I am honoured to call you friends.

To my great teachers: Gabrielle Bernstein, Kate Courageous, Pamela Ball, Heidi Nicole, Ruby Fremon, Iman Aghay, Kimra Luna, Marianne Williamson, Oprah, Eckhart Tolle, Dr. Wayne Dyer, Louis Hayes, Danielle Laporte, Esther and Jerry Hicks, and Abraham. Thank you for shining your light and helping me find my way.

To all of my phenomenal and generous GoFundMe Campaign supporters: THANK YOU from every corner of my heart for all of your help in bringing this book to life. I cannot begin to express what it means to me to have all of you stand beside me as this dream comes true. Thank you, thank you, thank you! Each of you have changed me forever:

Ron, Patti, Vince, Eleesha, Helen, Amir and Milena, Lindsay U., Rosalie, Melody, Lissette, Andrea L., Shelley and Wayne, Michelle M., Kerissa, Jeanne, Andrea W., Akri, Samantha, Sara, Alex H., Lilia, Kathie, Jill E., Shohreh and Ali, Kim M., Leantara, Melinda, Bernice and my Aussie Family, Kate S., Stephanie B., Christian, Allie, Alice, Cindy, Melanie D., Jackie, Jenness, Jennifer N., Kim and Dave, Brooke C., Sarah A., Marie-Lou, Suzanne S., David W., Marisa, Cristiane, Marissa P., Chutima, Christy H., Danielle M., Jill D., Melissa D., Roberta M., Pauline, Moe, Ruby, Heidi, Chris, Jodi B., Dalia, Brianne, Cheri, Rita, Ann, Ashley, Graciela, Sandi, Angela, and Jason.

About the Author

Iman Gatti, author of *Cracked Open – Never Broken*, is an empowerment coach, transformational speaker, and Certified Grief Recovery Specialist™. Through her work she helps people overcome self-limiting beliefs, heal past wounds, and step fully into their limitless potential. Committed to serving her community, Iman works with women recovering from domestic violence and is the founder of Lunch Bags of Love, which helps provide meals to Edmonton's homeless community.

To learn more about working with Iman, or to inquire about an appearance, please visit ImanGatti.com.

Book Bonus

Congrats on getting through my memoir! I know it was a long and emotional read and I am so grateful to have you with me on this journey.

As a way to say thank you for your support, I have created a free training just for you!

Please head over to my website and sign up to receive this free bonus available only to my loyal readers.

You can get your free Book Bonus here:
www.ImanGatti.com/book-bonus

I hope it serves you well!

Please let me know what you think, say hello and stay in touch by connecting with me in the following ways:
Facebook.com/imangatti
Instagram: @imangatti

Wishing you so much peace and ease in your journey.

Big Juicy Love,

Iman